SURVIVAL AT STAKE

Also by the Author

For a Moment of Taste: How What You Eat Impacts Animals, the Planet and Your Health

Praise for *Survival at Stake*

'Engaging and highly readable, *Survival at Stake* shows why it is essential that we reform our relationships with other animals to safeguard our environment and ensure good public health.'

—**Dr Andrew Knight**, veterinary professor of animal welfare and ethics, founding director of the University of Winchester Centre for Animal Welfare, adjunct professor in the School of Environment and Science, Griffith University, Queensland

'*Survival at Stake* targets some of the most pressing crises facing us: the stagnation of medical research, the rise in pandemics and antibiotic resistance, and climate change and environmental destruction—and presents us with food for thought and a disaster exit ramp.'

—**Dr Aysha Akhtar**, MD, MPH, CEO of Center for Contemporary Sciences, author of *Our Symphony with Animals*

'We are nothing without good health so a huge cheer to *Survival at Stake* for doing the homework that allows us to see how not only to survive, but to thrive.'

—**Dr Nandita Shah**, recipient of the Nari Shakti Puraskar, founder of SHARAN, author of *Reversing Diabetes in 21 Days*

'The sooner we humans accept that we have to live by higher standards than we have been, towards all life, plants, fungi, creatures from land and sea, the sooner we will get into balance with nature and take the pressure off all ecosystems. My advice is to follow the useful guide in this book to help save our own species and the planet.'

—**Jennifer (Jenny) Helen Jones**, The Baroness Jones of Moulsecoomb, member of the House of Lords (UK), affiliated with the Green Party

'Compassion is good economics, good science, even the best weapon against climate change. *Survival at Stake* shows us there is hope for humans if we can learn to treat other species with respect and understanding.'

—**Maneka Sanjay Gandhi**, Member of Parliament, Lok Sabha,
member of the Bharatiya Janata Party,
author of *Heads and Tails*

'There is absolutely no doubt that a vast array of diverse nonhuman animals (animals) are sentient and have rich and deep emotional lives. The important question is not *if* animals are emotional beings, but *why* emotions have evolved and why it is essential to pay careful attention to these well-established scientific facts in all of our interactions with them. We also know that caring for nonhumans spills over into caring for humans, and Poorva Joshipura's wise words show that when we treat other animals with respect, dignity and compassion, it's a win-win for all. *Survival at Stake* is a must-read for a global audience, and animals around the world will thank us for doing so.'

—**Dr Marc Bekoff**, PhD, professor emeritus of ecology and
evolutionary biology, University of Colorado Boulder,
author of *The Animals' Agenda*

'Whatever you think you know about the instant world emergency, you don't, not the half of it, until you read between the covers of this book. At one and the same time, it's global reach, combined with its terrifying detail, astonishes, informs and shocks. As humans we have no right, bestowed by any secular or spiritual authority to treat our planet and all life upon it as if it were our property to be exploited as we wish. We are not owners, nor superiors, but custodians with duties of care and respect. By the time you finish reading, you will not be able to sit still any longer. Silence and inaction are not options where survival is at stake.'

—**Michael Mansfield**, King's Counsel barrister,
author of *The Power in the People, Not the People in Power*

'Animal and human well-being are intertwined, and Poorva makes that crystal clear. She convinces us that we simply cannot afford to continue to turn a blind eye to animals' suffering, and the repercussions this is having on the world we share with them. Be kind and think where your food is coming from, anything that involves blood, tears and suffering is not meant to be on our plate.'

—**Mimi Chakraborty**, actress, singer,
Member of Parliament, Lok Sabha,
member of the All India Trinamool Congress

'*Survival at Stake* may be the most fascinating and troubling book you will ever read. Tracing the path that brought us HIV, Covid-19 and other killers, it shows exactly how to protect against future threats. More than a wake-up call, it is an alarm bell for environmental and health risks, along with a well-mapped escape route. The real gift of this book is its optimism. It shows how the steps that protect our health and those that protect our planet and the animals with whom we share it are one and the same.'

—**Dr Neal D. Barnard**, MD, FACC, adjunct professor of medicine,
George Washington University School of Medicine,
president, Physicians Committee for Responsible Medicine,
Washington, DC,
author of *The Power of Your Plate*

'Joshipura inspires us to be solutions-driven in our fashion and other choices so as to effectively tackle cruelty to animals, pollution and other grave problems we face today.'

—**Nicole Rawling**, chief executive officer and
co-founder of Material Innovation Initiative

SURVIVAL AT STAKE

How Our Treatment of Animals Is Key to Human Existence

Poorva Joshipura

HarperCollins *Publishers* India

First published in India by HarperCollins *Publishers* 2023
4th Floor, Tower A, Building No. 10, DLF Cyber City,
DLF Phase II, Gurugram, Haryana – 122002
www.harpercollins.co.in

4 6 8 10 9 7 5 3

P-ISBN: 978-93-5699-472-0
E-ISBN: 978-93-5699-464-5

Typeset in 11/15 Minion Pro at
Manipal Technologies Limited, Manipal

Printed and bound at
Thomson Press (India) Ltd

This book is produced from independently certified FSC® paper
to ensure responsible forest management.

For my parents,
who are ruthlessly kind
and
Ender and Omi
who deserve a kind world and a healthy future

'Whoever is kind to the creatures of God, is kind to himself.'

—Prophet Muhammad (PBUH),
Hadith: Bukhari

CONTENTS

FOREWORD

As I write this, India is dealing with the aftermath of deadly monsoon rains and flash floods; tens of millions of people face food insecurity and potential famine in East Africa as a result of drought; and wildfires are devastating swaths of Europe—events that are caused or worsened by climate change related to heat and dry vegetation. July 2023 will likely rank as the hottest month ever recorded; at least twenty-two countries have experienced suffocating temperatures of 50°C Celsius or higher. Meanwhile, a new report from Harvard Law School and New York University warns that the next pandemic could start on a US meat or fur farm—but the way things are going, it could start anywhere.

Today, Earth and all the animals—including humans—who live on it are in crisis. And that's why Poorva's book is so vital, especially for my children Avyaan and Samaira, for your children and for our future generations. This book comes at a crucial time. Scientists warn that we do not have much time before the numerous environmental and public health threats facing us become even more catastrophic.

Young people deserve a kinder, cleaner and healthier world than what it is currently on a path to becoming. That's why, when I'm not acting, I'm working with People for the Ethical Treatment of Animals (PETA) to encourage schoolchildren to consider the importance of keeping elephants and other animals in their jungle homes and of ensuring that those homes are safe. I also invest in brands and companies that care for people and our planet.

In fact, these days much of my time and energy is devoted to animal welfare, conservation and environmental action. This is because it is urgent and because I have a moral obligation to help animals and a parental duty to safeguard my children. And so, I contribute the best I can to making a difference through working with the United Nations and other effective organizations.

I know Poorva has written this book because she feels a responsibility to act, too. She has personally visited slaughterhouses, laboratories and other operations where animals are used—places she finds devastating and frightening—but she has done it so that she can knowledgeably tell us what's really going on. She wants us to know what animals' wellbeing means for our own.

The premise of this book is that it's not just nice to consider animals, it is necessary for our own preservation. To not do so would be to harm ourselves and could even mean our demise. She explains the important role every animal plays in nature—from a tiny beetle to a huge beluga whale—how our fates are intertwined, how animals face many human-caused threats in every corner of the world, and how those threats, in turn, affect our own welfare. These threats include the bulldozing of rainforests for land on which to produce animal-derived foods, the effluents created by the leather industry that leads to cancer in tannery workers, the decimation of life in the sea and its effect on the planet's oxygen levels, the butchering of wild animals for meat or capturing them for use in laboratories, the outbreak of zoonotic diseases, the poisoning of insects and the risk to our food sources.

Poorva also writes about who animals are and what we know about them today. For instance, bees are self-aware, fish use tools and cows grieve. She explains how they are all similar to us in all the ways that matter—every one of us can feel pain and suffering.

Today's 'new normal' is pandemics and epidemics, climate change and pollution, endangered animals and extinction, and injustice and societal violence. But it doesn't have to be this way. Poorva equips us with the knowledge to make informed choices and helps us to navigate our mindset—from one of exploiting nature to that of recognizing ourselves as only one part in the vast orchestra of life. She gives us hope that with more respect for the world around us, the dangers we face today can melt away. To help us find our way, the book ends with a guide that includes easy steps we can take to heal our own species and help our home recover.

I hope you read this book and then pass it on.

Dia Mirza
Actor,
UN Secretary General's Advocate for
Sustainable Development Goals
and UN Environmental Programme Goodwill Ambassador

INTRODUCTION

So hell-bent are most of us on insisting that we are not animals, despite the fact that we poop and reproduce and other evidence to the contrary, that People for the Ethical Treatment of Animals (PETA) and its global entities recently erected billboards starring award-winning actor Joaquin Phoenix in major cities from New Delhi to Los Angeles reading 'We Are All Animals', including in New York City's famous Times Square.

Phoenix was a natural choice to front the campaign. In his Oscars acceptance speech after winning the Best Actor Award for *Joker*, he said, 'I think, whether we're talking about gender inequality or racism or queer rights or indigenous rights or animal rights, we're talking about the fight against injustice. We're talking about the fight against the belief that one nation, one people, one race, one gender, one species, has the right to dominate, use and control another with impunity. I think we've become very disconnected from the natural world. Many of us are guilty of an egocentric world view, and we believe that we're the centre of the universe. We go into the natural world and we plunder it for its resources. We fear the idea of personal change, because we think we need to sacrifice something; to give something up. But human beings at our best are so creative and inventive, and we can create, develop and implement systems of change that are beneficial to all sentient beings and the environment.'[1]

One month and one day after Phoenix's speech, the World Health Organization (WHO) declared Covid-19, a disease that many scientists believe came about from going into the natural world and plundering it, a pandemic.[2] The WHO continues to try to trace the origins of Covid-19 to the best degree possible, but a leading view of virologists[3] is that it is a zoonotic spillover—that is, it has *spilled over* from an animal or animals to humans. Today, the Joker is reminding us that we are part of the natural world, and in 2003, it was 'The Batman', better known as Linfa Wang, a biologist and executive director of PREPARE (Programme for Research in Epidemic Preparedness and Responses) in Singapore, who helped determine SARS probably infected humans from bats through an intermediary animal host, civet cats.[4] Now, numerous scientists have come to the same idea: Covid-19 likely emerged in bats,[5] found an intermediary animal host, and then spread to humans thanks to China's colossal wildlife trade (for meat, furs and traditional medicines).[6]

Wild animals from a marketplace in Guangdong are the believed origin of SARS in humans,[7] and the now infamous Huanan Seafood Wholesale Market in Wuhan provided a similar opportunity for the emergence or spread of Covid-19. (One theory is that Covid-19 developed on a wildlife farm and was then transported to the Huanan market, where, thanks to the opportunity provided, it exploded.[8]) Experts tell us crowded markets like these, where live animals, often of a variety of species, are caged next to and on top of one another, allowing their bodily fluids to mix easily and where they are often cut apart, provide the perfect environment in which viruses can percolate, adapt and jump species, including to our own.

It's not just our treatment and use of wild animals, however, that should be of concern. In 1997, the first-ever human infections of the H5N1 strain of bird flu—which has plagued poultry farms from India to Europe and beyond—coincided with it being found in chickens at farms and live animal markets in Hong Kong.[9] Crowding, particularly in factory farms, facilitates disease spread. When humans get infected with this strain, the mortality rate is many times worse than what it is for Covid-19: about 60 per cent.[10]

The second line of the Joaquin Phoenix PETA advertisement reads, 'End speciesism'. For most of us, our relationship with non-human animals (henceforth, 'animals') is based on an assumption of human superiority—or speciesism, a bias in favour of our own species, just as racism is typically a bias in favour of one's own skin colour, and sexism a bias, usually referred to in relation to men, in favour of their own gender. And as is historically the case with other 'ism's, speciesism is today so prevalent that it is usually regarded as truth, with other perspectives often dismissed and even ridiculed. This is traditionally so especially in Western cultures. 'They're just animals' we may say as we cut them to pieces for taste, peel off their skin for shoes, poison them in product experiments, beat them for entertainment and use them for other human desires, and everyone will understand exactly what we mean. That is, that we consider their being animals alone enough to justify anything we may do to them for any reason.

Or, as Phoenix put it, 'we believe that we're the centre of the universe'. Ingrid Newkirk is the founder of PETA entities worldwide. Her work was featured in the 2007 HBO documentary named along the same theme as the Phoenix ad—*I am an Animal: The Story of Ingrid Newkirk and PETA*. In a speech given a few years ago, she said, 'Animals' interests are being ignored because allowing their oppression is advantageous. And that will continue as long as people are allowed to get away with the idea that only humans deserve consideration of their interests.'[11]

But now, Covid-19 has given the world a stinging wake-up call: that speciesism, or rather an 'egocentric world view', can form the basis for much of our own suffering and that it is not, in fact, advantageous to consider only the microcosm of certain business benefits while disregarding animals' well-being. In other words, ignoring the larger picture comes at our own peril. Indeed, by December 2020, the pandemic had already cost the global economy the equivalent of USD 6.7 trillion, and in the first half of 2020, working hours equivalent to 555 million full-time jobs worldwide were lost.[12] That year, the Centre for Risk Studies at the University of Cambridge Judge Business School warned that the pandemic's bill could amount up to USD 82 trillion in losses over the next five years.[13] In contrast, the meat industry, for example, turns over just about USD 1 trillion a year.[14]

Global lockdowns showed us with painful clarity that the fear of 'personal change' and the 'need to sacrifice something' that Phoenix spoke about will be forced upon us if we do not start living in a way more harmonious with nature. Elizabeth Mrema, executive secretary of the United Nations Convention on Biological Diversity, put it plainly in a conversation with *The Guardian*: 'The message we are getting is if we don't take care of nature, it will take care of us.'[15]

A more scientific sounding word for speciesism is anthropocentrism. Arguments in favour of anthropocentrism, the philosophical belief that 'we're the centre of the universe'—that we are the most important creatures on Earth and that nature exists merely for us to use—were made by ancient Greek philosophers, helping to pave the way for how we largely tend to view and treat animals and the planet, even today.

Certain influential early thinkers considered animals as lacking intelligence and consciousness. Aristotle, for instance, assumed animals lacked rationality and fit between humans and plants in a natural hierarchy, with humans on top. Aristotle understood all three to have life, animals to be able to sense the world around them and believed humans alone possess the ability for rationalization (including reason and language).[16] In *Politics*, Aristotle expressed that, '[A]fter the birth of animals, plants exist for their sake, and that the other animals exist for the sake of man, the tame for use and food, the wild, if not all at least the greater part of them, for food, and for the provision of clothing and various instruments. Now if nature makes nothing incomplete, and nothing in vain, the inference must be that she has made all animals for the sake of man.'[17]

Hundreds of years later, in the 1600s, French mathematician, scientist and philosopher René Descartes contended that animals simply mindlessly, and without consciousness or self-awareness, react to stimuli—like machines.[18] Anyone who has a relationship with a dog or a cat would recognize this as a deeply flawed conclusion, but today anthropocentric arguments are still used to justify violence against animals.

Crispon Sartwell, associate professor of philosophy at Dickinson College, Pennsylvania, wrote a piece for *The New York Times* titled, 'Humans Are Animals. Let's Get Over It.' In it, he hilariously describes Western philosophy's obsession with trying to convince ourselves that we are not animals. He wrote, 'The Great Philosopher will, before addressing himself to the deep ethical and metaphysical questions, pause for the conventional, ground-clearing declaration: "I am definitely not a squirrel." This is evidently something that needs continual emphasizing.' Sartwell ponders, 'But if we truly believed we were so much better than squirrels, why have we spent thousands of years driving home the point?'

Sartwell observes that the same arguments used to differentiate animals from humans are, in fact, also made to draw a line between 'beastly' humans and those who are deemed to be civilized. He points to a passage in *Politics* by Aristotle that reads, 'Where then there is such a difference as that between soul and body, or between men and animals (as in the case of those whose business is to use their body, and who can do nothing better), the lower sort are by nature slaves, and it is better for them as for all inferiors that they should be under the rule of a master.'[19] What a convenient excuse for the enslavement of humans if some can be labelled, by this logic, like animals, and if animals are neither reasoning nor self-aware. I am reminded of the words of American civil rights activist Martin Luther King Junior: 'Injustice anywhere is a threat to justice everywhere.'[20]

Dominant as speciesism may be, it is just a philosophical stand. Take Jains for instance, who have regarded animals—all animals, no matter how large or small—as conscious and worthy of respect for thousands of years. Jains live by the principle of ahimsa, that is, to live without causing harm to any living being. Jain monks take great care not to harm even the tiniest insects as they walk or inhale. Meanwhile, in Hinduism, which also has the concept of ahimsa, a revered god is not always in human form but can have animal features: Lord Ganesha with the head of an elephant and Hanuman, who appears in the form of a monkey in temples, which are often thronged by wild ones in India.

Jains and other religions, cultures, communities, organizations, and individuals who are merciful to animals encourage the challenging of speciesist views. They help question the widely held notions that animals are essentially unthinking or unfeeling, and encourage us to reconsider how we regard and behave towards animals—a task that we increasingly recognize as a must, as their well-being, as Covid-19 reminds us, is inseparably linked to our own. This is not a new concept to Jains. A Jain considers harming others, including animals, as harming oneself.[21]

As is the case with all faiths, not all Jain beliefs are backed by science (ahimsa can even extend to bacteria).[22] But today, more and more scientists are discovering Jains may have been on to something all along—including about insects.

For instance, scientists tell us bumblebees can recognize an object by touch or sight, as humans can across senses. We do this by imagining the object in our brains and it is likely bees do this too. Scientists are conservative about labelling bees as conscious as the concept is not well-defined, yet they cannot help but admit this demonstrates a likelihood of consciousness in bees. Bees can also learn by observing other bees, recognize human faces and do basic math.[23]

Scientists now tell us animals can be cleverer than us, too. Dr Arthur Saniotis, an anthropologist with University of Adelaide's School of Medical Sciences, has remarked, 'For millennia, all kinds of authorities—from religion to eminent scholars—have been repeating the same idea ad nauseam, that humans are exceptional by virtue that they are the smartest in the animal kingdom. However, science tells us that animals can have cognitive faculties that are superior to human beings.'[24]

When we consider that different species of animals require different abilities to thrive in their natural environments, this makes sense. A gibbon does not need to know how to file taxes, but she must be able to recognize which branches are the strongest at a glance—gibbons travel up to 15 metres with each swing and move faster than 55 kilometres an hour across the jungle canopy.[25] What if intelligence tests were based on this or some of the countless other impressive traits animals have that we don't? They are typically not, only because humans create these tests with just human qualities in mind.

Dolphins and other toothed whales use echolocation for navigating the ocean and finding food,[26] elephants appear to communicate over miles through foot-stomping,[27] tigers and many other species leave complex messages through olfactory markings,[28] pigeons use the Earth's magnetic field to find their way over vast distances[29]—the list goes on. Humans cannot naturally do any of these or many other things animals can do. We can only attempt to understand the full breadth of how animals make use of the information they gather through the unique ways they perceive the world.

Maciej Henneberg, professor of anthropological and comparative anatomy at University of Adelaide, says, 'The fact that they [animals] may not understand us, while we do not understand them, does not mean our "intelligences" are at different levels, they are just of different kinds. When a foreigner tries to communicate with us using an imperfect, broken, version of our language, our impression is that they are not very intelligent. But the reality is quite different.'[30]

In the *New York Times* article mentioned previously, Sartwell writes that we have long been fixated on how we are different from animals, and that these differences may be no greater than how animals differ from each other. And that perhaps it's high time we focused on how similar we are to animals. Indeed, doing so may allow us to better connect with the natural world.

Scientists now know chickens show signs of self-awareness, can count, have a variety of vocalizations with different meanings (in other words, talk) and can even be deceptive.[31] They have shown us through ethically questionable experiments that fish express feeling pain—not in an automaton type of way—but human-like, such as by rocking[32] and hyperventilating,[33] and that when given a choice, crustaceans choose to avoid pain.[34] They also tell us that fish, along with many species of animals use tools[35]—a trait once considered only human. And that ravens, elephants, chimpanzees and lions are among the animals who use rationality to make decisions.[36] Indeed, ravens are so bright that at a mere four months old, they perform comparable to adult chimpanzees and orangutans in various tests.[37]

Marc Bekoff, professor emeritus of ecology and evolutionary biology at the University of Colorado, Boulder, has extensively studied animal behaviour and minds. In a paper published in 2000 in *BioScience* he wrote, '[C]urrent research provides compelling evidence that at least some animals likely feel a full range of emotions, including fear, joy, happiness, shame, embarrassment, resentment, jealousy, rage, anger, love, pleasure, compassion, respect, relief, disgust, sadness, despair, and grief.'[38] Since then, we've learned a lot more about the emotional capabilities of animals of many species.

If we have dogs or cats at home, we can see they experience joy from play and know that play is essential for their physical and mental well-being. But now we know fish also play. Gordon Burghardt, a professor at the University of Tennessee, Knoxville, defined play as 'repeated behavior that is incompletely functional in the context or at the age in which it is performed and is initiated voluntarily when the animal or person is in a relaxed or low-stress setting.' Over years, he and his colleagues recorded cichlid fish species playing, as he defines it, with a thermometer and other objects.[39]

Now a new study shows octopuses not only feel pain physically, but also appear to feel it emotionally—like mammals. Neurobiologist Robyn Crook from San Francisco State University applied the same method that was used for testing pain in rodents on octopuses. She reports octopuses' behaviour demonstrates that they appear to experience a negative emotional state, like rodents do, when in pain.[40]

Today, much evidence also indicates animals grieve. Mother cows and buffaloes are commonly separated from their calves on dairy farms so that the farmers can sell their milk. As male calves cannot produce milk, around the world, they are commonly used for veal or outright killed.

John Avizienius, who works on farm animal issues for the UK Royal Society for the Prevention of Cruelty to Animals (RSPCA), remembers a cow who was visibly upset for almost two months after her calf was taken away. She would stand by the pen where she last saw her calf and bellow, moving from there only by force. Day after day, she would stop at the pen. Calves mourn being separated from their mothers too. Researchers have observed they cry and can stop being interested in food.[41]

Some species even have rituals regarding death. Shifra Goldenberg was a doctoral student at the Colorado State University when she captured an elephant mourning ritual on film. After a matriarch of an elephant herd in the Samburu National Reserve in Kenya died, Goldenberg filmed how elephants returned weeks later to fondle and smell the bones.[42]

Dante de Kort also caught an animal funeral on tape. He was eight years old when he set up a camera near a dead collared peccary (pig-like animal) in the US for a science fair project. His recording revealed that over ten days, until coyotes ate the remains, other peccaries nuzzled, sniffed at and even slept near the body.[43] While we cannot ask these elephants or the peccaries how they felt, their behaviours indicate loss.

And do animals fall in love? How nice it would be if we could ask Wisdom, the world's oldest known bird. She is a Laysan albatross who recently hatched a chick at the impressive age of seventy. She's just a few years younger than my own mother. She has been raising chicks with her partner Akeakami since 2010, having outlived others.[44]

Dr Claudia Vinke is with the Behavioural Clinic for Animals, Faculty of Veterinary Medicine at Utrecht University. In an article about whether animals fall in love, she wrote, 'There is the longing to be together (forming a bond), being in love itself (a period of no inhibitions in order to enter into an intimate relationship with someone) and sexual cravings (lust).'[45] She points out animals certainly form bonds—Wisdom and Akeakami surely have—and like for many of us, sex plays a role. Many animals also engage in long, even monogamous relationships. This includes bald eagles, who will find the same partner every mating season, and macaroni penguins, who dance upon seeing each other again.[46] Something surely makes these animals desire to stay with the same partner year after year. Why should we assume their motivations are wildly different from why many of us do?

Mark Rowlands, professor of philosophy at the University of Miami, argues various animals even demonstrate morals.[47] There are numerous videos and stories of animals helping other animals or animals helping humans on the internet that support this view. One of the more famous ones is of a gorilla who protected a young boy who had fallen into her enclosure at a zoo,[48] another is of a parrot who cried 'Mama, baby!' thereby saving the life of a choking girl,[49] yet another shows elephants working together to free a calf who was stuck in a mud pit.[50] There are videos of dogs helping other dogs, such as one from Chile in which a dog worked to drag another dog who had been hit on a highway to safety.[51] A similar scene was captured on video between two dogs in Istanbul.[52] In another video, a monkey in India appears to successfully revive another monkey who had been electrocuted by biting and hitting him and dipping his body in water.[53] In an experiment, rhesus monkeys kept hungry would not electrically shock other monkeys to get food.[54]

Rowlands told *LiveScience*, 'I think what's at the heart of following morality is the emotions. Evidence suggests that animals can act on those sorts of emotions.'

It shouldn't come as such a shock to us that animals, like us, feel pain, experience emotions and are not simply machines who mindlessly react to stimuli—that they have cognitive acumen, they *think*. As the Joaquin Phoenix PETA billboard says, 'We Are All Animals'. Today, it is scientifically recognized that we are primates who share a common ape ancestor with bonobos and chimpanzees,[55] making them our cousins.

But we are also fish. You read that right. Evolutionarily speaking. We descended from tetrapods as did other amphibians, reptiles and mammals—and indeed, we are tetrapods (as are birds, even though it means 'four feet'). We evolved from a fish-like creature who lived in water.[56] Through gradual changes the first land vertebrates emerged. Palaeontologist Neil Shubin, author of *Your Inner Fish*, which is about our 375-million-year-old ancestor, observes our hands bear a resemblance to fossil amphibian fins and our various other body parts correspond to ancient jellyfish and other fish-like animals.[57]

Now there are efforts to prove not only that humans are animals, but that animals are persons, of a sort. That's because with the recognition of animal consciousness, intelligence, emotion and even morality, must come our own moral responsibilities toward other species. We cannot continue to operate as if animals are unthinking, unfeeling beings—machines—when science today tells a different story.

And so, there have been efforts in various courts to grant certain species the legal status of 'non-human persons'. This doesn't mean that they are declared human or will now be allowed to vote—it means they can be represented in court for their own interests and rights. In India, in 2018, the Uttarakhand High Court deemed the status of a 'legal person or entity' to animals in that state, declaring 'they have a distinct persona with corresponding rights, duties and liabilities of a living person'. The bench explained the status was 'to protect and promote greater welfare of animals, including avian and aquatic, [and for this] animals are required to be conferred with the status of legal entity/legal person'.[58] Also in India, in 2019, the Punjab and Haryana High Court declared all animals 'legal persons' and citizens of the states their 'guardians'.[59] In 2015, a court in Argentina granted an orangutan the status of legal 'non-human persons'. This set the stage for lonely orangutan Sandra to be shifted to a sanctuary after spending much of her life in a solitary enclosure at the Buenos Aires Zoo.[60]

If we accept that we are animals, interconnected to other species, similar to them in ways that matter and are a part of, rather than holding dominance over, nature, then we can begin to open our eyes to why our treatment of animals, and how we use them, affects us—from the largest elephant to the smallest bee.

And of course, bees are key to human survival. In fact, if bees die, so may we. They pollinate many of the crop species that feed us. Yet, bee populations are declining at an alarming rate for reasons such as human-caused climate change, habitat loss and our use of pesticides. But just as how kindly we treat bees is inextricably linked to how considerate we're being to ourselves, so is how we treat other animals.

THE PANGOLIN, THE BAT AND THE CIVET CAT

Three days before the end of 2020, one of the most challenging years many of us have faced in our lives, I stood in my kitchen, wondering whether to have coffee or tea when I coughed. It wasn't really a cough though, I reasoned; I was just clearing my throat.

I poured a brew into my favourite mug and switched on the news. I had been stuck in London for much of the pandemic, and that's where I was. The television screamed: 'The UK has recorded its highest number of new daily infections! The new UK variant appears more contagious! Ambulances are being forced to queue outside hospitals!' Gosh, this is bad, I frowned, as I coughed again. Ahem, ahem—I purposefully cleared my throat, an attempt to prove to myself I was doing just that.

Except, as the day went on, every so often, I kept being forced to clear my throat. I googled the symptoms I had read about so many times before: 'a new, continuous cough—this means coughing a lot for more than an hour, or 3 or more coughing episodes in 24 hours (if you usually have a cough, it may be worse than usual)', the UK National Health Service (NHS) website said.[1] *Am I coughing a lot, am I having coughing episodes?* I pondered. The cough could hardly be called that at the time—it was only occasional, mild. Plus, the country had been in lockdown and I had been strictly following the rules. I hadn't met anyone or been anywhere besides the grocery store. There, I had worn a mask, and when I had got home, I had washed my hands. Not terribly worried, I went to bed.

The following day I was catching up on emails, and the next thing I knew, I was waking up on the couch. *How did I fall asleep? What the heck, that never happens. How long was I out?* I got up and rummaged through my drawers, looking for the thermometer I had purchased at the start of the pandemic, months earlier. I finally found it and put it in my mouth.

It read 37.8°C. That's a fever. Now I was a little nervous, especially as the UK vaccine rollout was new and hadn't yet hit my age group. *But people still have colds and flus*, I told myself. *Surely, that's all it is.* But as I monitored my fluctuating fever throughout the day, I grew more concerned. By the time I went to sleep again, my cough was persistent and my fever had climbed to 39°C.

On New Year's Eve, I paid for a rapid test, wanting to know fast what ailed me. Three hours later, I found out: it was Covid-19. Our brains try to protect us from pain, so my first reaction, despite having symptoms and knowing better, was disbelief. *These tests can be wrong.* I ordered a slower test provided by the NHS, which confirmed what I already knew. I considered whether to tell my family. They were in another country and it would worry them greatly, but then again, what if I had to be hospitalized? What if I died?

As anyone who received a Covid-19 positive result at that stage in the pandemic or has a loved one who did knows, each day thereon passed with tremendous anxiety as you monitored symptoms and hoped things didn't get worse. A *New York Times* article I had come across then read, 'While every patient is different, doctors say that days five through 10 of the illness are often the most worrisome time for respiratory complications of Covid-19 … Younger patients who develop complications may begin struggling a little later, as late as days 10 to 12.'[2] I am neither young nor old. I marked days five, ten and fifteen on my calendar as a countdown to, I hoped, better health. I ultimately decided to tell family members, and they called frantically, every day, until I recovered.

Although I googled obsessively about Covid-19 when I caught the disease, as if I would find some miracle news that would make me feel less fearful—*maybe they discovered a medicine that helps since the last time I checked*—I already knew plenty about the illness. Not so much regarding how it manifests in the human body, but about how such diseases typically emerge. In fact, I had been giving media interviews about this for much of that year.

It was because in my previous book, *For a Moment of Taste: How What You Eat Impacts Animals, the Planet and Your Health*, which I had written before anyone knew what Covid-19 was (although it was published after), I had warned it is a 'ripe time for a pandemic of deadly flu'. I'm not a psychic and own no crystal ball. I don't need to—we've had ample deadly warning shots and experts have long been crying themselves hoarse that we're in grave danger if things don't change.

Most new emerging diseases affecting humans over the last several decades—a whopping 75 per cent—are zoonotic.[3] That is, they spread from animals to humans and, worryingly, the frequency of pathogens circulating in animals spilling over to humans and the variety of them has been accelerating, particularly over the last ten years.[4] Among zoonotic diseases are SARS, HIV, Ebola, various bird flus, swine flus, likely Covid-19 and many more. As disease detectives, we only need to ask ourselves what's changed recently that would increase the likelihood of humans catching animal diseases. The answer is simple: our intensified and relentless meddling with nature. Today, as experts warn, our constant generation of plentiful opportunities for pathogens to pass between species and to our own is nothing short of 'playing with fire'.[5]

Many virologists say that we should have seen Covid-19 coming. Only about seventeen years before it was first identified, there was SARS, which, like Covid-19, is a respiratory disease. Both Covid-19 and SARS stem from the coronavirus family of viruses and disease trackers largely believe the first infections of humans occurred similarly: through wildlife who are commonly caged and cut apart in live animal markets (referred to as 'wet markets' by many, with the phrase coming from the water and ice used to keep items fresh, but in reality not all wet markets are wildlife markets and some vendors only sell produce).

At the time of writing, over 6.9 million people worldwide have died from Covid-19,[6] and counting. That's essentially like striking Libya off the map.[7] SARS too was a pandemic of global concern—it spread fast to over thirty countries, resulting in the deaths of some 11 per cent of people who caught it.[8] Through coordinated efforts, quarantine and World Health Organization (WHO) involvement, by July 2003, SARS was fortunately contained.[9]

While SARS and Covid-19 symptoms are similar, Covid-19 proved far trickier to control. It spreads earlier in the illness and more easily than SARS,[10] and as we now all know, often without any symptoms present whatsoever. Indeed, I seemed to get it from proximity to someone who, unless they were simply reckless, believed themselves to be healthy enough to walk around a grocery store.

Initial SARS cases pointed to live animal markets and restaurants in Guangdong, China, and those who sold or handled wildlife for meat. A team led by renowned virologist Yi Guan of Hong Kong University and researchers from the Centre for Disease Control Shenzhen, China, found coronavirus nearly identical to the SARS in humans in masked palm civets (nocturnal, arboreal animals commonly referred to as civet cats) and a raccoon dog (who are not raccoons at all but part of the dog family) in a market in Guangdong. There, they also found antibodies against SARS in Chinese ferret badgers.

People connected to this and other similar markets in Guangdong were also tested for antibodies matching with SARS indicating previous infection. As a result, numerous civet cat dealers and dozens of other wildlife handlers tested positive for them.[11]

Two patients with SARS were associated with a restaurant in Guangzhou, the capital of Guangdong province. One was a twenty-year-old server, the other a forty-year-old customer who had sat close to civet cat cages. The restaurant served civet cat meat, and while the server said she never ate it, she worked near the animals and their dead bodies. Researchers tested six civet cats at the restaurant who had been purchased from a nearby animal wholesale market, and all were found to be infected with the SARS-like coronavirus.[12]

China was under the world's spotlight and facing pressure to act on SARS. It banned the hunting, sale and movement of wild animals in southern China[13]—a positive move—but also embarked on a frenzied killing spree of civet cats, badgers and other animals. Feng Liuxiang, who was with Guangdong's health bureau, proudly declared, 'We will kill all the civet cats in Guangdong markets, which number about 10,000. We will start a patriotic health campaign to kill rats and cockroaches in order to give every place a thorough cleaning for the lunar New Year.'[14] Local reports described caged civet cats and other animals were being drowned, and a man from the Guangzhou Hygiene Supervision Bureau anonymously told press, 'We first put them in disinfectant to sterilize them, then electrocute them, then burn them.'[15]

Local animal protection advocates condemned the cruel killings, while WHO warned that destroying civet cats in a haphazard, rushed manner could lead to more SARS infections or even prevent additional discoveries about the source of the disease.[16] Nevertheless, China was on a lethal mission.

The wildlife trade ban came into effect at the end of April of 2003, and by August of that year, a person could be forgiven for thinking it was little more than a show. China's Forestry Administration issued a circular stating dozens of species of wildlife, including civet cats, could be used as pets and for meat so long as they were raised on farms, rather than caught in the wild. A forestry department official said this was to support the wild animal farming industry.[17] Business as usual.

Today, scientists consider civet cats to be just the intermediary host,[18] the 'mixing vessel' as they often call them, between bats and humans for SARS. 'Mixing vessel' animals can connect two species who may otherwise rarely meet and allow diseases to adapt to be able to better infect and spread between other animals and humans. A perfect chance for such a mix is where a variety of species come together, such as a crowded farm, certain restaurants and live animal markets.

Just as early cases of SARS led to markets in Guangdong, early cases of Covid-19 led to a market in Wuhan: with patients located around the Huanan Seafood Wholesale Market. Swabs taken from surfaces and items in the market after it was forced shut on 1 January 2020, particularly from the section where wildlife were traded, tested positive for SARS-CoV-2 (that is, the virus that causes Covid-19). The physical link to the market was so striking, a team of top scientists from the US, the UK, Canada, Netherlands, Belgium and Australia banded together on a paper confidently titled 'The Huanan Seafood Wholesale Market in Wuhan was the early epicenter of the COVID-19 pandemic'. It was published in *Science* in July 2022.[19]

The market was known locally as the place to go to for exotic fare. Shortly after the world's attention was focused on it, a price list apparently from one of the market's vendors circulated on the web listing over one hundred items of either live animals or products made from them such as foxes, deer, camels, crocodiles, ostriches, wolf puppies, giant salamanders, snakes, rats, peacocks, porcupines—and even the previously problematic civet cats.[20] Coronaviruses exist in a large number of animals and frequently mutate. In fact since the pandemic began, at least thirty species have been found to be susceptible to Covid-19. China's business as usual strategy meant a similar route thought to be followed by SARS was still laid out for this disease.

When the public focus turned to a live animal market as a possible origin for Covid-19, in a video by American news site Vox, Dr Peter J. Li, associate professor of political science at the University of Houston-Downtown, said, 'It was not a surprise at all. And I think it was not a surprise to many scientists. The cages are stacked one over another. Animals at the bottom are often soaked with all kinds of liquid. Animal excrement, pus, blood.'[21] Animals are sold at such markets following often long and stressful transport and many arrive at the destination sick or injured—further adding to the already perfect setting to spread disease.

Another popular theory is that SARS-CoV-2 escaped from the Wuhan Institute of Virology, which studies coronaviruses avowedly for public safety. There is inconsistency in how people think this occurred. For instance, some say Covid-19 was created purposefully and secretly there as a biological weapon, others that the kind of research happening at this laboratory was dangerous and got out of hand, or that a fieldworker became infected by a wild bat, or a researcher accidentally infected themselves in the facility.

In an August 2022 piece he wrote for the Conversation, Professor Edward C. Holmes, one of the authors of the *Science* paper, argues against some of these ideas stating, among other things, 'For the lab leak theory to be true, SARS-CoV-2 must have been present in the Wuhan Institute of Virology before the pandemic started. This would convince me. But the inconvenient truth is there's not a single piece of data suggesting this. There's no evidence for a genome sequence or isolate of a precursor virus at the Wuhan Institute of Virology. Not from gene sequence databases, scientific publications, annual reports, student theses, social media, or emails. Even the intelligence community has found nothing. Nothing. And there was no reason to keep any work on a SARS-CoV-2 ancestor secret before the pandemic.'[22]

As of 26 July 2023, the US intelligence community says 'there is no evidence that the coronavirus research at the Wuhan lab could have been a precursor to the virus that causes Covid…' according to an article in *The New York Times*.[23] The piece explains per latest American intelligence, Wuhan laboratory workers who fell sick—something proponents of the laboratory leak theory point to—may not have had Covid-19 after all but something else especially as not all symptoms they experienced matched this disease. It also shares that five US intelligence agencies favour the view that Covid-19 infected humans through a natural route rather than a laboratory incident.

Meanwhile, in a lengthy *The New York Times Magazine* piece[24] published at the end of July 2023 that takes readers through all of the popular Covid-19 origin theories in detail by science writer David Quammen called 'The Ongoing Mystery of Covid's Origin', he shares his considered view that, 'I agree it's important to remain open-minded toward a lab-leak possibility, but most of the arguments made in support of that possibility boil down to conjecture from circumstance and unsupported accusations.'

He also refers to a *The Sunday Times* piece about the idea that Covid-19 is an engineered weapon. He observes, 'The reporters didn't name their intelligence sources or supply evidence to make their allegations concrete, but if they did, it would be explosive news.' Quammen's full article is well worth a read.

In this chapter, I focus on the speculation with the most substantial publicly available evidence so far. And the clues that point to animals who were sold at the Huanan market are significant. It is also the speculation that aligns with how other animal coronaviruses have infected humans in the past. And ultimately, whatever is concluded regarding the origin of Covid-19, if anything is ever conclusively decided at all, SARS and numerous other illnesses show tremendous zoonotic disease risk from markets like Huanan. This makes understanding the dangers they pose important regardless of the origin of Covid-19—a truth that may never be found due to active secrecy on China's part at the start of the pandemic to either protect its image, safeguard its wildlife product industries or as some claim (with little publicly available proof so far), because secret work on this coronavirus was taking place.

Notably, wildlife were quickly confiscated and removed from the Huanan market before anyone external could investigate,[25] and Chinese authorities' initial response was to deny that its vendors sold live mammals or illegal wildlife,[26] contrary to evidence that it did.

Nevertheless, the study published in *Science* in July 2022 describes research that found SARS-CoV-2 divided into A and B lineages before February 2020. We know today that there are different types of Covid-19, that is, distinct variants, and this is the same. This paper reads, '[A]ll of the circumstantial evidence so far points to more than one zoonotic event occurring in Huanan market in Wuhan, China, likely during November–December 2019.'[27] Holmes explains, 'Further analyses suggest the A and B lineages were the products of separate jumps from animals. This simply means there was a pool of infected animals in the Huanan market, fuelling multiple exposure events.'[28]

Today, the search is still on to try to identify the specific, most plausible animal origin of Covid-19. Bats are a natural reservoir of coronaviruses and do not get ill from them, but it is generally considered unlikely for them to have infected us with Covid-19 directly. So far, a direct SARS-CoV-2-like bat virus with the capability of affecting human cells has not been found.[29] That's where a mixing vessel comes in, and research as of March 2023 points to racoon dogs as a strong candidate[30] (remember them from SARS?). Just as civet cats have been identified as the probable mixing vessel that led to SARS in humans, camels are considered the mixing vessel for

MERS, another respiratory disease affecting humans, also caused by a coronavirus and also thought to originate in bats.[31]

Pangolins are small, gentle, endangered creatures who roll into a ball when they feel threatened and resemble artichokes. As recently as August 2022, researchers published a paper in *International Journal of Molecular Sciences* stating their view that, 'Based on our comparative analysis, we support the view that the Guangdong Pangolins are the intermediate hosts that adapted the SARS-CoV-2 and represented a significant evolutionary link in the path of transmission of SARS-CoV-2 virus.'[32] (The Guangdong specification is because that's where the samples deemed to fit were collected from. There are eight species of pangolins in Asia and Africa.)[33]

In tracing where the animals who were sold at the market came from, as mentioned earlier, scientists are considering whether Covid-19 developed somewhere else, such as on a wildlife farm and then ended up at the Huanan market,[34] where the crowding and general market conditions provided an excellent opportunity for disease spread. Bats were apparently not for sale at the Huanan market[35] and, as per one study, pangolins were not either.[36] But pangolins are commonly smuggled into China for trade,[37] and some farmed animals sold at the Huanan market were from areas in China where bats and pangolins infected with coronaviruses comparable to SARS-CoV-2 had been discovered.[38]

Dr Diana Bell is a professor of conservation biology at the University of East Anglia in the UK. She and her colleagues have long been sounding the alarm that the wildlife trade—one of the most lucrative illegal trades in the world after drugs, human trafficking and counterfeiting[39]—puts human health and biodiversity in jeopardy. She has warned that today's zoonotic disease crisis is due to, in large part, wildlife trafficking. This includes species being crammed or transported together and otherwise mixing thanks to this trade, and new regions being targeted for wildlife capture when animal populations decline.[40] None of these activities are limited to China.

Pangolins are the most trafficked mammals in the world. They are used for meat not only in China, but also in Vietnam and for both African and Asian traditional medicine. They are commonly trafficked from Africa to Asia through a network of organized, international gangs, and the trade is growing.[41]

Whether animals are caught or reared and traded for meat, fur, to be kept as pets, for traditional medicine over myths about virility or other supposed benefits, or for any other purpose, the risk of zoonotic disease exists. In February of 2020, China took steps to curb the sale and consumption of much wildlife. At that time, it was reported that nearly 20,000 wildlife farms breeding a huge variety of species such as civet cats, peacocks, ostriches, bamboo rats, wild boar, foxes, pigeons and many others had been closed.

But wild animals are not only used for food. Their use for other purposes such as traditional medicine, fur and leather (including for items sold abroad), was still allowed.[42] Today, China seems to be easing these restrictions.[43]

Due to past experience with SARS, the world's attention was on the dangers of live animal markets and the wildlife trade as soon as Covid-19 emerged. And yet, since WHO declared the pandemic, PETA entities have filmed such blood and urine-soaked, faeces-ridden and crowded markets in full swing in numerous Asian countries. In these markets, most workers and customers handled the animals or their body parts with their bare hands; animals were often found to be dying or sick; and they were stabbed and sliced while fully conscious.

Most of India's indigenous wild animals are protected under its Wildlife Protection Act, 1972, and 2022 amendment from hunting and capture, but PETA India has released video footage of wildlife meat markets thriving in parts of the country taken both before and after the start of the pandemic.[44] Their footage documents vendors at various markets selling the charred or raw remains of wild animals—including monkeys, wild boars, porcupines and deer. It shows frogs clamouring for air in plastic bags, buckets full of live eels jostling for space as well as mice and various birds such as pigeons and quails in cages stacked on top of each other and ducks in pen-like enclosures waiting to be sold or killed. For the species protected under India's wildlife legislation, PETA India has reported the trade to relevant authorities, including the country's Wildlife Crime Control Bureau, and has pushed for enforcement. At the time of writing, there is, however, no corrective government action to report.

Also in India, dogs are not listed as a species that can be eaten by the country's Food Safety and Standards Authority, and while it is nowhere near as common as the use of other species for food, dogs *are* killed for meat there. PETA India and Humane Society International (HSI) have both released separate footage of dogs confined to cages or sacks with their mouths tied or being struck on their heads with heavy clubs for meat in India, with some material shot before and other video shot after the pandemic began.[45] Recently, a bench of the Gauhati High Court officially allowed the sale and consumption of dog meat in an Indian state.[46] HSI warns, 'A significant threat to human health, the dog meat trade has been linked to outbreaks of trichinellosis, cholera and rabies.'[47]

Similarly, in April 2020, just weeks after WHO declared Covid-19 a global pandemic, PETA Asia shot video footage in business-as-usual live animal markets in Indonesia and Thailand.[48] In the film clips, a variety of species, living and dead, can be seen. In Indonesia, this included live chickens and cats and butchered wild boars, snakes, dogs and rats. At a market in Bangkok, netted bags of live frogs were placed in a tray next to those cut open and dead. Live birds and turtles were also sold.

By that month, there was a growing international call for the closure of live animal markets. Much of that pressure came from the US. Dr Anthony Fauci, the former chief medical advisor to the US president, remarked on the American show *Fox & Friends*, 'I think we should shut down those things right away. It boggles my mind how when we have so many diseases that emanate out of that unusual human-animal interface, that we don't just shut it down. I don't know what else has to happen to get us to appreciate that.'[49] More than sixty American bipartisan lawmakers signed a joint letter to WHO, World Organization for Animal Health (OIE) and the UN demanding a worldwide ban on live wildlife markets and measures to stop the international trade of live wildlife.[50]

Yet, ironically, American live animal markets remain in operation, including in New York City, now infamous for the lives lost during the pandemic. Local animal protection groups, some politicians and public health advocates have been running campaigns for years to shut them down. Among other concerns, the markets put consumers at risk of contracting salmonella, E. coli, campylobacter and other infections.[51] There are over eighty live animal markets and slaughterhouses running in New York City alone keeping live chickens, ducks, sheep, cows and other species to slaughter on site, even in the open street.

Video footage of these markets that can be seen on PETA US' website shows disturbing scenes of sick and distressed chickens in cages stacked on top of each other, dying birds kept among the living and conscious animals' throats being slit. It also shows customers handling live animals with their bare hands, chickens left to bleed in buckets, carcasses strewn on the streets, dead animals spilling out of garbage sacks and blood pouring out on roads.[52]

We know from bird flu and swine flu, some variants of which can infect humans from chickens or pigs, that a focus purely on wildlife markets for pandemic prevention is flawed. Indeed, in November 2022, there was an outbreak of bird flu in a market in Queens, New York.[53] But in California's live animal markets, wild animals such as live frogs and turtles can also be found.[54] California Senator Henry Stern has remarked, 'The trade in wildlife both import as well as sales really poses a threat to our ecosystems, our public health, and the biodiversity in this state.'[55]

Most Asian markets actually do not sell wildlife.[56] But just weeks after its April 2020 visits to markets in Indonesia and Thailand, a PETA Asia investigator visited nearly a dozen more live animal markets alive and kicking in Indonesia and Thailand again, as well as in China, Cambodia, the Philippines and Vietnam.[57] Different species, live or dead, were found being sold for various purposes in each country. Among them were chickens, ducks, fish, dogs, rabbits, monkeys and more. At some markets, civet cats and bats were being sold for food.

PETA Asia went back to Asian markets in 2021, a full year after the start of the pandemic. This time, to those in China, Indonesia, Vietnam, Thailand, the Philippines, Laos and Sri Lanka, where animals were sold for meat, traditional medicine or to be used as pets to live the rest of their lives in a cage or in chains.[58] Once again, a huge variety of sick and stressed animals crowded into adjacent cages were found. Among them were bats, ferret badgers, civet cats, different kinds of birds and monkeys in Indonesia. A caracal cat with hardly any room to turn around, pigs and sick ducks, chickens and other birds in Thailand. Rabbits and birds in Sri Lanka, charred bats and butchered pigs, rodents and squirrels in Laos and sick chickens in the Philippines. Dead dogs, birds and pigs in Vietnam. And a variety of sea animals and chickens in China.

Live animal markets exist in other parts of the world too. Vice TV engaged Jimena Ledgard, a journalist in Peru, to document live animal markets there.[59] She focused on a market in Iquitos, a town that was ravaged by Covid-19. The market sells a huge variety of species from the adjacent Amazon jungle, including taricaya turtles and yellow-footed tortoises who are considered vulnerable, caimans (alligator-like reptiles) for leather and meat, guinea pigs, leaf cutter ants and more. She also visited a farm breeding taricaya turtles and yellow-footed tortoises that claims to be involved in conservation but sells most of the animals' offspring to the Chinese market, and a restaurant where tourists can get the meat of any animal who could be caught in the Amazon or purchased from the market, no matter how threatened, as long as you asked in advance.

In Iquitos, some people believe zarapatera, a soup made with yellow-footed tortoise meat, can help against Covid-19, apparently missing the irony of using wild animal meat to protect against a disease largely believed to be linked to a wild animal market. Evidently, China missed the irony, too, when Tan Re Qing, a medicine containing bear bile, was recommended by its government health agency for Covid-19, in support of its wildlife farming industry.[60] The move came just weeks after the country took steps to stop the production and consumption of wildlife for its probable role in spreading the disease.

Bear bile is obtained from Asiatic black bears, who are endangered, and brown bears. Only bear bile from farmed bears is allowed in China and the import of bear bile is also illegal. However, the product from the legal trade and illegal trade is the same, and so wildlife traffickers were quick to promote their bear bile as a treatment for Covid-19. In fact, consumers prefer bile from wild caught bears, considering it more authentic. Bile from wild and captive bears enters the market from within China itself, as well as Laos, Vietnam and North Korea. Bear bile is also sold in numerous other countries.

Tens of thousands of bears are reared on farms in the region to have bile removed from their gallbladders. Animals Asia has rescued hundreds of bears from the industry. They describe that the bears are never allowed to leave cages that can be so small, they are hardly bigger than the size of the animals' bodies, restricting essentially all movement. Bears who are forced into the cages as cubs can spend up to decades in the extreme confinement, to be released only upon death. Seen essentially as bile-making machines, many of the bears are nearly constantly hungry and thirsty.

The bile is extracted using a choice of various invasive, painful methods. This can be through drugging and jabbing the bears, cutting an opening into the bears' bodies for metal tubes or the permanent insertion of a catheter. Other bears may live their lives strapped into a rusting metal jacket that is to keep the catheter secure (despite its use being illegal in China). One of the bears rescued by Animals Asia, Oliver, spent three decades in one. The bears often die from cancerous tumours or from being left to starve to death once they stop producing enough bile.[61] In addition to medicine, bear bile is used in a variety of products like toothpaste and tea.

Not to be left behind, a company making traditional Chinese medicine reportedly donated nearly USD 140,000 worth of ejiao, gelatine from donkey skins, to numerous Chinese hospitals, pitched as a Covid-19 treatment. The Brooke, a UK-based charity, issued a public warning that the product risks the spread of more disease, including to other animals, as the skins are transported from countries around the world. The group pointed to equine influenza affecting donkeys across numerous African countries in 2019, believed to be linked to the donkey skins trade, and the risk of anthrax, which can also sicken humans.[62]

PETA Asia has documented the treatment of donkeys in both China[63] and Kenya[64] for ejiao. In China, these gentle creatures are bashed on their heads with a sledgehammer. Once they fall over, their throats are slit. Kenya's donkey slaughterhouses exist to supply to China. They kill donkeys transported in overcrowded vehicles over vast distances from other African nations, many of them arriving at slaughterhouses injured or already dead. Following immense public pressure, including from PETA entities and their supporters, and out of concern for their declining donkey populations, Kenya banned the commercial slaughter of donkeys in 2020. However, the ban was revoked in that same year.

Donkey slaughterhouses are not the only zoonotic disease risk ignored in parts of Africa. And while the world has not faced an international disease outbreak affecting humans from donkeys yet, we have suffered Ebola and HIV, both of which are believed to be linked to the hunting of wild animals. Yet, thriving wildlife markets can be found on the continent, while hunting also persists.

MONKEY BUSINESS

On 16 December 2020, while the UK was in lockdown, a dear friend living in another country whom I had been meaning to connect with over a Zoom chat sent me a photo of the two of us out and about in pre-Covid times. That is, when it was normal to socialize and life felt carefree. In the photo, we are making funny faces. I look fake-surprised. She looks fake-concerned.

Delighted to hear from her, I replied, 'Hey there. That feels like a hundred years ago. A different lifetime. In normal times it would feel like yesterday. How have you been?'

The next day, I got a lengthy message back. Happy to see a notification from her, I sat down to read it. It started out routine enough with the same kinds of gripes everyone had about that year, an update about her mother's health and then . . . 'It turns out, I am HIV+.'

I read those few words over and over before I proceeded with the rest. She had written about why she hadn't suspected it (trusting a partner) despite symptoms that she 'brushed off as random illness' until it could no longer be ignored. The virus activated hepatitis C that had long been dormant in her body, an infection she believes she got from a surgery in childhood. As this went untreated for almost a year, she developed cirrhosis of the liver. Hard to ignore indeed.

Much of the rest of the message read as if she was trying to console me over the news. Among other things, she told me her hepatitis C was under treatment and that her HIV was thoroughly managed with one daily pill resulting in a viral load so low that she could not pass it on to others. She said she was getting support from close friends.

She ended with her signature self-depreciating sense of humour: 'Honestly, with the exception of not being able to drink anymore, it isn't so awful.'

I replied thanking her for sharing the difficult life update and let her know that I'm there for her. I also reiterated what she already knew from her doctor better than I did—that HIV treatment is so advanced these days, particularly if started sooner rather than later, that those infected can enjoy good health and a long life.

For a long time afterwards, I couldn't get her out of my mind. I was afraid of the higher risk of a serious outcome if she caught Covid-19. She did ultimately catch the disease, but after being vaccinated, and it wasn't so bad. Now, her overall health has improved, but drinking alcohol is still off the table, which suits her just fine.

Today, HIV treatment is helping millions lead normal lives, but about 630,000 people still died from AIDS-related causes in 2022. That year, 1.3 million people around the world discovered they are HIV+, and 39 million were living with HIV. In total, some 40.4 million people have died from AIDS-related sicknesses and around 85.6 million have contracted HIV.[1]

Weeks after infection, some people experience flu-like symptoms, but not everyone does. Infected persons may not have any symptoms at all—for years. This delay allows HIV in individuals who do not regularly get tested for sexually transmitted diseases, or who do not have easy access to such tests, to go undetected, often until they become ill with an infection their bodies cannot fight.

When a person's immune system has become ravaged by HIV, they are said to be suffering from late-stage HIV (or AIDS) and can become unwell with AIDS-defining illnesses such as tuberculosis, cancer or pneumonia.[2] My friend, with her modern treatment, is unlikely to ever experience late-stage HIV, but my late pal Riyad Wadia had a different story. He was infected with HIV just over a decade after the AIDS epidemic began, when he was in his twenties. In a tribute article that appeared in the Indian publication *Mid-day*, his brother Roy revealed that Riyad had learned of his condition after a bout of poor health.[3] I do not know whether or what treatment he availed of then.

I met Riyad in early 2002 at Athena, a nightclub in Mumbai that has since closed, when I was twenty-five years old. I was in the city helping PETA India, which was a new organization there then, and back then I enjoyed nights out on the town. He would have been thirty-four.

We found ourselves standing next to each other at the crowded venue. I glanced over at him, noticing he was flashily dressed with a colourful scarf around his neck and dashingly good looking. He winked at me mischievously and said, 'Honey, I'm gay.' His audacity made me laugh, my laugh made him laugh and we began talking over the loud Bollywood music. I discovered he had just moved back to Mumbai from New York, and I told him excitedly, 'I grew up in the States!'

After that night, Riyad and I would regularly meet for evenings out. He was always fabulously dressed and I felt the pressure to keep up and tried my best. He was also guaranteed to be jovial and outrageously funny and we would party hop around South Bombay (people who live in the city still tend to call it that rather than South Mumbai).

On my twenty-sixth birthday, he took me to the now closed nightclub Voodoo, where legend has it that Led Zeppelin's Jimmy Page and Robert Plant gave an unplanned performance with local musicians in 1972. Back then, the venue was called Slip Disc. When I went there, it was a preferred spot, perhaps the only spot, for Mumbai's gay community. While there were not many women at Voodoo, I was happy to see there was at least somewhere gay men could be themselves in what was certainly then a largely conservative country—even if it was in the dark under pulsating lights. There, among the smell of sweat, cigarettes and spilled beer, Riyad and I danced the night away.

Riyad was as bold and intelligent as he was a joy to be around. His grandfather was the founder of Wadia Movietone, an illustrious film production company and studio based in the city. Among its successes was the blockbuster *Hunterwali*, India's first superhero film, released in 1935. It featured Fearless Nadia, progressively a female lead, as the main star. *Hunterwali* was so popular when it came out and Fearless Nadia's stunts in it so impressive, that she went on to act in numerous action films. Fearless Nadia eventually married Homi Wadia, Riyad's granduncle, in 1961, becoming Nadia Wadia (she was born Mary Ann Evans and was of Australian origin). In 1993, Riyad made a documentary about her called *Fearless: The Hunterwali Story*. He also made *Bomgay*, a short film based on poems by Ramachandrapurapu Raj Rao, author of *The Boyfriend*, which is about India's gay subculture. It is commonly referred to as India's first gay film.[4]

In the latter part of 2003, I became busy, or he did, or so I supposed, and months went by when I didn't hear from Riyad at all. It happens, I thought. I told myself I'll phone him soon and we'll be back to our merry ways. However, that never happened. Instead, I received a call from a mutual friend in December that year, asking me if I'd heard that Riyad had passed away.

Riyad never told me about his illness,[5] and I would have never guessed it—he seemed too happy to know he was going to die soon—fearless, like his grandaunt.

In the *Mid-day* article, Roy shared that Riyad had contracted abdominal tuberculosis and was in agony towards the end of his life. He lived in a beautiful flat across Mumbai's Worli Sea Face promenade, against the Arabian Sea. As Roy tells it, on 30 November 2003, Riyad ate lunch, went out on the terrace for fresh air and then felt drained. His mother sat with him on his bed. He told her, 'You know this is the end, Ma, don't you?' She told him not to say things like that. 'Ma, I can hear the sea calling me now. It's time to go.' She hushed him by singing 'Summertime', his favourite lullaby from when he was a child. And then in a moment, he was gone.

Now Onir, an Indian film director, is planning a biopic on Riyad. I hope he calls it *Fearless: The Riyad Wadia Story*. I cannot wait to see it.

Where did this disease that took away my beautiful friend, that has infected another and killed so many, come from? How did it spread? For that answer, we will have to travel to the jungles of Africa. However, first, let's start in the US.

On 5 June 1981, as Kim Carnes' hit song 'Bette Davis Eyes' topped the US music charts, the US Centers for Disease Control and Prevention (CDC) published a report about something unusual: five formerly healthy young men in Los Angeles contracting Pneumocystis carinii pneumonia (PCP), a critical lung infection, and other signs that something was seriously wrong with their immune systems. They were all gay and each died soon.

That very same day, Dr Alvin Friedman-Kien raised the alarm on Kaposi's sarcoma in numerous gay men in New York and California. Kaposi's sarcoma is a rare cancer that affects the skin and causes patches in the mouth. As a dermatologist, Friedman-Kien would have noticed purplish, bruise-like lesions in such patients. It, too, indicates a weakened immune system.

After this, throughout that year, reports of PCP, Kaposi's sarcoma and other infections that occur in people with severely weakened immune systems, in mostly gay and bisexual men, began to pour in from around the US. Meanwhile, New York immunologist Dr Arye Rubinstein reported five babies with signs of weakened immunity. Most of these children had mothers who were sex workers and used drugs.[6]

(Most HIV worldwide has been transmitted heterosexually,[7] but in some countries gay men are disproportionately affected.[8] One of the reasons for this is the type of sex gay men may engage in. While unprotected vaginal sex with an infected partner can result in an HIV infection, anal sex carries greater risk for it, particularly for the receiving partner.[9])

The caseload became so numerous that by the end of 1981, hundreds of people—337 to be exact, including over a dozen children—were reported to be infected with this strange immunity-damaging condition there. By New Year's Eve, 130 of those individuals were dead. By 31 May 1982, the crisis had so developed that the *Los Angeles Times* ran a front-page story titled: 'Mysterious Fever Now an Epidemic'.

Some researchers began to call the illness gay-related immune deficiency (GRID), which fed into the false and dangerous impression that it only affects members of the gay community.[10] This notion stigmatized anyone who was not heterosexual, resulting in open discrimination and violence, and helped the disease blow up out of control.

By September 1982, the term acquired immunodeficiency syndrome (AIDS) was in use, but it did not remove the stigma. About a month after the renaming, journalist Lester Kinsolving asked then US President Ronald Reagan's press secretary, Larry Speakes, about

AIDS at a publicized press conference. In doing so, he referred to it as the 'gay plague', resulting in uproarious laugher by other press present in the room. Speakes' reply was a joke rather than a plan. He simply said, 'I don't have it.' More laughter followed.[11]

With homophobia coming from the top and coverage of homophobic views by the mainstream American press, unsurprisingly, in the 1980s, hate attacks on gays and lesbians skyrocketed in the US. They ranged from verbal abuse to murder and were reported by rights groups as becoming increasingly cruel as the AIDS epidemic continued.[12]

In 1982, the CDC defined AIDS as: 'A disease at least moderately predictive of a defect in cell-mediated immunity, occurring in a person with no known cause for diminished resistance to that disease.'[13] Keywords here being 'no known cause'. There was still a lot to learn. For a long time yet, members of the public falsely thought you could contract AIDS from essentially just being near a gay person through things such as public toilets, sharing dishes, hugging or holding hands.

Scientists are cautious about stating things conclusively without absolute proof. It took over a year into the ongoing pandemic for the WHO to declare Covid-19 airborne.[14] Likewise, it wasn't until 1984 that a paper came out in *The American Journal of Medicine* stating, 'The finding of a cluster of AIDS patients linked by sexual contact is consistent with the hypothesis that AIDS is caused by an infectious agent.' In other words, as the title of the paper says, 'Patients linked by sexual contact'.[15] By then, it was also observed that HIV appeared to be blood-borne, which meant blood transfusions, sharing needles contaminated with blood for either medical purposes or taking drugs also puts people at risk of contracting the virus.

By the end of that year, over 3,500 Americans had died from AIDS, while at least 7,700 had gotten sick from it. But the common view was still that it was a 'gay disease', affecting 'immoral' people like drug-takers and prostitutes. It is widely believed that this prejudiced outlook delayed US government's response. In fact, it wasn't until late 1985 that Reagan even uttered words about AIDS himself—at least publicly. He finally did so in reply to a reporter's question. Under pressure, in 1987, the US finally began creating awareness about AIDS.[16] Even the awareness campaigns were often homophobic or at least so moralizing that they had reduced effect, not just in the US, but around the world.

For instance, Margaret Thatcher, who was the UK Prime Minister at the time, tried to curb public health warnings about AIDS that she thought were in poor taste and would harm teenagers' minds.[17] This meant people were not always getting the information they needed to protect themselves. In an article about this for *The Conversation*, Dr João Florêncio, a senior lecturer at the University of Exeter, wrote, 'Marked by a fear, on the part of the Thatcher and Reagan governments, that speaking directly to homosexuals could be seen as endorsing "deviant" homosexual behaviour, the often moralistic—and publicly-funded—health campaigns released during the peak of the Western AIDS crisis ignored the specific realities of those most affected by the epidemic.'[18] The public service announcements commonly advised things like not having sex at all or only having sex with one person, with sermonizing messaging such as promiscuity means AIDS, rather than helping the public learn about more practical safer sex practices.

While all this effort, even though sluggish and imperfect, was going on, work to figure out where HIV came from was too. Today, over two-thirds of people with HIV and around 90 per cent children infected by it live in Sub-Saharan Africa.[19] There are lots of factors at play as to why this is, including not the least of which is that Africa is HIV's continent of origin.

Now we know that there is HIV-1 and HIV-2. They differ genetically by more than 55 per cent.[20] They are so different that a test may only pick up one or the other, except where the test was specially developed to detect both. HIV-1 is far more common than HIV-2, accounting for 95 per cent of all HIV infections. The progression of HIV-2 is slower than HIV-1, and the illness is less deadly.[21] HIV-2 is more common in west Africa and countries nearby than anywhere else, though, and it's also increasing in India.[22] But how are there two of them?

In October 1988, *Scientific American* ran an article titled 'The Origins of the AIDS Virus' by Max Essex and Phyllis J. Kanki. Both researchers are still with the Harvard T.H. Chan School of Public Health. It read, 'The AIDS virus is not unique. It has relatives in man as well as other primates.'[23]

They described how laboratories using primates for experimentation in the US were reporting Asian macaque monkeys sick with something that resembled AIDS—ultimately dying.[24] They called it SAIDS—simian AIDS. The virus responsible came to be called simian immunodeficiency virus (SIV) and upon study, the authors wrote SIV 'was clearly related to HIV'. They had to see if SAIDS was affecting Asian macaques in the wild to rule out something to do with the laboratory environment causing infections in these animals. And as it turned out, they could not find SAIDS in wild Asian macaques.

Meanwhile, central Africa was reporting an HIV and AIDS crisis. So the researchers started looking for HIV-like viruses in wild primates there instead and began testing high-risk human populations, such as sex workers, to see what they could learn.

They examined blood samples from all sorts of African primates and discovered signs of SIV infection in more than half of the samples from African green monkeys. Samples from thousands more of these monkeys from different parts of Africa showed that 70 per cent of them were infected with SIV, but that it did not make them sick (like coronaviruses in bats). Perplexing. Why not? The researchers surmised that the virus may have, over a long period of time, adapted to coexist peacefully with these animals. They also guessed Asian monkeys were infected by African monkeys in captivity and that the Asian ones got sick because the virus was novel to their bodies. An amazing discovery, but although African green monkey SIV was evidently related to HIV, it was not a strong enough match with the HIV scientists knew about at that time for it to be considered its precursor. It was, however, more of a match for something else.

These researchers and others found many Senegalese sex workers were infected with something much more like the African green monkey SIV than the human HIV. So much so that Essex and Kanki wrote that 'the reactivity of the prostitutes' antibodies to SIV antigens was indistinguishable from that of antibodies in the blood of SIV-infected macaques and African green monkeys.' Indistinguishable!

African green monkeys are one of six vervet monkeys. Some vervet monkeys are heavily hunted for meat[25] or killed by crop farmers who consider them a nuisance, creating opportunities for humans to come into contact with monkey blood. They are also used as 'pets' and people in the regions they inhabit clash with them, such as when they bound through their gardens or disturb them in other ways.[26] And so, an African green monkey infecting a human at some historical point is an entirely plausible idea.

This breakthrough led to the understanding that this illness was different to the HIV that people in other parts of Africa, the US and most other parts of the world were suffering from. It came to be called HIV-2. The search was still on for the precursor of the other HIV, which would be called HIV-1, and a more detailed study on the full genome of African green monkey SIV by Japanese scientists cast doubt on them being the direct ancestor of HIV-2.[27] The search continued there too.

This is not so strange despite the initial excitement over how similar African green monkey HIV was to Senegalese sex worker HIV when we consider what we know now—that SIV has been found in over forty-five primate species in Africa, with infection rates as high as over 75 per cent in some populations. SIV has not been found in any non-human primate on any other continent.[28] That still left a lot of options for potential direct ancestors to HIV-1 and 2.

In his book, *Spillover: Animal Infections and the Next Human Pandemic*, science writer David Quammen, who I also mentioned in Chapter 1, describes all of these disease-tracker developments and more in the history of HIV in great detail, including how American scientists trying to infect rhesus macaque monkeys with leprosy from a sooty mangabey monkey accidentally infected several of them with SIV. They developed SAIDS and died.

This led to the discovery that sooty mangabeys, like African green monkeys, can be SIV positive but not get sick, including those in the wild. Here again, SIV from African monkeys (sooty mangabeys) killed Asian monkeys (rhesus macaques). Upon further scrutiny of sooty mangabey SIV, it was discovered that it is very close to HIV-2, leading scientists to deduce that sometime in the decades before, a sooty mangabey infected a human in west Africa with SIV, resulting in HIV-2.[29] These monkeys, too, are butchered and eaten, killed for raiding crops and used as 'pets', providing opportunities for infection.[30]

Today we also know there are numerous different types of HIV-1 and HIV-2. There are four groups of HIV-1 but the one most people are concerned about is group M, since that is the version responsible for most human infections. Meanwhile there are eight HIV-2 groups, with only subtypes A and B with the widest spread.[31] All of the HIV-2 groups are similar to the SIV in sooty mangabeys, while all of the HIV-1 versions look like the SIV found in apes (with one group matching that found specifically in gorillas). As Quammen reveals in his book, these versions are so distinct, it is believed they infected humans from primates in separate events![32]

On 18 January 2002, *Scientific American* published an article titled, 'First Case of AIDS-like Virus in a Wild Chimpanzee'. By then, an HIV-1 like virus had been found in wild-caught chimpanzees in captivity.[33] The article describes how chimpanzee urine and faeces was tested by researchers who discovered the virus in a healthy twenty-three-year-old male chimpanzee who lived at the Gombe Stream National Park in Tanzania—a place you may know through the work of Jane Goodall. The SIV in this chimpanzee was determined to differ enough from HIV-1 that it was concluded humans were not directly infected by chimpanzees from this subspecies, but it was a clue.[34] At that time, it was believed SIV was rare and harmless in chimpanzees—but it was all about where you looked and how long you observed.

Chimpanzees in the part of Cameroon closest to the Republic of the Congo were found to have a high prevalence of SIV—an SIV that resembled HIV-1 group M.[35] Bingo! And to everyone's surprise, a chimpanzee in a laboratory developed AIDS and died.[36] Ultimately, researchers observing chimpanzee communities in Gombe Stream National Park over nearly a decade discovered SIV infected chimpanzees had a ten to sixteen times higher death rate than those who were not infected. One of the female chimpanzees died of what looked like end-stage AIDS.[37]

On 12 June 2003, an article in *National Geographic* read, 'Scientists now say that the simian immunodeficiency virus (SIV) in chimpanzees (Pan troglodytes), which is believed to have been transmitted to humans to become HIV-1—the virus that causes AIDS—didn't start its life in chimps. Instead, it was a product of separate viruses jumping from different monkey species into chimps, where they recombined to form a hybrid virus, according to a new study.'[38]

In other words, it seems a chimpanzee became a mixing vessel of SIVs from the red-capped mangabey and the greater spot-nosed monkey, perhaps through hunting episodes.[39] The idea being as the disease was relatively new to their bodies, it was killing them, like it kills Asian monkeys, and like it can kill us.

Today, while precise details of how and when continue to be researched and discussed—it is scientifically accepted that humans were first infected with the various HIV strains through monkeys and apes (depending on the type), with the most plausible theory being through hunting. In his book, Quamenn elaborates on how a scientific timeline process points to the first infection of a person, likely a hunter, by a chimpanzee with what became HIV-1 group M was around 1908. He also shares various theories on how this particular type of HIV spread more than the rest.

A few years ago, journalist Evan Williams travelled to Cameroon for a documentary for *Unreported World*, which is broadcast by the UK's Channel 4, about the trouble facing that country's great apes.[40] It showed how in a market in Yaoundé, Cameroon's capital, various species of animals from the nearby rainforests are openly sold to be eaten, such as monkeys, anteaters, porcupines and snakes, and that on special order, chimpanzee and gorilla parts can also be unlawfully obtained.

On its website, Ape Action Africa, an organization in the region that rescues primates orphaned by the wild animal meat (bushmeat) trade, explains, 'Great apes, such as gorillas and chimpanzees, are particularly at risk from the bushmeat trade because they have a very slow reproductive rate, females usually only giving birth every 3 to 5 years. Hunting them is illegal but the meat is prized as a delicacy and the high prices mean that the law is constantly broken.'[41]

Most meat, 80 per cent of it, eaten in Cameroon is wild animal meat.[42] But today, the killing of wildlife there and in neighbouring areas is not simply led by village demand. Rather, it has become a booming business to supply to urban markets and to those who consider wild animal meat a gourmet endeavour, including buyers in Western countries.[43] The group describes, 'Today, hunters penetrate deep into the forests on the back of logging trucks, armed with rifles, and kill whole families, often smoking the dead animals to avoid detection when they return to town.'[44] About ten years ago, it was said, up to 3,000 gorillas were killed in southern Cameroon alone every year.[45]

Indeed, the *Unreported World* documentary features a poacher who admits entire gorilla families may be shot when they are found together. Many young gorillas and chimpanzees, however, are not considered large enough to be worthwhile for meat and end up in the pet trade. We can imagine how horribly that typically pans out since they are wild animals, mentally disturbed and suffer behavioural issues from seeing their parents killed. The director of Ape Action Africa, Rachel Hogan, told Williams that these animals grieve. In relaying the story of a particular infant gorilla, she said, 'She would sit, and she would cry, and she would call out for her mother.'

The logging and bushmeat industries go hand-in-hand. As with bushmeat, much of the logging that occurs in Cameroon is illegal.[46] Paths cleared to allow the felling of trees are used by poachers to go further into the forests to capture and kill wildlife. Logging trucks are then used to smuggle loads of up to 200 kilograms of meat from gorillas, chimpanzees and other wild animals.[47]

The Baka are forest dwellers who have been permitted to eat non-apes in Cameroon. Felix Biango, a Baka, told Williams that they do not kill outlawed animals for themselves, but do so for the urban markets and the wild animal meat trade. He also narrated a story of nearly an entire village that died after some members found a dead gorilla in the forest to bring back to eat. The only person spared was the one who didn't eat the meat. Ape Action Africa veterinarian Babila Tafon suspects this may have been an Ebola outbreak.[48]

It is a good guess, as this incident is far from isolated. As with HIV, the existence of various distinct Ebola viruses indicates separate outbreak events. Currently, out of six known Ebola virus species, four can cause Ebola in humans.[49] And where Ebola outbreaks in humans have occurred, locals and scientists have often shared accounts of nearby dead gorillas and chimpanzees. Patients have sometimes had stories to share of recently butchering apes.[50]

In the early 2000s, outbreaks of Ebola were affecting villagers living at the border of Gabon and the Republic of the Congo. Researchers ultimately counted hundreds of dead gorillas nearby, with numerous testing positive for Ebola. Based on findings and knowledge of the region, Peter Walsh, an ecologist who was with the Max Planck Institute for Evolutionary Anthropology in Germany at the time, estimated 5,500 gorillas would have been killed by Ebola then.[51]

As gorillas and chimpanzees face a high mortality rate, they are not considered the likely natural hosts for Ebola viruses. Today, certain fruit bats are considered the likely natural hosts.[52] Ebola can spread to humans, and among humans, through close contact with blood, bodily fluids, organs or secretions of infected animals or people. The list of risks can include infected gorillas, chimpanzees, fruit bats, monkeys, forest antelopes and other animals—dead or alive.[53]

A paper published in 2020 by *Global Health: Science and Practice* reveals Ebola had killed about 15,266 people by then since its discovery in 1976, mostly in African countries, and that figure continues to rise.[54] On average, the fatality rate from catching an Ebola virus is around 50 per cent, with case fatalities sometimes reaching as high as 90 per cent.[55] Patients may suffer fever, pains, fatigue, abdominal problems or other symptoms, such as those horrifying ones most of us have heard about, like haemorrhaging, bleeding and red eyes.

HIV and Ebola are not the only diseases we can contract from primates. Before a colleague and I went to Kenya many years ago, we had to take a yellow fever shot. That's because it is transmitted to humans by mosquitoes via primates (human or non-human). When yellow fever becomes severe, it can be fatal.[56]

Simian foamy virus (SFV) is also very common in certain primates. For example, nearly all (97 per cent) western red colobus monkeys and up to 100 per cent of chimpanzees in the wild carry the virus. It can be transmitted via bites to humans, and many hunters butchering apes are believed to be infected.[57] This is unfortunate for them because its consequences in humans are currently not well understood.

Yet, primates and other wild animals continue to be killed in parts of Africa, including for the voodoo religion, for which animal sacrifice is common. A *Vice* documentary on west Africa[58] wildlife markets showed whole dead bodies of baboons available for sale. It also showed parts of chimpanzees, different monkeys and other animals such as a hippopotamus, an elephant, a baleen whale and many others displayed on tables—all believed to offer the buyer protection. But viruses pay no heed to religion.

In Lagos, Nigeria—a country notorious for wildlife trade to Asia—the Epe Fish Market, a wildlife meat market, was closed down at the start of the Covid-19 pandemic, but had reopened just a few months later. There, many species of animals from the nearby jungle are sold including dead pangolins, tortoises and snakes. A vendor told a journalist that they are not concerned about diseases from the animals because they have been eating and selling this meat for a long time, and so far, nothing has happened (as far as they know).[59]

The WHO, World Organisation for Animal Health (OIE) and United Nations Environment Programme (UNEP), however, appear to disagree with this risk assessment at least to some degree. That's because in April 2021, in response to Covid-19, they urged governments to 'suspend the trade in live caught wild animals of mammalian species for food or breeding purposes and close sections of food markets selling live caught wild animals of mammalian species as an emergency measure...'[60]

This move came after months of pressure demanding these agencies encourage the closure of such markets. The pleas came from the over sixty American lawmakers mentioned in the last chapter, celebrities such as Paul McCartney[61] and Ricky Gervais,[62] members of the public who sent appeals to the WHO through an action alert that appeared on the websites of PETA entities and various other advocacy groups who made their voices heard. Media reports from around the world also highlighted health risks live animal markets pose.

There are problems with the WHO, OIE and UNEP guidance though. Farmed wild animals are susceptible to disease, particularly when kept in crowded, filthy environments as is routine, and mammals and wild species are not the only animals who carry zoonotic disease. The guidance also included the disclaimer 'unless demonstrable effective regulations and adequate risk assessment are in place', which essentially means they were really not recommending a ban on the trade in live caught wild mammalian animals either.

PIGGY WENT TO MARKET

You probably know the nursery rhyme 'This Little Piggy'. It goes:

This little piggy went to market,
This little piggy stayed home,
This little piggy had roast beef,
This little piggy had none.
And this little piggy cried 'wee wee wee' all the way home...

Eric Zorn, a columnist for the *Chicago Tribune*, would sing these lines to his children while wiggling their toes. It always struck him as strange that this little piggy had roast beef. 'Is there no solidarity in the barnyard?' he mused.

Later, he stumbled upon a post about the nursery rhyme on Twitter that read, 'I'm 22 years old and I just realized that "This little piggy went to … market" doesn't mean he went food shopping.'

Until that moment, Zorn, too, had always imagined the pig wandering down a grocery store aisle like a human, on two hind feet, basket hung over a front leg. It was only then that he understood the rhyme is about pigs being sent to slaughter, ending up at the market as meat.

Zorn wrote about his unsettling realization: 'Wee-wee-wee becomes the fearful yet ultimately fruitless cry of a creature that realizes it, too, was born to be sold and eaten.'[1]

Grim.

Grim also that a little piggy on a farm could, in fact, have roast beef—well, of sorts. Pigs are mostly plant-eaters, but they as well as chickens and other animals reared on today's factory farms are commonly fed the pulverized remains of other animals, blood and other slaughterhouse waste and even faeces to cut costs on feed.[2]

This is because that's what factory farms—intensive, crowded animal farming systems—exist to do—cut costs, just about at *any* cost, to maximize profits and fuel the demand for animal products. On average, a meat-eater now consumes double what they would have about fifty years ago.[3] And today, over 70 per cent of farmed animals are factory farmed (that is, over 64 billion land animals out of the over 92 billion used for food each year[4]). In the US, the figure is 99 per cent.[5] On these farms, up to thousands of animals are confined to cages, crates or sheds in warehouses.

The European Union (EU) lifted a ban on feeding some farmed animals, specifically non-ruminant animals, the remains of other animals in 2021. This is to allow farmers to do things such as feed chickens with pig remains.[6] European farmers argued they need to be able to feed farmed animals cheap animal remains in order to be competitive against non-EU countries where farmed animals are fed animals—what the industry calls processed animal protein (PAP).

Feeding cattle and sheep with PAP from mammals has been prohibited in the EU since 1994 and feeding farmed animals the remains of other animals had been banned there since 2001 over cross-contamination concerns. The bans were in response to the bovine spongiform encephalopathy (BSE) crisis going on around that time.[7]

BSE is a progressive neurological disorder of cattle, also known as 'mad cow disease', and the human version, variant Creutzfeldt-Jakob disease (vCJD), is believed to come from eating infected beef. vCJD has killed hundreds of people, after first often making them blind, unable to control movements and lose brain function.[8]

BSE is thought to have come about by farmers feeding cattle the remains of infected sheep or other infected cattle. The US Food and Drug Administration explains, 'A cow gets BSE by eating feed contaminated with parts that came from another cow that was sick with BSE.'[9] Meanwhile, the US CDC says, 'BSE possibly originated as a result of feeding cattle meat-and-bone meal that contained BSE-infected products from a spontaneously occurring case of BSE or scrapie-infected sheep products … There is strong evidence and general agreement that the outbreak was then amplified and spread throughout the United Kingdom cattle industry by feeding rendered, prion-infected, bovine meat-and-bone meal to young calves.'[10] Scrapie is a similar fatal disease of sheep and goats. In other words, BSE is believed to be thanks to making herbivorous cows cannibalistic meat-eaters.

The EU is maintaining a ban on feeding cows and sheep animal remains and on cannibalism.[11] But if the European Fat Processors and Renderers (EFPRA) are to be believed, 'the European rendering industry fulfils the highest regulatory standard worldwide',[12] which means elsewhere the industry may not be as 'careful'. The WHO advises that certain risky cattle tissues such as the brain, spinal cord, eyes and intestines be left out of animal feed as a measure to prevent BSE. But even the US, where a person might expect standards similar to those in Europe, engages in worrying practices. In his book, *How to Survive a Pandemic*, Dr Michael Greger describes how there, pulverized pigs may be fed to cattle, cattle to chickens and chicken excrement fed back to cattle. He describes how from a disease risk perspective, this is not so different to making cows cannibals.[13]

Piernicola Pedicini, an Italian Member of European Parliament (MEP), is worried. He said, 'I personally don't see any good human or animal health related reason to lift this ban … I am afraid there are only economic objectives behind it.' He also expressed doubt over adequate controls over what remains make it into animal feed.[14]

Apart from their stomachs being used as waste disposal, farmed animals are also the living embodiment of pharmacies. Around the world, almost 75 per cent of antimicrobial drugs on the market are used to rear animals for meat, eggs and dairy.[15] That means far more antibiotics are used on farmed animals than for ourselves. This overuse of drugs is contributing to antimicrobial resistance and the development of superbugs—when medicines we need to treat illnesses from bacteria, viruses, fungi and parasites become less effective or stop working altogether and when new resilient forms of infections arise.

The WHO warns, 'Antibiotic resistance is one of the biggest threats to global health, food security, and development today.'[16] It also points out, globally, approximately 700,000 people lose their lives every year from drug-resistant diseases.[17] In India, it is said sepsis related to such infections kills almost 60,000 newborn babies every year.[18] The WHO has warned if steps are not taken for change, 'drug-resistant diseases could cause 10 million deaths each year by 2050', and that 'by 2030, antimicrobial resistance could force up to 24 million people into extreme poverty.'[19]

Antibiotics are used on factory farms for reasons such as growth, instead of cleanliness, and to keep animals alive in severely crowded, disease-prone conditions. In an article on the subject, Dr Emanuel Goldman from the Department of Microbiology, Biochemistry and

Molecular Genetics at the Rutgers New Jersey Medical School writes, 'In order to have sufficient animal flesh available for those who want it, farms have to become "factories", with animals crowded into confined areas to maximize the amount of meat per unit of space. In this crowded environment, disease can spread like wildfire. But if the animals are routinely fed antibiotics, bacterial diseases that could decimate them are prevented. Thus, antibiotic use makes possible the existence of factory farms.'[20]

However, not all bacterial diseases are decimated—some arise from the strongest bacteria that become resistant to the onslaught of antibiotics, resulting in problems such as from salmonella, campylobacter, listeria, E.coli O157:H7 and others. All of these and more are from meat, egg or dairy foods. Even when plant foods are contaminated by these germs, upon a closer look, the culprit is usually animal manure used for fertilizer.[21] In 2015, during its first worldwide estimate on the subject, the WHO revealed that up to 600 million people suffer from food-borne diseases and 420,000 die from them every year.[22] The WHO had previously warned that animal-derived products are the number one cause of illnesses from contaminated food.[23]

A couple of years ago, World Animal Protection (WAP) released its findings on antibiotic resistance genes (ARGs) in rivers and streams near pig factory farms in the US, Canada, Spain and Thailand. WAP focused its attention on pig farms because they are notorious for keeping pigs in severely crowded, intensive conditions and due to their extreme use of antibiotics. Many of these antibiotics are administered when the pigs are just weeks old.

Their study highlights the release of ARGs and superbugs into the waterways of local communities. The group explains, 'ARGs are the building blocks for superbugs; they create antimicrobial resistance, the resistance of common bacteria to antibiotics critically important to people. This means some antibiotics are already ineffective in some parts of the world; while in future, routine procedures like caesarean sections or cancer treatment will become dangerous worldwide.' Alarmingly, their findings include ARGs with resistance to 'last line of defence' antibiotics vital to keep critically ill human patients alive.

The group's report warns, 'Waterways can be flash points for toxic pollutants and create reservoirs where superbugs accumulate and mix. However, there is no international standard describing the concentration at which superbugs in the environment become dangerous to people. Consequently, no one is held responsible, and farm discharge of antibiotics and superbugs into waterways are unmonitored. This is despite the UN identifying superbug contamination as one of the most important emerging global environmental issues. Furthermore, most countries don't monitor antibiotic use directly on farm animals.' No water treatment method exists to remove superbugs.[24]

In 2022, the EU passed several prohibitions on the routine use of antibiotics in farmed animals. They include those aimed at stopping their use in place of poor hygiene and management and in preventative treatment in groups of animals. Where infection or disease is found, controlled antibiotic use will be permitted if deemed necessary. While well intended, the European Public Health Alliance has raised concerns about compliance since Europe continues to use factory farming systems for pigs and other animals.[25] And antibiotic use in farmed animals remains rampant elsewhere around the world.

China produces about half of the world's pork[26] and increasingly, there and elsewhere, 'megafarms'—facilities with over 10,000 female pigs to be used for breeding[27]—and other large farms are becoming commonplace. In fact, according to National Hog Farmer, a pork industry website, as of 2020, thirty-four facilities worldwide housed at least a whopping *100,000* sows,[28] with China and the US both having eleven farms operating at this extreme level.[29]

The world's largest pig farm on a single site is a new twenty-six storey skyscraper with two adjacent buildings run by Hubei Zhongxin

Kaiwei Modern Farming in Hubei province, China. It is planned with the capacity of keeping 650,000 pigs at a time and slaughtering 1.2 million pigs a year.[30] In the US, Smithfield, owned by China's WH Group, is the biggest pork producer rearing 21.7 million pigs across farms worldwide in 2021.[31]

Dirk Pfeiffer, chair professor in the Department of Infectious Diseases and Public Health at City University of Hong Kong is worried. He warns, 'The higher the density of animals, the higher the risk of infectious pathogen spread and amplification, as well as potential for mutation.'[32]

In crowded indoor facilities, poor air quality is a major problem with stench and noxious gasses from the animals' waste penetrating the environment. Dust is also formed from the animals' faeces, food and dander—containing hazardous agents such as toxins, fungi and bacteria. Sustained exposure to their own waste and other air pollutants often leaves pigs suffering from respiratory infections, which can prove fatal, and other health ailments. The air pollution is also hard on workers who can suffer conditions such as pulmonary disease.[33]

Barring some countries, gestation crates (also called sow stalls) are commonly used to confine pregnant pigs, usually throughout their nearly four-month pregnancy.[34] In India, following work by PETA India, over twenty states and union territories have issued internal circulars against the use of such crates by their pig farms.[35] They reference the country's Prevention of Cruelty to Animals (PCA) Act, 1960, which makes it illegal to keep or confine 'any animal in any cage or other receptacle which does not measure sufficiently in height, length and breadth to permit the animal a reasonable opportunity for movement'. Gestation and farrowing crates do not allow this movement. However, there is inadequate enforcement of this law. For instance, both gestation and farrowing crates are sold for use in India.[36]

Gestation crates are metal cages essentially the size of the pig's own body, with concrete or slatted floors, leaving her unable to turn around or to even stand up without difficulty and lying in her own waste. Farrowing crates are what pigs are transferred into to give birth and typically kept in for several weeks until their piglets are taken away. They are fundamentally the same as gestation crates, except for some side room for piglets.

The severe confinement deprives pigs of everything natural and important for them, including even basic movement, socialization with other pigs, ability to regulate their body temperatures (such as by wallowing in mud), foraging for food, building a nest in which to give birth, raising their young, moving away from their own bodily waste, protecting their young or even adjusting against piglets who may painfully nibble at their teats. The sows also feel constantly hungry. They are bred for rapid, unnatural growth but are only fed just enough for their weight and pregnancy, not appetite.

Male pigs used for breeding are also typically kept individually in metal pens. These pens can be small, resulting in similar miserable experiences to female pigs. Pigs reared for meat are commonly kept in groups in larger pens, but the overcrowding can lead to injuries and fights. Pigs on factory farms also routinely face mutilations, usually without painkillers, such as castration, removal of certain teeth with pliers, notches cut into their ears and the slicing off of their tails. Most of this is done to try to address the very problems intensive farming causes—such as injuries during fights or that result from severe stress.[37]

Stress is a major problem for pigs. The relentless confinement, inability to engage in innate behaviours and unnatural diet leaves many pigs acting bizarrely, such as incessantly biting at their bars and making repetitive empty chewing movements. What's worse, some pigs are genetically predisposed to stress. That's because pigs used for meat are bred for certain traits such as unnatural and fast growth, requiring less food intake for 'efficiency' and carcass leanness. This specialized breeding has left many pigs suffering from porcine stress syndrome (PSS)—a condition where pigs are extremely sensitive to stress. Pigs with PSS can face difficulty breathing, skin discoloration and a heightened body temperate when stressed—particularly during handling and transport. They suffer heart attacks more frequently and die more commonly, too.[38]

Stress can significantly impair animals' immune function.[39] This and filth, terrible air quality, overcrowding, breeding for unnatural traits, breeding animals for genetic uniformity and drugging set the perfect stage for disease development, spread and disaster. So when disaster strikes, we shouldn't be surprised.

It is estimated that the 2009 H1N1 swine flu pandemic killed up to over 575,000 people in just the first year that it circulated alone, worldwide.[40] In the same book mentioned before, Dr Greger explains this swine flu took root in an intensive pig farm in the US,[41] and its development can be further traced back to the 1918 influenza pandemic that killed at least 50 million people around the world.[42]

The 1918 pandemic, also called the Spanish flu (even though it did not originate in Spain), was the deadliest in the history of anyone alive today. Dr Greger shares it was caused by an H1N1 bird flu virus that infected humans, either directly or through another animal host, like pigs.[43] One theory is that the pandemic started in farmed animals such as chickens or pigs in Kansas, US.[44] However, more likely than pigs giving it to us, we gave it to pigs. Evidently, before that year, flu in pigs was unheard of.[45]

Then in 1998, a reassortment of this virus that had been circulating in pigs for decades combined with human and bird flu viruses creating a triple-animal reassortment virus. (Reassortment means gene swapping in cells infected with different influenza viruses.) Although it was first found on a pig farm in the American state of North Carolina, it fast spread to other parts of that country and the world through the transportation of pigs from farm to farm and for slaughter.[46]

Author of numerous books on viruses and retired University of Edinburgh professor Dorothy Crawford notes, '...overcrowded farms are a hotbed of genetic mixing for flu viruses'.[47] Similarly, former executive director of the Pew Commission on Industrial Animal Farm Production, Bob Martin, warns, 'Industrial farms are super-incubators for viruses'.[48]

Even so, by 1998, Dr Greger writes North Carolina's pig population was exploding at ten million, a 400 per cent increase from just six years before. Around the same time, the number of pig farms there was rapidly shrinking. That means there were far more pigs packed per farm—around twenty-five times more he says—than just some years before.[49] Just over a decade later, the 2009 H1N1 swine flu pandemic was born out of the triple-animal reassortment virus circulating in pigs around the world combining with a Eurasian swine flu.[50]

Around the time that the triple-animal reassortment virus was found on a North Carolina pig farm, on the other side of the world, fruit bats were being displaced by forest burning in Indonesia. Some ended up roosting in trees adjacent to an intensive Malaysian farm with more than 30,000 pigs, dropping bitten-into fruit into the pigs' enclosures. The bats' bodily fluids contained Nipah virus. This virus, which causes no harm to bats, began fast infecting pigs causing loud, bloody coughs, twitching and convulsing and often a rapid death. Thanks to pig transport, the virus spread to pigs throughout the country and to Singapore,[51] before finally being controlled through the decimation of one million pigs in the region.[52]

Through pigs, the Nipah virus infected many other species of animals, including humans. Its fatality rate in people is somewhere between 40 to 75 per cent. It can be transmitted to humans from animals but is also transmittable from human to human. Infected persons can suffer from a range of symptoms including fever, vomiting, dizziness, severe respiratory problems, encephalitis, seizures and coma. Many survivors suffer long-term neurologic problems.[53]

Nevertheless, apparently, we still don't learn. African swine fever, which does not affect humans but spreads quickly amongst pigs, killed off around half of China's massive pig population in 2018 and 2019[54] and now continues to plague China and the rest of Southeast Asia.[55] The mega multistorey pig farm is among the giant pig farming facilities springing up in China to replace the smaller farms that could not survive this fever crisis—although we now very well know high density means high disease risk.

Unsurprisingly, in 2020, Chinese researchers reported the discovery of a new pandemic potential kind of swine flu. It was named G4, and its ancestor is the H1N1 strain that caused the 2009 pandemic. The virus has infected humans from animals but had not yet infected person-to-person. The concern, however, is that as more humans are infected, G4 could adapt to better human-to-human transmission, thereby potentially triggering a pandemic.[56]

A similar concern exists about influenza A viruses H5N1 and H7N9 bird flu, which have up to 60 per cent[57] and 40 per cent[58] mortality rates respectively in humans. Right now, neither H5N1 nor H7N9 does well transmitting between people. The CDC warns, however, that, 'Influenza A viruses circulating among poultry have the potential to recombine with human influenza A viruses and become more transmissible among humans. If HPAI Asian H5N1 viruses gain the ability for efficient and sustained transmission among humans, an influenza pandemic could result, with potentially high rates of illness and death worldwide. Therefore, the HPAI H5N1 epizootic continues to pose an important public health threat.'[59] Similarly, Dr Amesh Adalja, senior scholar at the Johns Hopkins Center for Health Security and emerging infectious disease expert, warns that were H7N9 to develop better human-to-human transmission, a pandemic caused by it 'could well be worse—perhaps much worse—than the great pandemic of 1918.'[60] HPAI means highly pathogenic avian influenza. 'High rates of illness and death' indeed. With mortality rates like that, H5N1 or H7N9 as a pandemic could wipe out much of humanity.

Recently, an eleven-year-old girl from Cambodia[61] and separately an eleven-year-old boy from India died of H5N1 bird flu.[62] In fact, more than 700 human infections with Asian HPAI H5N1 viruses have been reported to the WHO since November 2003.[63] Meanwhile, over 600 people have died of H7N9 since 2013.[64] In most cases, infected persons had contact with sick or dead chickens or were in contaminated environments.[65] The UN also warns that improper cooking can risk infection of H5N1 bird flu and that 'the virus can be found inside and on the surface of eggs laid by infected birds.'[66]

The HPAI Asian H5N1 virus is now considered endemic in chickens in India, Bangladesh, China, Egypt, Indonesia and Vietnam with outbreaks in chickens also regularly occurring elsewhere.[67] In these countries and others, chickens from farms have often been transported to live poultry markets to be butchered on site for fresh meat. Live poultry markets are believed to be a major source of H5N1 and H7N9[68] infections in humans. It is common to see sick chickens in them. A few years ago, China announced an intention to phase out live poultry markets over health concerns[69] and Egypt is talking about enforcing a law aimed at preventing this practice.[70]

As mentioned in the Introduction, the first outbreak of sickness from the H5N1 virus in humans took place in Hong Kong in 1997. It was contracted from chickens, and six of the eighteen people who caught it died. The illnesses in humans occurred around the same time as chickens on farms and in markets in the region became ill from the virus. In fact, nearly 20 per cent of chickens who ended up at markets there at the time were found to be infected. To try to control the outbreaks, 1.5 million chickens were killed.[71]

Human infections of various forms of avian influenza have also been reported in Russia and other places in recent times. In Russia, seven poultry farm workers were reported to have contracted H5N8 bird flu, the first known infections of this form in humans.[72] In China, a fifty-six-year-old woman died from H3N8 bird flu,[73] the first person to do so, and a forty-one-year-old man became the first person to contract H10N3 bird flu.[74] Outbreaks of various types of bird flu in chickens are not restricted to Asia and countries nearby. For instance, in December 2022, WATTPoultry reported that in Europe, 'Over the 2021-2022 epidemic seasons, 2,467 outbreaks [of avian influenza] were recorded on poultry farms...' warning, 'Europe's largest avian influenza outbreak to worsen'.[75] Meanwhile, the CDC has reported on numerous incidences of 'North American lineage avian influenza viruses' or 'North American reassortant viruses' in the US.[76]

Chicken farms can be even bigger than pig farms. Farms confining chickens for eggs may keep more than a million birds.[77] As an example of the scale, in 2020, a fire broke out at a farm in the US state of Nebraska, killing 400,000 chickens there who were being used for eggs. The facility, run by Michael Foods, houses about four million chickens crammed into twenty barns at a time.[78] (Mass deaths from fires are a common occurrence in crowded farmed animal facilities. In December 2022, it was reported that since 2013, over 6.3 million farmed animals in the US alone have been killed in fires, most of them chickens. They are thought to largely occur from electrical malfunctions or problems with heating devices.[79])

The FAIRR Initiative, a UK-based collaborative investor network, reiterates concerns about overcrowding in intensive farming of animals and other issues stating, 'The very environment of factory farming inherently creates the ideal conditions for disease. Cramming large numbers of animals into confined spaces with poor sanitation generates a hotbed for harmful pathogens. Furthermore, heightened stress levels and unnatural diets in livestock contribute to weakened immune systems, which increases susceptibility to disease.'[80]

Similarly, in a 2020 paper published in *Neuroepidemiology*, Drs David O. Wiebers and Valery Feigin, both neurology academics, observe that a 'well-recognised source for increasingly lethal human zoonoses is the massive overcrowding of animals for human consumption in industrial "factory farm" environments—also known as concentrated animal feeding operations.'

They caution, 'Intensive confinement of unprecedented numbers of chickens in these facilities to lower cost has provided a fertile ground for the development of an ever-increasing supply of new pathogens. And while bird flu was once a very rare disease among chickens, today we see outbreaks occurring every year. Transmission of these diseases from chickens to humans was almost non-existent 25 years ago; now serious outbreaks are occurring regularly—more in the past 15 years than in the entire 20th century.'[81]

Billions of hens used for eggs worldwide are housed in battery cages. These bare wire cages house up to ten birds per cage, allotting so little space to each bird that they cannot even spread a wing or turn around. The cages are then stacked on top of each other in tiered rows.[82] In Europe, battery cages have been replaced by 'enriched cages', which give the birds more space, but not much more. Animal Aid reports, 'Despite the claims of improved conditions, enriched cages provide only an additional 50 cm^2 of space per hen compared with traditional battery cages. This is smaller than the area of [a] beer mat.'[83]

Overcrowding is not always avoided at so-called free-range facilities either. The UK's *Daily Mail* reported on one such facility with 'up to 16,000 hens crammed into a shed.'[84] Meanwhile, a PETA

US eyewitness visited a cage-free shed at Hilliker's Ranch Fresh Eggs in California. The owner called it 'Chicken Disneyland'. The reality, however, was very different. PETA US reports, 'The shed was so crowded that the hens couldn't spread their wings. The eyewitness could barely see the floor through the flock.'[85]

Compassion in World Farming (CIWF) tells us that more than 70 per cent of chickens reared for meat worldwide (referred to as 'broiler' chickens by the meat industry) are raised in factory farm systems in sheds that can house up to tens of thousands of birds. In them, just like for chickens reared in battery cages, the birds may be allotted a space about the size of a standard sheet of paper.[86]

As a writer for the *Daily Mail* observes, overcrowding is very stressful for the birds. Their journalist notes, 'When you force thousands of bored birds to live together like this, their stress levels rise. Hens peck at each other's feathers, or worse, at their vents—the holes through which they defecate and lay eggs. Occasionally they turn to cannibalism.'[87] Instead of simply giving them more space, the egg and meat industries generally try to tackle stress-induced behavioural issues by slicing off a portion of chickens' beaks, causing often acute and chronic pain.[88]

The severe crowding combined with the bleak environments in which the chickens are forced to live, prohibit nearly all forms of natural behaviour vital for the birds' well-being. This is true for hens in enriched cages, too. The UK's Royal Society for the Prevention of Cruelty to Animals (RSPCA) shares its official view that enriched cages 'offer few benefits to laying hens' over battery cages because of the lack of space. They say the 'severely restricted movement' makes it hard for the birds to use the nest box, perch or dustbathing facilities fitted into these kinds of cages.[89] They were incorporated in response to criticisms by the public about barren battery cages. The lack of exercise and being bred to be either unnaturally high egg producers or fast growing with meaty builds wreaks havoc on their bodies, too.

The believed wild ancestor of chickens commonly used for eggs lays only up to fifteen eggs a year. Chickens deliberately bred for high egg production today lay over 250.[90] Meanwhile, since 1925 to now, the number of weeks a chicken used for meat was allowed to grow to become what is considered suitable weight for slaughter has decreased from sixteen weeks to six.[91] And, thanks to selective breeding, chickens today are quadruple the size of chickens in the 1950s, yet are given only half the feed of just decades before.[92]

And so, hens used for eggs often suffer health problems related to their reproductive systems as well as osteoporosis, bone fractures and other ailments. Poor bone health is particularly due to the calcium load required for egg production, exacerbated by the hens' inability to move in cages.[93] Meanwhile, chickens used for meat often suffer painful skeletal deformities, heart and lung problems, fatigue and other issues from their fast growth.[94]

In his book, Dr Greger writes, 'In intensive confinement production, crowding, stress, and filth go hand in hand.'[95] In tiered cage systems, waste from the birds on top falls on the ones below.[96] In sheds, the birds' live in their combined urine and faeces resulting in a heavy concentration of gasses such as carbon dioxide, carbon monoxide and ammonia as well as dust and pathogens. The ammonia damages the birds' eyes and respiratory systems and burns their bodies.[97] Birds in cages face similar burned eyes and chronic respiratory disease problems[98] from the manure pits that form below.

Due to poor air quality and associated risks, poultry, pig and other factory farm workers often wear protective equipment. Such precautions offer them varying degrees of protection, depending on the gear chosen, from factory farm pollution, but unfortunately there's no such thing as an N95 mask for planet Earth.

CODE RED

One of the most famous Biblical stories is that of the Great Flood and Noah's Ark. As the story goes, God was so let down by humanity's violent and corrupt ways that he decided to flood the world and destroy nearly everyone in it, with waters that submerged even the tallest mountains—a cataclysmic purge. Only Noah—a righteous man—and those he saved on his ark under the instruction of God were spared.

God had directed Noah to build the ark of wood and to make it a particular size. He told him to take his wife, sons and their wives with him when the floods came, along with a pair, male and female, of 'every kind of bird, of every kind of animal and of every kind of creature that moves along the ground'[1] so that they could create new life on Earth. The torrential downpour lasted for forty days and forty nights, killing every person and animal on land, and leaving the ark on the mountains of Ararat.

Once the rain stopped, Noah sent a dove from the ark to explore, but the animal returned, having nowhere to land. After a week, Noah released the dove again, who came back carrying an olive leaf—the imagery now regarded as a sign for peace. Waiting a week again, he freed the dove once more, who did not return. Noah understood this to mean the land was dry and safe for his family and the animals he had on board.

The Quran also contains a similar story of a worldwide flood. There are also ancient Babylonian tales of huge floods,[2] a story in which Lord Vishnu, the Hindu God, saves the world from a destructive flood[3] in the avatar of a fish and other old stories from the folklore of various cultures about evil people being drowned or the cleansing of bad from Earth.[4] Geomorphologist David Montgomery's scientific examination of many such legends have found them to be often based on some truth.[5]

American film director Darren Aronofsky's high-grossing film *Noah* is based on the story of the Great Flood, but it was criticized for not adhering to the Biblical portrayal. Aronofsky is reported to be an atheist and was not seeking a scriptural depiction anyway. He rather remarked it was 'the least biblical film ever made' and described the chief character in the film as 'the first naturalist ... who saved and cared for all the varied species on the planet.'[6] A *Time* article reads, '*Noah* is as much a parable for the modern threat of climate change as it is an Old Testament morality play.'[7]

Aronofsky, whose film uses computer-generated imagery rather than real animals, applied his artistic licence to use *Noah* to make a commentary on today's environmental issues. The film's villains are those who want to dominate the Earth and animals, including by butchering and eating them, and in contrast its heroes are those who see their purpose as guardians rather than plunderers. Aronofsky told *The New Yorker*, 'There is a huge statement in the film, a strong message about the coming flood from global warming.'[8]

Exploration on whether there was an ancient global or local flood has led to various theories—including one regarding flooding of the area that is now the Black Sea around 7,500 years ago[9] and another that widespread flooding was caused by an enormous comet colliding into the planet.[10] Whatever event or events may have happened that found themselves in ancient tales, the incidences were not human-contributed, unlike the regular environmental calamities of today.

In recent years, we have faced extreme weather events, and in particular floods. There were the floods in Pakistan that killed 1,700 people and submerged a third of the country. The devastation was estimated to cost over USD 14.9 billion.[11] Bangladesh suffered what the International Federation of Red Cross and Red Crescent Societies (IFRC) called 'one of the worst floodings ever seen'. An estimated 7.2 million people were in need of emergency relief as 94 per cent of Sunamganj town and 84 per cent of Sylhet district were underwater.[12] India was also affected by this and other floods in these years. Floods in the Indian state of Assam killed 197 people there.[13] Malaysia endured the worst flooding in its history.

It's not just Asia: Heavy rains killed 600 people in Nigeria. Australia faced its wettest year in 164 years.[14] Storm Christoph destroyed homes, submerged cars and led to hundreds of people being evacuated in north-west England and Wales.[15] Torrential rain resulted in flooding devastation in Germany leaving around 200 dead, 700 injured and many missing.[16] One survivor said it left damage looking like a bomb went off. This list is far from exhaustive. Significant flooding events occurred in other countries in recent years too.

Of course, urbanization, infrastructure and other factors help determine the extent of damage caused by flooding in any given place. But the UNEP says climate change plays a major role. They explain, 'Floods are made more likely by the more extreme weather patterns caused by long-term global climate change. Change in land cover—such as removal of vegetation—and climate change increase flood risk.'[17] Meanwhile, a study published recently in *Nature* states, 'Flooding affects more people than any other environmental hazard…' and that up to nearly a quarter more people worldwide are at risk of flooding since 2000. The percentage of those affected is expected to considerably rise by 2030.[18]

It hasn't only been floods plaguing the planet in recent years. In 2022, a bomb cyclone winter storm hit the US and Canada killing at least fifty-nine people and plunging 1.8 million homes into darkness and bitter cold without electricity.[19] The year before, a winter storm in the US state of Texas killed an estimated 700 people during the worst affected week, over four times more than the official state count, according to an assessment by *Buzzfeed News*.[20] India and Pakistan faced extreme heat, with Ahmedabad city reaching land-surface temperatures of about 65°C. Meanwhile, hundreds of forest fires ravaged India's Uttarakhand and Himachal Pradesh. China experienced its worst heat wave in sixty years. Numerous parts of Europe and Africa faced extreme drought.[21] The US suffered a severe hurricane that killed at least 114 in just one state[22] and Japan faced a typhoon resulting in four million people being evacuated from their homes.[23] The list goes on.

In August 2021, the Intergovernmental Panel on Climate Change (IPCC), which functions under the UN, released a report produced by hundreds of the world's most reputed scientists stating 'it is unequivocal' that the climate crisis is caused by human actions and that it is affecting the whole globe. It said some climate effects were already irreversible; that heatwaves, torrential rain and flooding have become more routine and severe in recent decades; that hurricanes and typhoons appear more regularly; and that drought is increasing in most places. The report warned that things are on track to deteriorate to disaster if we don't ward off average global heating above 1.5°C—the maximum global temperature rise determined by scientists to give us a fighting chance against even worse, and more irreversible, effects of climate change.[24]

Previously, the IPCC had created a special report on what can be expected if we cross the threshold of global warming of 1.5°C above pre-industrial levels to just 2°C. Apart from even more frequent and intense weather extremes, sea levels are expected to more substantially rise by 2100. This means flooding, destruction of housing and other infrastructure, job loss and other problems for those in coastal areas. Vector-borne diseases such as malaria and dengue fever are also expected to increase, as will the regions they affect, farmers will suffer more reductions in crops and food availability and water resources will decrease. Innumerable more people will suffer climate-related risks and poverty at 2°C versus 1.5°C, forests will face degradation and more plant and animal species will go extinct. Oceans will become more acidic and experience decreases in oxygen levels—immensely affecting marine life. And as problems get worse, the report warns we can expect a domino effect—such as with sea levels continuing to rise and ocean acidification from greater carbon dioxide levels worsening the harmful effects of warming.[25]

The UN Secretary-General António Guterres said the 2021 IPCC report was 'a code red for humanity' explaining that already the 1.5°C threshold is 'perilously close'. IPCC experts say we still have time to protect ourselves against the worsening effects of climate change, but not much time. The UN states promisingly, 'Strong and sustained reductions in emissions of carbon dioxide (CO2) and other greenhouse gases could quickly make air quality better, and in 20 to 30 years global temperatures could stabilize.' Guterres echoes, 'Inclusive and green economies, prosperity, cleaner air and better health are possible for all, if we respond to this crisis with solidarity and courage.' But at the rate things are going, IPCC scientists predict 2°C will be crossed during this century while we, our children, or certainly our grandchildren are still alive.

According to the report, the warming we are now seeing is happening at a rate unmatched in thousands of years with global surface temperatures increasing particularly rapidly since 1970. The global mean sea level has risen faster since 1900 than in any century in thousands of years. Meanwhile, methane and nitrous oxide greenhouse gas concentrations in the last few years surpassed those over the last 800,000 years, while carbon dioxide levels are higher than at any time in millions of years.[26] Now, scientists are warning we are likely to surpass the 1.5°C limit, at least temporarily, by 2027 thrusting us into 'uncharted territory'.[27]

All of this means we are living in a potential geological epoch of our own creation—the Anthropocene, or rather the age of time when human activity began to significantly impact the planet. There is debate on when the Anthropocene started. Some argue it should be considered to have begun around 50,000 years ago, when woolly mammoths, giant kangaroos and other large animals began to go extinct, with the key culprit believed to be hunting and other human activity. Others point to more recent things in human history such as plastic pollution, coal burning, nuclear bomb tests, modern wars, the clearing of forests for agriculture and the domination of land use for systems linked to the use of animals for meat, eggs and dairy.[28]

An expert group that presented the concept to the International Geological Congress in 2016 said the epoch should begin around 1950. This idea seems to have strong support thanks to the rapid warming over the last several decades and accelerated sea level rise, unprecedented recent greenhouse gas emissions, new deforestation at an alarming speed and the recent mass extinction of species—the Anthropocene extinction.

Chris Rapley, professor of climate science at the University College London, told *The Guardian*, 'Since the planet is our life support system—we are essentially the crew of a largish spaceship—interference with its functioning at this level and on this scale is highly significant. If you or I were crew on a smaller spacecraft, it would be unthinkable to interfere with the systems that provide us with air, water, fodder and climate control. But the shift into the Anthropocene tells us that we are playing with fire, a potentially reckless mode of behaviour which we are likely to come to regret unless we get a grip on the situation.'[29]

At the time of writing, the Anthropocene remains unofficial, but scientists are now fast working to zero in on a date[30] and conversations surrounding it remind us how significantly our actions impact the Earth.

The Anthropocene extinction is also called the sixth mass extinction,[31] as there have been five mass extinctions before. Conservation group World Wide Fund for Nature (WWF) explains, 'Unlike the mass extinction events of geological history, the current extinction challenge is one for which a single species—ours—appears to be almost wholly responsible.'[32] A paper that appears in the journal *Proceedings of the National Academy of Sciences* on the subject reads, 'The ongoing sixth mass extinction may be the most serious environmental threat to the persistence of civilization, because it is irreversible. Thousands of populations of critically endangered vertebrate animal species have been lost in a century, indicating that the sixth mass extinction is human caused and accelerating.'[33]

Apart from species being inherently worthy, biodiversity is crucial to our own survival. For instance, bats pollinate over 500 species of plants,[34] frogs play a role in mosquito control, rabbits and moles dig soil allowing plants to grow, rhinos and elephants disperse seeds from the plants they eat. Hundreds of species of birds pollinate plants too,[35] and so on.

According to a report by the UK's Royal Botanical Gardens, Kew, developed in collaboration with hundreds of scientists, nearly 40 per cent of plant species are now also at risk of extinction. The report warns, 'Never before has the biosphere, the thin layer of life we call home, been under such intensive and urgent threat. Deforestation rates have soared as we have cleared land to feed ever-more people, global emissions are disrupting the climate system, new pathogens threaten our crops and our health, illegal trade has eradicated entire plant populations, and non-native species are outcompeting local floras.'[36]

Meanwhile, a 'State of the World's Forests' report by the Food and Agriculture Organization of the United Nations (FAO) states, 'Deforestation and forest degradation continue to take place at alarming rates, which contributes significantly to the ongoing loss of biodiversity. Since 1990, it is estimated that some 420 million hectares of forest have been lost through conversion to other land uses…'[37] Plants are needed for reasons including food, medicines and clothing while forests are key to life on Earth. Trees release oxygen, induce rain through a process called transpiration, and absorb carbon dioxide.

Today, systems linked to animal agriculture—that is those related to the breeding, rearing and slaughter of animals for meat, eggs and dairy and other animal-derived products—occupy nearly half of the global surface area—*nearly half*![38] At the same time, 83 per cent of all agricultural land is occupied by facilities linked to the rearing or feeding of animals used for food.[39] We breed so many animals for various human purposes and have decimated so much wildlife and their habitats to rear them that today, 96 per cent of the world's mammals are humans and the species we use as livestock—with farmed animals making up 60 per cent of this. Similarly, most birds on Earth—70 per cent of them—are farmed chickens, turkeys and other birds raised for meat.[40]

Thanks to factory farming, the world chicken population is so fast-rising that in 2020, there were 33.1 billion chickens on Earth—130 per cent more than in just twenty years before. In the same time span, there were over 48 per cent more goats, 23 per cent more ducks, 18 per cent more sheep and 15 per cent more cattle.[41] So prevailing is the farmed chicken in the world today that some say the animals' bones, which are fossilized and found wherever humans exist, should be regarded as the key marker for the Anthropocene.[42]

This imbalance crisis has worsened in recent decades. In 2014, WWF and the Zoological Society of London scientists told us that half of the world's wild animal population, including those in oceans and rivers, was lost in just the forty years before.[43] They largely blamed the killing of animals for human consumption and the destruction of habitats, while climate change also played a role.

A group of scientists who published a paper in *Science and the Total Environment* titled 'Biodiversity conservation: The key is reducing meat consumption', warn meat, egg and dairy consumption is the largest threat to most plant and animal species through the land cleared to rear animals for these industries and grow the crops to feed them and their other environmental impacts. It reads, 'Livestock production is the single largest driver of habitat loss, and both livestock and feedstock production are increasing in developing tropical countries where the majority of biological diversity resides.'[44]

Gidon Eshel, research professor of environmental physics at Bard College, told *Science*, 'Now we can say, only slightly fancifully: You eat a steak, you kill a lemur in Madagascar. You eat a chicken, you kill an Amazonian parrot.' That's because the research team studied projections and found that fifteen countries that are the richest in plant and animal life are expected to clear up to 50 per cent of their biodiverse terrain for the production of animal-derived foods by 2050. The scientists warn that if this ruthless habitat destruction takes place, it, along with other environmental impacts of meat, egg and dairy production, will be the number one reason for extinctions.[45]

Already in Brazil, an area larger than the size of all European Union forests combined is used to raise cattle for beef and leather.[46, 47] There, forested land rights can be secured through land usage. This is often achieved through clearing land for cattle or for crops to feed farmed animals by cutting down and burning trees. Monitoring of the Andean Amazon Project (MAAP) reported almost 1,000 fires burned in the fire season of the Amazon rainforest in 2022, with most taking place in the Brazilian Amazon. A huge majority of the fires in the Brazilian Amazon at this time were human-caused fires in newly deforested areas.[48] Amazon Conservation, a group that works to protect this rainforest, also reports on illegal fires in that rainforest and warns of the risk of these fires getting out of control, as they often do.[49] For example, in 2020, of the 2,500 fires that blazed in the Amazon between late May and early November, over 40 per cent spread outside already deforested areas into the rainforest.[50]

'Meat Atlas', a report by Heinrich-Böll-Stiftung, Friends of the Earth Europe and BUND, reveals 'cattle graze on 63 percent of all deforested land' in the Amazon and that at least two-thirds of deforestation there is for cattle.[51] Soy production to feed cows, pigs, chickens and other animals has also devastated the Amazon through deforestation. While this destruction reduced[52] following the Amazon Soy Moratorium—an agreement signed by relevant parties in 2006 and renewed in 2016 indefinitely[53]—it has shifted the problem.

The moratorium followed revelations by Greenpeace linking meat sold by companies such as McDonald's to likely deforestation in the Amazon for soy. It is aimed at ensuring soy production in the region does not involve new deforestation, that slave labour is not used and indigenous areas are protected.[54] While certainly a good move, the moratorium falls short as it does not protect the biodiverse adjacent Cerrado dry forest, which is now being destroyed for soybean production.[55]

Indeed, deforestation causes a great deal of conflict over land in that part of the globe, as indigenous and local communities are squeezed out for animal agriculture related industries, resulting in the murder of hundreds of land rights activists. In fact, land used for cattle and to feed them is the key cause of disputes over land in South America. There are also battles for water.[56] It is easy to understand how water scarcity results in clashes considering recent figures show water shortages affect more than three billion people worldwide.[57]

Water Footprint Network estimates that it takes over 15,000 litres of water to produce one kilogram of beef—with most of it for crops that are fed to cattle—as compared to 322 litres to produce one kilogram of vegetables.[58] Meanwhile, the rearing of animals for food uses up a mammoth one-third of all the world's freshwater.[59] And while up to 828 million people in the world lack enough food to eat[60] one-third of the world's cropland is used to feed cattle,[61] chickens and other animals reared for food. Up to more than 90 per cent of worldwide soy production is used to feed these animals.[62] Researchers have found that if humans were fed with crops direct instead of channelled through animals, an additional four billion people could be fed.[63]

The relentless fires and loss of trees in the Amazon means terrible things for its inhabitants and for all of us. The rainforest is the largest in the world, the planet's most biodiverse region, home to one in ten species on the planet.[64] Its health is not only vital for those who live there, but also for the health of the world. In a report about the Amazon Soy Moratorium from a few years ago, Greenpeace explained, 'Holding one fifth of all the fresh water in the world, the Amazon contains 53% of the Earth's remaining tropical rainforest cover. It also provides 20% of the oxygen we breathe and is estimated to hold between 90-140 billion tonnes of C02.'[65]

It was a carbon sink—a vital protector against the climate crisis. Yet today, scientists tell us the Amazon releases more carbon dioxide than it absorbs with a 2021 study revealing it emitted almost 20 per cent more in a decade.[66] The key culprit—fires often purposefully ignited to make room for cattle and soy production, with the situation worsened by the effects of climate change. The dire state of affairs is now essentially creating itself, since less trees means less rain, higher temperatures and droughts—perfect conditions for more fires, and thus less trees, and so on. Ironically, climate change and the effects on rainfall will impact the agriculture for which much of the land was cleared.

Environmental advocates tell us all of this makes the need to tackle greenhouse gas emissions even more of a 'burning' issue than it already was, with it being imperative to take an honest look at where these emissions are coming from, and have it reflect in decisions we make. According to the FAO, meat, egg and dairy production is responsible for about 14.5 per cent of global greenhouse gas emissions. A new detailed analysis in *Sustainability* argues this figure is now out of date, and that it should be regarded as 16.5 per cent at a minimum instead.[67] By one comparison, even the 14.5 per cent amounts to greater emissions than all the world's transportation systems combined.[68] Meanwhile, a recent study published in *Nature Food* reveals animal products account for almost 60 per cent of greenhouse gas emissions from food production.[69]

'Meat Atlas' exposes how just twenty meat and dairy companies emit more greenhouse gases than either Germany, Britain or France. The year before 'Meat Atlas' was released, a report by the US-based Institute for Agriculture and Trade Policy (IATP) revealed that emissions from the world's largest dairy companies combined match those of the UK.[70]

A comparison on whether dairy or meat is worse for the environment found that cheese ranks the worst, after beef and mutton, in greenhouse gas emissions partly because of the vast amounts of milk required to make cheese. The shocking emissions contribution is especially thanks to methane belched out by the ruminant animals bred to make cheese and other dairy.[71] The US Environmental Protection Agency says, 'Methane is more than 25 times as potent as carbon dioxide at trapping heat in the atmosphere.'

And that, 'Over the last two centuries, methane concentrations in the atmosphere have more than doubled, largely due to human-related activities.'[72]

India is the world's largest milk producer[73] and has the world's largest cattle population.[74] Most of the milk it produces is consumed domestically.[75] Recently, concerned about the dairy trade's contribution to climate change and common Indian dairy industry practices like supplying cattle to the beef industry to kill and the destruction or abandonment of male calves since they cannot produce milk, PETA India sent an appeal to Amul, the country's largest dairy body. The group asked Amul to consider selling plant milk.

The request made ecological sense: a University of Oxford study found a glass of dairy milk to be nearly three times worse for greenhouse gas emissions than milks made from plants. The study also showed dairy milk trumped almond, oat, soy and rice milks in water and land use.[76] What's more, a study by Indian Institute of Technology Delhi and the Deenbandhu Chhotu Ram University of Science and Technology, Murthal, warned methane produced by India's livestock population can considerably warm the climate.[77] Instead of considering the reasons behind PETA India's request, Amul publicly attacked the group and plant milk.

PETA India retaliated by defending its request, pointing out many meat and dairy giants around the world now sell or invest in plant-based versions of meats, milks, yoghurts or other traditionally animal-based items if for no other reason than good business—to meet growing consumer demand. This includes biggies such as Tyson, Danone, General Mills, Unilever, Smithfield and many more.[78,79] Restaurant and fast-food chains are adjusting their offerings too. McDonald's, KFC and Burger King all offer vegan (wholly plant-based) burgers in some markets, for instance.

That's because today, whether Amul likes it or not, consumers are increasingly appreciating the need to eat in respect of the Anthropocene. These individuals know that to have a healthy planet and to feed a growing human population, something has to give—and these or other concerns, such as health and animal welfare, are increasingly reflected in the foods they choose to eat. The need for sustainable eating is echoed by EAT, a 'science-based global platform for food system transformation'.

The EAT-Lancet Commission on Food, Planet, Health brought together dozens of scientists from around the world to examine the question, 'Can we feed a future population of 10 billion people a healthy diet within planetary boundaries?' They concluded, 'The answer is yes, but it will be impossible without transforming eating habits, improving food production and reducing food waste.' In a report, the commission puts forward several strategies, including a global commitment 'to shift toward healthy diets' and to 'reorient agricultural priorities … to producing healthy food'. The commission explains they mean 'increased consumption of plant-based foods—including fruits, vegetables, nuts, seeds and whole grains—while in many settings substantially limiting animal source foods' and producing 'a variety of nutritious foods that enhance biodiversity rather than aiming for increased volume of a few crops, much of which is now used for animal feed.'[80]

Numerous expert sources specifically recommend vegan eating to help the Earth. Researchers at the University of Oxford tell us eating this way can reduce our individual carbon footprints from food by up to 73 per cent.[81] An article that appears on the UN Climate Change website titled 'We Need to Talk About Meat', quotes University of Oxford's Joseph Poore as saying, 'A vegan diet is probably the single biggest way to reduce your impact on planet Earth, not just greenhouse gases, but global acidification, eutrophication, land use and water use. It is far bigger than cutting down on your flights or buying an electric car.'[82]

In 2010, the UNEP released a report stating, 'Impacts from agriculture are expected to increase substantially due to population growth increasing consumption of animal products. Unlike fossil fuels, it is difficult to look for alternatives: people have to eat. A substantial reduction of impacts would only be possible with a substantial worldwide diet change, away from animal products.' *The Guardian* summarized the report as concluding, 'A global shift towards a vegan diet is vital to save the world from hunger, fuel poverty and the worst impacts of climate change.'[83] Fuel poverty means when people are unable to afford their energy requirements such as heat for those living in cold climates.

The Academy of Nutrition and Dietetics, which is 'the world's largest organization of nutrition and dietetics practitioners' has also chimed in affirming, 'Plant-based diets are more environmentally sustainable than diets rich in animal products because they use fewer natural resources and are associated with much less environmental damage.' They add encouragingly, 'Vegetarians and vegans are at reduced risk of certain health conditions, including ischemic heart disease, type 2 diabetes, hypertension, certain types of cancer, and obesity.'[84]

But while the EAT-Lancet commission warns, 'A radical transformation of the global food system is urgently needed', there is still little concrete action at the world-leader level to influence eating habits. In October 2021, the UK government momentarily included guidance to change public behaviour like a tax on food with a high-carbon footprint in a strategy document before it was quickly deleted.[85] In Spain, the consumer affairs minister, Alberto Garzón, was attacked by officials who are supposed to be his political allies for daring to say, 'Eating too much meat is bad for our health and for the planet' in a video on Twitter.[86] And at COP27, the recent United Nations climate change conference, meat and other animal-derived food was served—a lot of it—while discussions on how the production of animal products accelerates climate change were left off the agenda.[87]

In the lead-up to COP26, which took place a year before COP27 and where meat was also served, more than one hundred non-governmental organizations and key figures joined hands to appeal to the world's governments to put the impact of food and animal agriculture on the conference's agenda.

Their joint statement read, in part, 'Our planet is in crisis. The issue of food and agriculture impact needs to form a central part of the discussion and world leaders need to be ready to bring about serious change. If the way we eat does not change substantially, as a matter of urgency, we will fail to meet climate targets and the science says the repercussions will be catastrophic. Global meat and dairy consumption must be greatly reduced if we are to achieve the United Nations' Sustainable Development Goals (SDGs).'[88]

The UK-based charity Compassion in World Farming has blasted world leaders for being 'terrified of taking on the powerful vested interests that drive expanding global consumption of meat and dairy' and for being 'reckless and irresponsible' by ignoring this elephant in the room.[89] Nevertheless, it seems, for now, protecting the planet from the environmental consequences of animal product production remains largely up to the individual.

All these environmental problems with the use of land animals for food has many people looking to the sea. Which reminds me, whether any sea creatures were included on Noah's Ark is debated by those who believe in the tale by faith. Some argue that marine animals were not included because they would have survived the Great Flood. Others speculate that if there was a mixing of freshwater and seawater, most aquatic species would not have survived.[90] Was the Great Flood dangerous for fish then or not? While we have to leave that question for speculation, today, scientists tell us that our modern environmental plight and our treatment of sea creatures is linked, and that despite how the old saying goes, there are actually not plenty more fish in the sea.

IN NEED OF A SEA CHANGE

In *Death of a Whale: The Challenge of Anti-Whaling Activists and Indigenous Rights*, Captain Paul Watson, founder of Sea Shepherd Conservation Society, describes watching a whale die. It was the moment that led him to commit to a 'lifelong service to the citizens of the sea.' Sea Shepherd is a marine conservation organization famous for its direct action approach and popularized through the *Whale Wars* series about its work on the Animal Planet TV channel.

He describes, it was 1975, when he and Robert Hunter climbed into an inflatable boat to confront a Soviet whaling fleet hunting sperm whales. Robert Hunter is the late co-founder of Greenpeace. They careened their small craft so as to position it between eight terrified whales and a huge whaling vessel. This was an act of tremendous bravery—sperm whales can grow to nearly 18 metres in size and weigh up to nearly 40 tonnes. A little Zodiac boat would be nothing against a huge wave caused by a panicked whale trying to save her own life or the flick of a whale's tail.

Paul and Robert believed the whalers would back off—not possibly killing people over whale parts, but their confidence was quickly shattered. The ship released a harpoon that only just missed them and burst a female whale open. In response to the mayhem, a bull whale shot in and out of the sea. Paul and Robert braced themselves for an attack (and certain death) by an upset creature, bigger than the size of a bus.

That didn't happen. Instead, a bold whale went for the ship. As he launched his enormous body towards the vessel, the whalers fired another harpoon that lodged in his skull. The whale let out a scream and showered the ocean with a river of blood as his body fell back into the sea. Suddenly, the injured whale ascended out of the ocean, looming over Paul and Robert's boat. They had no time to get out of the way. But the whale did not come crashing down on them—instead he slipped back into the water, and as his head floated up towards the surface, his eye met Paul's as he died.

Paul believes the whales could distinguish between friend and foe. He wrote, 'The gaze of the whale seized control of my soul and I saw my own image reflected back at me. I was overcome with pity, not for the whale but for ourselves. Waves of shame crashed down upon me and I wept. Overwhelmed with horror at this revelation of the cruel blasphemy of my species, I realised then and there that my allegiance lay with this dying child of the sea and his kind.'[1]

In a tribute to Robert Hunter on its website, Greenpeace reminds us that in the 1960s and early 1970s, environmental protection was a radical concept. They write, 'There was no ecology movement, as there is today, no environment ministers, no ecology field trips in high schools, or courses in universities.' Greenpeace was founded in 1971, and among their first campaigns was 'Save the whales!'[2]

Could these whales have understood Paul and Robert were trying to protect them? Whales are so intelligent that some scientists have pondered whether they are smarter than humans. Of course, the intelligence of different species is hard, and even unfair, to compare—our smarts exist for wholly different survival needs. Sure, humans have built cities, but as neuroscientist Dr R. Douglas Fields wrote in *Scientific American*, 'One wonders how different life on earth might have been if humans, big brains and all, had flippers instead of hands…'[3]

Size isn't everything when it comes to intelligence, but nevertheless, whales have very big, complex brains. Sperm whales have the biggest brains of any creature on Earth. It is theorized that larger brains come with some advantages,[4] and considering the mental capabilities of other animals such as elephants, dolphins and porpoises, who also have large brains, perhaps it is so.

Meanwhile, orcas have denser cerebral folding than humans—indicative of rapid information processing—and the most complex insular cortex of any species. The insular cortex is responsible for self-awareness and emotion.[5] That whales *feel* would be tough for anyone to deny after news of the mother orca who kept her dead baby by her side for a heartbreaking seventeen days.[6] But could this brain structure mean they feel even more deeply than us?

Whales also form bonds and take care of those who need help. A few years ago, beluga whales in Canada included a lost narwhal in their group.[7] They have language—sperm whales speak in rhythmic clicks—and different whale communities have different dialects. They have song—humpback whales compose tunes with each other that change over time.[8] They have cultural traditions and tastes—for instance, orcas in different parts of the world and even individuals have different food preferences[9]—and they have learned behaviour—orca mothers and grandmothers teach calves how to hunt.[10]

In other words, whales are intelligent, emotional creatures who deserve not to be harmed, simply for being who they are. Yet, they were so intensely hunted in the 1970s that the population of large whales reduced by some 66 to 90 per cent.[11] Today, although commercial whaling was largely banned in 1986, they are still hunted in some places like Japan, Norway and Iceland. Iceland had announced an intention to end whaling in 2024 due to falling demand for whale meat, however, the latest news is that commercial whaling will continue there.[12] And since 1986, Japan hunted whales on the excuse it was doing 'research', but in 2019, the country blatantly resumed commercial whaling, removing itself from the International Whaling Commission (IWC), which had prohibited hunting.[13]

But leaving them be for their inherent worth is more of an animal rights view. What do whales have to do with protecting the environment? Evidently, a lot.

Whales are Greta Thunbergs with flippers. They are nature's climate activists—existing, in part, to protect the Earth. When land animals die, carbon is released into the atmosphere, soil or rocks. However, things are a little different in the ocean. When whales die, they move carbon accumulated in their bodies over their lifetimes (bowhead whales live to over 200 years!) down to the seafloor where it can stay for hundreds of years.[14]

Whales are such tremendous carbon stores; they greatly outdo trees. So much so, that the International Monetary Fund says 'one whale is worth thousands of trees', with a single great whale's contribution to protecting our planet valued at about USD 2 million. A great whale on average absorbs 30 tonnes of carbon dioxide when they die. A tree, in comparison, absorbs up to just over 21 kilograms of carbon dioxide a year.[15]

Everyone knows trees produce oxygen, but so do whales. At least, indirectly. Scientists tell us that at least 50 per cent and up to 80 per cent of oxygen on the planet comes from the ocean[16] mostly thanks to plankton—microscopic plants, algae and bacteria that photosynthesize and drift along tides and currents. The microscopic Prochlorococcus species makes up to 20 per cent of the world's oxygen, more than all tropical rainforests combined![17]

Where there are whales, there are phytoplankton (tiny marine algae), which take nutrients from the animals' excrement. Phytoplankton are eaten by small zooplankton, who are consumed by larger zooplankton, who are consumed by fish, who are consumed by sharks—you get the picture. It is from phytoplankton that other life in the ocean exists.[18] But without whales, phytoplankton populations decline—and they have been declining in global waters for over seventy years. And so, without whales, other marine life suffers. (Since the population of great whales has been gradually recovering, scientists have observed that more whales appears to mean more fish.[19] This is because whales spread nutrients all the time—even while breeding, as their placentas may be eaten, and even when dead—as they provide food to creatures at the bottom of the sea.)

Just over a decade ago, scientists warned phytoplankton had decreased by an alarming 40 per cent since 1950.[20] Apart from being affected by whale populations facing decades of hunting, phytoplankton populations are impacted by climate change, particularly rising sea surface temperatures, and ocean acidification[21] resulting from excess carbon dioxide.[22] This is caused in large part by fossil fuel burning and deforestation[23] (and undoubtedly exacerbated by the lack of enough whales to act as carbon regulators).

In addition to being carbon stores, whales help the ocean store more carbon simply by moving around and excreting iron and nitrogen, which aids not only phytoplankton but also other marine plants, all of which remove carbon from the atmosphere through photosynthesis.[24] It's not just whales—the movement of all animals in the ocean contributes to necessary circulation and the spreading and mixing of nutrients, the force of which is like that provided by wind, waves and tidal movements.[25]

Other sea life are carbon stores, too. And the same rule that applies to whales, applies to big fish. When left alone, their bodies sink to the ocean depths when they die along with the carbon they accumulated. However, fisheries significantly change this.

A recent study published in *Science Advances* reveals fisheries have released over 662 million tonnes of carbon dioxide into the atmosphere in some seventy years. A writer for environmental website Mongabay compared this to the amount 188 coal-fired power plants would release in a year stating, 'These emissions come from the release of carbon in fish bodies into the air when they're eaten or disposed of on land instead of in the sea, and from vessels' fuel consumption, and they contribute significantly to global warming and climate change.'[26] The hard truth evidently being there is no Earth-safe tuna meat. The removal of big fish such as tunas, mackerels, sharks and billfishes by the fishing industry was factored into the researchers' calculations.

The authors of the study point to the decimation of fish populations by industrial fishing fleets thereby removing astronomical amounts of 'blue carbon' from the ocean (carbon stored by the world's ocean and coastal ecosystems). Meanwhile, huge amounts of fossil fuels are burned as the fleets travel vast distances to capture fish. The authors say this is enabled through government subsidies without which an estimated 'more than half of the high-seas fishing grounds would be economically unprofitable'. They conclude, 'Therefore, overexploiting fish stocks has likely reduced or even annihilated the contribution of marine vertebrates to blue carbon sequestration over vast ocean areas since decades.'[27] Bad news for us.

Big fish play a role in ocean health and, therefore, planet health, in other ways too. Sharks, tuna and other big fish are predators. However, unlike humans, they do not do things like take fishing vessels with weighted trawl nets the size of several football fields out to catch fish, dragging them across the seafloor, capturing and destroying coral reefs and everyone and everything in their path. Instead, they help maintain a healthy ocean environment.

This includes the effect they have just from being intimidating. For instance, sharks help keep seagrass meadows healthy by scaring turtles into moving along. Turtles eat seagrass, but without sharks, they can munch away in one area to the point of destruction.[28]

Seagrasses have been called 'the lungs of the sea'. They are plants, so they photosynthesize and release oxygen. They trap sediments and particles, keeping the water quality healthy. They act as filters, helping protect coral reefs. They also protect the ocean floor from the effects of strong currents and storms. Without these services, marine animals' activities would be disrupted. They also help baby fish and little fish hide from big fish, provide a place to lay eggs, protect small creatures from currents and offer food and homes. When dead seagrass decomposes, it provides food for crabs, worms and other creatures, and when it decomposes more, it releases nutrients absorbed by seagrasses and phytoplankton.

Now Elton John's song Circle of Life will be stuck in my head.

They are also incredible carbon absorbers. Just one acre of seagrass can sequester as much carbon as that emitted by a car that's travelled over 6,200 kilometres.[29] In addition to the threat created by fisheries capturing big fish, seagrasses face many human-caused dangers such as pollution and habitat destruction.

Sharks and other fish are also good for coral reefs, most of which are under threat. Since the 1970s, shark and ray numbers have plummeted by over 70 per cent.[30] A coral reef can regrow and recover, but this process can take twenty-five years.[31]

When shark numbers suffer from fishing, the number of mesopredators (smaller predators) rise. This results in a decline in herbivorous fish, allowing algae to overgrow.[32] These helpful plant-eating fish also face a direct threat from fishing.[33] Too much algae on reefs means the blocking of sunlight and an opportunity for potentially harmful microbes to thrive. The harmful microbes reduce oxygen or cause reef disease.[34]

Parrotfish are particularly helpful for coral reefs. There are about ninety different species of them found in tropical waters and areas around them. These colourful fish spend most of their day chomping on algae. While doing so, they consume bits of coral and do the wonderful service of excreting out sand. According to the University of Hawaii at Mānoa, 'Scientists estimate that up to 70% of the sand on white sandy beaches in the Caribbean and Hawaii has been excreted by parrotfish. A large adult parrotfish can excrete nearly one tonne of sand per year.'[35] Wow. Thanks, parrotfish!

Sadly, parrotfish are being captured in such large numbers to be put on plates that algae populations are smothering coral reefs, particularly across the Caribbean. In describing a study of how parrotfish keep coral reefs healthy, marine conservation ecologist Katie Cramer said, 'Parrotfish have a positive and critical role in coral health. Using the fossil fuel record to analyse the natural state of reefs before human disturbance, we have conclusively shown that if we want to protect corals we have to protect the parrotfish from overfishing.'[36]

The situation for coral reefs is worsened when combined with other threats they face. This includes being damaged by human construction, recreation or fishing gear; the harvesting of coral itself such as for jewellery or to plonk a piece into an aquarium; climate change and ocean acidification; and pollution. The pollution comes in many forms—garbage and plastic waste, chemicals and industrial discharge, smothering by sedimentation resulting from things such as construction on the coast and agriculture, and pathogens and excess nutrients from animal waste from factory farms—and other sources.[37]

Coral reefs are hugely important. They teem with diverse forms of life. Coral Reef Alliance says, 'Coral reefs are believed by many to have the highest biodiversity of any ecosystem on the planet—even more than a tropical rainforest. Occupying less than one percent of the ocean floor, coral reefs are home to more than 25% of all marine life.'[38] It is thought there may be up to millions of species yet to be discovered who live among coral reefs.[39]

And as should by now come as no surprise, knowing what we know about how other marine life works, the species who live in and near the reefs have a symbiotic relationship with each other. In addition to the herbivorous fish (and snails) keeping the algae in check and various-sized predators keeping each other and herbivorous fish in balance, cleaner fish and shrimp pick parasites off other fish and crabs and sea cucumbers do a good job cleaning up debris from the reef and ocean floor. Worms, molluscs and other animals act as filtration systems while sponges act as hiding spaces and homes and provide food.[40]

Is it any wonder then that when a coral reef destroyed by blast fishing in the Spermonde archipelago in Indonesia was restored, scientists described the fish there as 'singing'? Blast fishing is an atrociously damaging practice in which explosives are used to stun or kill fish. Because it reduces everything in the area to debris, coral reefs are unable to grow. To overcome this challenge, the Mars Coral Reef Restoration Project placed metal frames on the seafloor, with fragments of live coral, which permitted growth.

Now, scientists are hearing fish sounds they have never heard before in the restored reef, such as 'trills, whoops, croaks, foghorns, and growls' and what sounds like radio static from shrimp eating. Marine biologist Dr Tim Lamont told the BBC the variety of noises produced had 'as much as the diversity of birdsong'.[41] An unhealthy reef depressingly goes silent as it deteriorates.

Coral reefs also protect us. The US National Oceanic and Atmospheric Administration says, 'Coral reef structures ... buffer shorelines against 97 percent of the energy from waves, storms, and floods, helping to prevent loss of life, property damage, and erosion. When reefs are damaged or destroyed, the absence of this natural barrier can increase the damage to coastal communities from normal wave action and violent storms.'[42]

Fishing drove most types of tuna to the brink of extinction by 2011[43] and now sharks and rays are fast disappearing from the world's oceans, being caught for fins, meat and liver oil and by people who recreationally catch fish. Aggressive and modern methods of fishing allowing colossal numbers of animals to be caught, illegal and unregulated fishing and fishing that's not reported—have all contributed to the number of sharks in oceans falling. Dr Richard Sherley of the University of Exeter told BBC News, 'For every 10 sharks you had in the open ocean in the 1970s, you would have three today, across these species, on average.'[44]

An estimated 100 million sharks are killed worldwide each year, including because of the shark fin trade. For shark fin soup, a pretentious dish eaten in certain Asian countries, sharks' fins are typically sliced off while the animals are still alive as this one body part is more profitable than the rest. They are then often tossed back into the ocean bleeding where they sink, now unable to swim, and suffocate, are killed by other fish or die of blood loss.[45]

(In contrast, despite what watching *Jaws* might have us think, sharks kill about six humans per year.)[46]

They are also caught as bycatch, or rather by accident along with other fish deliberately targeted by fishing vessels. Bycatch animals can include any who are unintendedly hooked, entangled or trapped in nets and fishing gear, such as sea turtles, seals and seabirds. The Fish Forward Project, worked on jointly by WWFs in various countries and co-funded by the EU, exists for 'raising awareness of social and environmental impacts of fish consumption.' They explain, 'a large amount of [bycatch] is either thrown back into the sea as "rubbish", dead, dying or seriously injured, or disposed of on land' warning, 'this commercial, unselective fishing is therefore one of the biggest threats to marine species.'[47]

In a 2009 paper that appeared in *Marine Policy*, researchers defined bycatch as 'catch that is either unused or unmanaged'. With this definition, they conservatively estimated that more than 40 per cent of global marine hauls are bycatch![48] That means for every fish eaten, another animal has likely died.

The Consortium for Wildlife Bycatch Reduction, founded by Duke University, University of New Hampshire and other organizations, says the problem is so severe that 'In some fisheries, the percentage of bycatch far outweighs the amount of target catch,' while giving the example, 'for every shrimp caught by nets dragged behind trawls in the Gulf of Mexico, over four times its weight is bycatch'.[49] And according to various WWF reports, bycatch figures include at least 300,000 small whales, dolphins and porpoises; over 250,000 turtles; 345,000 seals and sea lions; 720,000 seabirds; tens of millions of sharks and other sea animals. The organization warns 'many of these species are endangered or on the brink of extinction'[50] and calls bycatch 'the biggest killer of whales'[51]—surpassing the number killed on deliberate hunting missions. In fact, the IWC says bycatch and entanglement in fishing gear is 'the single, most direct threat to cetacean populations and welfare'.[52]

So much of a threat that there are only a few hundred North Atlantic right whales left. Experts blame them being trapped in fishing equipment and hit by ships. These whales were also previously heavily hunted.[53] What's more, bycatch has driven the baiji, a freshwater porpoise who lived in China's Yangtze River, to likely extinction. In Mexico's Gulf of California, there are now only about ten vaquita porpoises, who continue to be threatened by nets.[54]

Numerous albatross species[55] are threatened with extinction because of longlining, a fishing technique using nets up to 100 kilometres long, with up to thousands of baited hooks hanging from them, to capture tuna, swordfish and other targeted fish. The hooks become embedded in the animals' mouths or elsewhere on their bodies, injuring them further as they struggle to escape. Fish and other animals who are caught in longlines can be trapped for days until they are hauled up on boats.[56]

Tuna and swordfish are huge. Bluefin tuna can weigh up to 680 kilograms and be 3 metres long. Meanwhile, swordfish can reach 450 kilograms and be nearly 5 metres long. Such large animals are not easy to handle, and so fishers sink pickaxes anywhere on to the animals' bodies where they can get a grip, to yank them on deck. This could be in their fins, sides and even eyes.[57]

Albatrosses and petrels, who are among the birds who get caught in longlines, are also at risk from the fishers themselves. Fishers operating in the south-west Atlantic use blades to slice the beaks off live albatrosses to hurriedly remove them from hooks. The birds are then chucked in the ocean where they die.[58] Meanwhile, fishers using various methods of fishing have been observed hitting birds with weapons to try to stop them from getting to bait. Birds are also severely injured or killed through fishers' rough handling.

The UK's Natural History Museum describes research undertaken to understand the extent of this problem revealing, 'The data showed records of birds with these types of injuries occurring across the coastal waters of Brazil, Uruguay and Argentina. These records included 16 birds from four species, two of which are globally threatened, being intentionally killed or mutilated. The records indicated that birds had suffered head trauma, broken limbs, wounds or bill mutilation. In addition to these a further 29 birds, from eight species, were recorded alive with serious bill mutations, most likely the result of fishermen intentionally cutting the birds' bills.'[59]

There are numerous other modern methods of fishing that indiscriminately catch animals. That's why today, WWF calls fishing 'the biggest threat to marine wildlife'. Apart from trawl nets and longlines, undiscerning fishing equipment includes gillnets and purse seines.[60]

A gill net is a sheet of netting that fish cannot see. Many fish get their heads stuck in the net and become even more constricted by it as they try to escape. The struggling can make it difficult for the fish to breathe as the net tightens around their bodies. The fish suffer lacerations from the net and become easy prey for predators. The gill nets can remain suspended in the water for days, causing prolonged suffering.[61]

Meanwhile, fish caught by the purse seining method find themselves enclosed in netting that can be 1 kilometre long. The netting and all the animals in it are then pulled up, like a drawstring handbag. It's not hard to imagine what happens inside the net—the fish begin to panic as the net closes in and the area gets smaller and overcrowded. As the fish try to escape, moving helter-skelter, they collide into one another and with the netting, causing injury. When they are brought on board as a mass, many fish are crushed.[62]

Seabird health is considered a good indicator of the conditions of marine ecosystems. Unfortunate, then, that seabird populations studied around the world have plummeted by 70 per cent since the 1950s.[63] The reasons include dramatic declines of species they rely on for food due to fishing, plastic and oil pollution, climate change and destruction of their habitats in addition to being caught as bycatch and harmed by fishers.

Many seals are also killed by fishers for doing what seals need to do—eat fish. In Scotland, officially, nearly 2,000 seals have been killed by fishers since 2011[64] to stop them from getting to farmed salmon in cages and to those trapped in nets. Unofficially, the death toll is thought to be far more. Recently, Scotland prohibited the shooting of seals by the fishing industry in most cases. This means non-lethal methods should be used instead (although Acoustic

Deterrent Devices have been near prohibited by Environmental Standards Scotland[65] as they are so strong that they cause stress and hearing damage in seals and other animals). The country wanted to continue exporting salmon to the US (the US is banning imports from countries that allow seals to be killed for fishing[66]). But it is thought Scottish fishers may kill seals in isolated areas when nobody is watching.

Shooting seals is a practice that is wrought with welfare problems. Shooting them in the water can result in a prolonged death. When they are shot in a way that just causes injury, the death is slow, agonizing. When mother seals are shot, pups die of starvation. Many pregnant seals are shot too.[67]

The existence of aquaculture or fish farms—factory farms for fish—in which huge numbers of salmon or other fish are raised in cages or tanks harms wild animals too. In its report, 'Until the Seas Run Dry, How Industrial Agriculture is Plundering the Oceans', Compassion in World Farming (CIWF) along with other agencies reveals 'almost a fifth of the world's total catch of wild fish is processed into [fishmeal and fish oil], of which 69% of fishmeal and 75% of fish-oil production are used to feed farmed fish.' These fish and fish products are even fed to non-carnivorous farmed fish for abnormally fast growth. They are also often fed to farmed chickens and pigs.

The report reveals the target species to feed to farmed fish are usually small forage fish (such as sardines, anchovies, mackerel and herring) and crustaceans like krill. But these are the animals that tuna, salmon, cod, sharks and whales need to survive. The group warns of 'knock-on effects on other marine life, including marine mammals and seabirds' and that feeding farmed fish wild-caught fish 'could have other unknown consequences given the extreme complexity of marine ecosystems and the impacts of climate change'.[68]

In an article about the eye-opening documentary *Seaspiracy*, on how fishing industries impact oceans and the planet, British journalist George Monbiot says the film highlights 'why we must treat fish not as seafood, but as wildlife'.[69] This is because just as hunting on land can lead to animals going extinct, so can hunting in the sea. Neither jungles nor oceans are a never-ending resource. In 2006, a study reported on in *Science* warned that per global trends at that time, all species of wild-caught marine animals are on course to collapse by 2050. 'Collapse' meaning a 90 per cent reduction of the species' baseline population.[70] (*Seaspiracy* covers the debate regarding estimations of fish populations in the next decades on its website at seaspiracy.org/facts, but the key point remains, wild fish populations are in trouble.)

A 2014 *National Geographic* magazine article cautioned that by then, already, 'Aquacultural pollution—a putrid cocktail of nitrogen, phosphorus, and dead fish—is now a widespread hazard in Asia...' And that, 'To keep fish alive in densely stocked pens, some Asian farmers resort to antibiotics and pesticides that are banned for use in the United States, Europe, and Japan.'[71] Drugs are commonly used in underwater factory farms for the same reasons they are used in factory farms above ground—to compensate for filth and severe overcrowding. They are also used to increase growth.

A couple of years ago, India's environmental magazine *Down To Earth* raised the fact that we should still be concerned. During an Antimicrobial Awareness Week, its journalists wrote, 'Diseases are a primary constraint to aquaculture and a variety of drugs are used to control the diseases. However, the imprudent use of these drugs in aquaculture is a contributing factor in the spread of anti-microbial resistance (AMR).' That, as you will recall, is when medicines we need fail to work.

The magazine went on to state, 'Since the majority of antimicrobials used in aquaculture are also employed in human medicine, their use has a significant impact on the development of AMR in other ecological niches, particularly the human environment. Researchers have reported an increase in the frequency of serious infections and treatment failures as a result of antimicrobial resistance being transferred from aquaculture to humans through the consumption of aquaculture products.' Regarding fish farming in India specifically, *Down To Earth* revealed, 'Misuse and overuse of antibiotics are pervasive…'[72]

India is the world's second largest shrimp exporter.[73] Its seafood customers include the US, the EU, Asian countries and the Middle East.[74] Consignments of antibiotic-laden shrimp are sometimes rejected. Concerned about this, in January 2022, the Indian Ministry of Fisheries, Animal Husbandry and Dairying sent a letter to the chief secretaries of the country's states and union territories urging them to stop antibiotic use in aquaculture.[75] However, in November of that same year, experts at an aquaculture and fisheries conference held in India discussed that monitoring is difficult. Dr George Ninan, director of India's Central Institute of Fisheries Technology, said, 'Most of the water bodies used for aquaculture are contaminated with AMR pathogens.' And that, '[I]n fisheries, people are adding all kinds of chemicals without knowing anything about their impact.'[76]

What happens in Asia should concern us all. According to a 2020 article in *Scientific Reports*, 'Asia contributes nearly 90% of global aquaculture production.'[77] But it's not just Asia where the use of drugs in fish farming poses an issue. Researchers looked at the aquaculture data of forty countries and determined that twenty-eight showed evidence of 'high-risk antibiotic contamination'.[78] To make matters worse, rising water temperatures due to climate change appear to aggravate certain fish diseases, which will likely result in even more antibiotic use.

Too much nitrogen and phosphorus from animal waste in waterways is bad news too,[79] especially when combined with various effects of climate change, such as high levels of carbon dioxide and heat.[80] Such conditions cause algae blooms, or a severe abundance of algae in the water. The blooms can produce toxins that kill fish and other animals and make humans sick or worse from eating fish containing toxins, swimming in toxic water or breathing in toxic droplets.[81] Blooms can also consume oxygen from the water, resulting in dead zones where animals cannot survive. They can also form stinking, septic pools.

Around the world—from America's Lake Erie[82] to China's Dianchi Lake[83]—animal waste from nearby livestock farms is turning waterways putrid and green. Waste from fish farms can cause algae blooms too. In their report on Scottish salmon farms, CIWF and OneKind state, 'Not only is salmon farming bad for animal welfare, but it is also damaging the environment. Organic and chemical waste from Scottish salmon farms is changing the chemistry of sediments and killing marine life on the seabed. Waste from farms can lead to poor water quality and harmful algal blooms, which deplete oxygen from the water, and can suffocate the farmed fish who cannot swim away.'[84]

You read that right—algae blooms from farmed fish waste harm farmed fish themselves. In 2019, around 83,500 farmed salmon from just one company died from a harmful algal bloom. That same year, in Norway, over 8 million fish trapped on farms died in a week because of algae blooms.[85] Phys.org, which covers science news, reports that between 1985–2018, 'A sharp increase in the poisoning of farmed fish and shellfish worldwide had led to speculation that toxic algae blooms were on the rise. But such incidents stemmed more from an increase in fish farming itself, which grew 16-fold over the 33-year period.'[86]

And as CIWF and OneKind state, fish farming raises animal welfare concerns—serious concerns. Scotland is among the top producers of farmed Atlantic salmon. In 2020, CIWF investigated twenty-two Scottish salmon farms using various technology and means, including drones and divers. On these farms, fish were confined to crowded barren underwater cages for up to two years.

They documented salmon with missing eyes and injured mouths, damaged gills and fins, cut and wounded, infected and diseased. On numerous farms, they found fish with portions of flesh missing, plagued with sea lice. Trapped in cages, the salmon cannot escape the parasites. The lice from caged salmon farms can increase infestations in nearby wild fish. There are treatments used for sea lice, but they involve taxing procedures that can kill the salmon themselves, such as chemical baths. Or the farms create welfare problems for other fish, such as when cleaner fish are introduced into pens to eat the sea lice. These fish are so poorly kept, they often die.

The salmon often die too. The CIWF and OneKind report reveals, 'In Scotland, farmed salmon mortality rates can be as high as 28.2% in the seawater stage and including mortalities from the freshwater stage would push this number even higher.' The chemicals and drugs used for reasons such as addressing sea lice and disease in farmed salmon make their way into the environment and are harmful to other life.[87] Alarmingly, a UK government Veterinary Medicines Directorate report revealed a 168 per cent increase in antibiotic use in Scottish salmon in 2021 as compared to 2017.[88]

Essere Animali is an Italian organization that has investigated fish farms in several European nations in recent years. The group claims its investigation of Italian sea bream, sea bass and trout farms in 2018 was the first investigation of fish farms in Europe. The similarities of the group's findings in other European nations indicate they can be considered representative of common fish farming practices on the continent.

Their video documentation from Italian farms shows sea breams used for breeding circling in a small tank, where artificial light is used to manipulate them into reproducing. It also exposes the crude process of artificial insemination, in which male and female fish are handled out of water and squeezed until eggs or milt squirt out of their bodies. It reveals severely overcrowded land and sea-based tanks and cages where fish are housed for up to eighteen months. And it shows them being removed from these receptacles by nets causing crushing and fish being shot through a chute into crates for transport at force.

The group also documented the variety of killing methods used, with one starting with fish being packed into boxes containing ice and water, gasping as the oxygen drops. An hour later, many of these fish are still alive as they are processed to be tied by their gills and tails into U-shapes to be taken to the market. Other fish left to suffocate are shown gasping hours after being hauled up out of their pens. Yet other live fish are hit on their heads against a metal container or with an iron bar.

The group's investigation of Greek sea bream and sea bass farms conducted with We Animals Media and released in 2021 also resulted in concerning findings. In Greece, there are dozens of cages at each of the country's hundreds of fish farms, housing millions of fish. The investigators filmed cages crammed with hundreds of thousands of fish swimming in endless circles, suffering from the effects of their own waste. The conditions end up being so poor, 20 per cent of the fish die before slaughter. As in Italy, these fish too are hauled up in crushing nets and dumped into containers filled with ice water where freezing or suffocating to death is agonizing and slow.

Most recently, in 2022, the group published a video in collaboration with CIWF of seven Spanish farms rearing trout, sea bass and sea bream. This video too depicts similar treatment, including thousands of fish crowded into tanks swimming in circles in their own waste. It exposes how fish fight to get to food tossed into their tanks, leading to injuries and death. And shows a cruel size grading system where fish are passed through rollers as they fight for breath. It uncovers fish being given electric shocks in icy water or in containers, a stunning method prior to slaughter that Essere Animali calls 'ineffective' as many fish continue to struggle for minutes and try to escape.[89]

Essere Animali has taken its #AncheiPesci (#FishToo) campaign to the European Parliament,[90] where the group is arguing for better treatment of fish for the fish themselves, but environmental impacts of fish capture and production mean no matter how different marine animals may seem from humans, their welfare is directly linked to our own.

This is true from a food consumption perspective too—a study found that today waters are so polluted that approximately 84 per cent of fish contain mercury levels so high that their meat is considered unsafe to eat.[91] Most mercury in oceans is the result of human activity, such as the burning of fossil fuels.[92] Exposure to mercury has been linked to cancer, heart issues and other serious health concerns and is considered extremely dangerous for pregnant women since it can affect the baby's brain development. Considering the health disadvantages of eating fish, which Washington DC-based Physician's Committee for Responsible Medicine (PCRM) warns contain cholesterol and saturated fat just as other animal-derived foods do, the doctors' group recommends flaxseeds, walnuts, chia seeds, hemp seeds, soybeans or wheat germ instead of fish for alpha-linolenic acid (an essential omega-3 fatty acid good for heart and brain health).[93]

The welfare of other animals who may seem very different from us—insects—the biggest, most diverse group of organisms on Earth,[94] is also wholly linked to our own.

BUTTERFLY EFFECT

There are many astoundingly stunning insects on Earth, and monarch butterflies are certainly among them, with their marigold-coloured wings lined with black and dotted with white at their rims—their beauty reminds us of flowers, of sunshine and instantly begets joy. These exquisite animals, however, offer more than just good looks—they are also part of the ecosystem as pollinators, are responsible for one of the most epic natural phenomena that happen in the world and their declining numbers signify trouble.

Monarch butterflies join different bats,[1] birds like hummingbirds, honeycreepers and sunbirds as well as various other species of butterflies,[2] bees, wasps, beetles, moths and other animals who are pollinators. (Houseflies and mosquitos are pollinators too!)[3] As pollinators, adult monarch butterflies aid in plant reproduction. They do this by landing on wildflowers for their nectar and transferring pollen between plants as they flutter from flower to flower.[4]

Many pollinators are important for humans, too. In fact, no pollinators would mean no chocolate! About three-quarters of the various food crops we grow need pollinators to some degree and about one-third of our food production comes from crops that need them. Many fruits, vegetables and nuts are among the crops partly reliant on pollinators, while certain fruits and cocoa beans are among the crops wholly dependent on them.

An article in *Our World in Data*, a scientific online publication run with the support of the University of Oxford, reads, 'Pollinator insects—bees, wasps, beetles, flies, ants and butterflies—play an important role in agriculture. We might associate crop pollination with honey bees, but a range of studies have shown that non-bee pollinators (such as butterflies, beetles and hoverflies) also play an important role in the pollination of fruits, vegetables, and oilcrops.'[5]

Monarch butterflies and their caterpillars are also food for birds and other insects.[6] Other pollinator species are eaten by reptiles, bats and other small animals.[7] These animals are, in turn, food for larger animals—with each thereby playing a key role in nature.

Eastern monarch butterflies make a spectacular one-way journey of up to nearly 5,000 kilometres from various summer breeding grounds in the US and Canada to a few forested mountains in Mexico, their overwinter destination. There, after travelling for two or three months, up to millions gather together on the branches of oyamel fir trees, causing them to bend, and making the sound of rain when they take flight again. The trees help regulate temperature and provide a protective environment for the monarchs.[8,9]

Fascinatingly, while most adult monarchs live for a little over a month, during which time they feed on nectar and lay their eggs on milkweed, by the fall of a year, a generation is born that postpones sexual maturity and can live for up to eight months.[10] This generation, called the 'Methuselah', are the ones who migrate to Mexico, a place they have *never previously been* to.[11] (Methuselah is a Biblical figure who is said to have lived for 969 years.)[12]

How do they do this? Scientists say they are led to Mexico by an 'internal compass'. Incredibly, these marvellous little beings are believed to use an internal body clock and the sun's position to figure out where to go. They are also thought to operate with a 'separation point' in their visual field that determines how they must travel to get back on track, for instance, should the wind blow them off course.[13]

Not a moment late, the monarchs begin arriving in the Mexican mountains during the Día de los Muertos (Day of the Dead),[14] a festival that takes place on the first two days of November. Dia de los Muertos originated in Mexico and is observed in much of Latin America, coinciding with All Saints Day and All Souls Day. The celebration has pre-Hispanic Aztec roots as goddess Mictecacihuatl, the Lady of the Dead, allowed spirits to meet living family again. This became intertwined with Catholic traditions[15] (Catholicism was first introduced, or rather forced, on to indigenous people in the region by Spanish *conquistadores*[16]).

Día de los Muertos observers create altars for their deceased loved ones. There, the dead's photos are placed, along with marigolds and objects such as candles, skull art made of sugar, bottles of mezcal and tequila, bread and perforated paper art—with each item carrying a purpose or meaning. For instance, the beautiful fragrance of the marigolds and their bright orange colour is thought to guide souls from cemeteries back to their family homes.[17]

The festival is jubilant and lively, not sombre, as it is in celebration of the lives ancestors lived, and a time to allow those deceased to return to share in the joy of their families again. Festival traditions, therefore, include parties and parades and Día de los Muertos celebrants often wear skull masks, flowers and monarch-butterfly-inspired garments.

Before the Spanish arrived in Mexico in the 1500s, Purépecha Indians noted the annual arrival of the monarch butterflies. It is their belief that upon death, most of us live on in Mictlán. There, it is said, we rest until we can reunite with our relatives. The monarchs were thought to represent the souls of loved ones returning for their yearly visit.[18,19]

In March, the monarchs begin to migrate northwards, and as they do, they lay eggs on milkweed, the only plant used by them for this purpose, after which the adult monarchs die. Their offspring then continue to move north, taking several generations to reach their ultimate destinations in the US and Canada.[20]

Today, the Mexican place of the monarchs, the Monarch Butterfly Biosphere Reserve, is a UNESCO World Heritage Site, aimed at protecting the monarchs, and thereby also protecting the significant role they play in local culture. And they do need protection—but safeguarding them in Mexico alone is not enough.

Historically, the Eastern monarchs arrive in Mexico by the millions, maybe even a billion,[21] but today these butterflies are in deep trouble. Over about the last forty years, their population has dropped by around 80 per cent. Western monarchs opt to spend their winters in the US state of California, rather than in Mexico. Both excellent choices if you ask me! But they too are in trouble—such trouble that they are edging towards extinction. Their numbers have plummeted by 99 per cent in that same duration.[22] The International Union for Conservation of Nature (IUCN) now classifies the migratory monarch butterfly as 'endangered'.[23]

Initially, conservationists thought illegal logging and deforestation in Mexico were behind the Eastern monarchs' decline. Areas were then shielded by being incorporated into the Monarch Butterfly Biosphere Reserve and problems were better addressed. However, now it is understood that to improve monarch numbers, protection must also happen elsewhere the monarchs go. In a story about the Eastern monarchs' plight, Vox aptly describes it as '[A] real-life butterfly effect: Pull a lever in one part of the world and it affects another. And that's what makes protecting monarchs so challenging. For decades, the leading approach to saving animals has been to set up reserves—refuges where they're free of harm. But that strategy simply isn't enough for species with complex and far-reaching migrations.'[24]

Chip Taylor is professor emeritus, ecology and evolutionary biology, at the University of Kansas and director of Monarch Watch, an education, conservation and research programme based at that university. Monarchs rely on milkweed to lay eggs across the American Midwest, and in the early 2000s, an email from a farmer about what was going on there worried him.[25]

Monsanto debuted Roundup Ready soybean in the mid-'90s. It is genetically engineered so not to be killed by glyphosate, the most commonly used herbicide worldwide. Within a few years, other crops resistant to glyphosate were also introduced.[26]

Taylor learned that in Midwestern US, farmers had begun using this new genetically engineered herbicide-resistant corn and soybean. This helped them use chemicals to get rid of weeds and other unwanted plants, including milkweed, which compete with their crops.[27] The chemicals destroy these 'nuisance' plants, but not the desired ones, and harm insects like honeybees and other animals.[28, 29]

By 2018, Tierra Curry, conservation biologist at the Center for Biological Diversity in the US, told the *Des Moines Register*, 'In the Midwest, nearly ubiquitous adoption of glyphosate-resistant "Roundup Ready" corn and soybeans has caused a precipitous decline of common milkweed, and thus of monarchs, which lay their eggs only on milkweeds.'[30]

Today, according to the US Department of Agriculture (USDA), over 90 per cent of corn and soybeans grown in the US are genetically engineered. This includes those herbicide-tolerant, insect-resistant, or both.[31]

Soy and maize are among the few crops that are described as dominating global agriculture.[32] Most—up to around 90 per cent[33] as stated in a previous chapter—of the soy produced worldwide is fed to animals raised for meat (including farmed fish), eggs and dairy,[34] while just 7 per cent is used for direct human food products such as tofu, soy milk, edamame beans and the like.[35] Most corn worldwide is used for animal feed too—about 70 to 80 per cent.[36]

In the US specifically, the USDA says, 'Corn is the primary U.S. feed grain, accounting for more than 95 percent of total feed grain production and use.'[37] Feed grain means any grain used to feed animals. Meanwhile, the American Soy Association shares, '[M]ore than 90% of U.S. soybeans produced are used as a high-quality protein source for animal feed.'[38]

The very transition of grasslands into land used for crops and industrial farms in the Midwest has also decimated nectar-producing plants like milkweed.[39] World Animal Protection notes, 'The production of corn and soy takes up more than a third of America's agricultural land, despite humans consuming less than 10 percent of it.'[40] Massive sheds housing factory-farmed animals also sprawl across the Midwest, having cleared the plants that once stood there.[41]

Grasslands are important. The WWF Plowprint report reads, 'Like forests, grasslands also play a critical role as carbon storing ecosystems … Grasslands also provide critical habitat for plant and animal life, livelihoods for rural communities, clean water, and fresh air.' The report reveals, across the Great Plains (which includes parts of Midwestern states), 'from 2018-2019 an estimated 2.6 million acres of grassland were plowed-up, primarily to make way for row crop agriculture.'[42] That's an area bigger than the size of Lebanon.[43] Almost half of this was for corn and soy.

The WWF report goes on to state, 'When grasslands are tilled, soil organic carbon stocks are immediately reduced by 30% on average, releasing vast amount[s] of carbon into the atmosphere. As abandoned croplands are restored, recovery of carbon stocks to levels comparable to the soil found in native prairies may take 350 years, though up to 50% recovery has been observed in the first few decades. Therefore, the optimal solution is to avoid conversion in the first place…'

Then there are the wildfires destroying the monarchs' habitats and everything in their path that have recently been burning through the Midwest and the Great Plains due to wind and drought, making vegetation perilously dry, thanks to climate change.[44] A couple years ago, a huge swath of the forested area, Boundary Waters Canoe Area Wilderness, in Minnesota state, went up in flames. Parts of that state were deemed to be suffering 'exceptional drought'—a designation achieved for the first time then. Around the same time, snow melting abnormally early in Wisconsin state contributed to wildfires raging so severely that people had to be evacuated from their homes. Climate change means the region is on course for more droughts and extreme heat, and thus more wildfires.[45]

Making matters worse, the variety of trees, including drought-resistant ones such as oak and pine, have reduced in the region due to historical logging and clearing land for farms. Adding to trees' woes—warmer temperatures and conditions like drought can cause plants stress, predisposing them to disease from fungi, bacteria, viruses and other contributors.[46] Warmer temperatures can also cause an imbalance in certain insect numbers,[47] which can negatively affect trees, especially when they are vulnerable. Abnormally cold temperatures and air pollution can harm trees too.[48] The resulting dead and dying plants add fuel to wildfires,[49] as they are available to burn, but also because they release more energy as heat in fires (the amount of this energy available depends on the amount of water they store, which is affected by climate change).[50]

There is also the direct effect of climate change on monarchs. The UNEP warns, 'Monarch Butterflies are very sensitive to changes in temperature as they rely heavily on this factor to prompt migration, hibernation and reproduction. Thus, changes in temperature due to climate change are expected to influence and potentially disrupt these critical stages of the butterflies' life cycle.'[51] For instance, it is the change in temperature that signals to the monarchs when to start moving north or south. Plunges in temperatures at butterfly hibernation sites could also mean they freeze to death. Too much rain means less time spent by the monarchs in laying eggs. The butterflies are also killed by severe storms.

Temperature affects monarchs' metabolism and flight efficiency too. Those born in the cooler weather common to the autumn temperatures of the US experience greater flight efficiency than those born when it's hot.[52] This means the monarchs born in cooler weather have to spend less energy to fly—a worry as temperatures rise.

The UNEP notes, 'Higher than normal temperatures also hinder the growth and quality of milkweed, the plant that Monarch caterpillars feed on. Current predictions indicate that milkweed populations will need to shift poleward to find the appropriate growing conditions. This raises the current concerns about whether the Monarch Butterflies will be able to adapt successfully to these changing sites and environments. Furthermore, it is thought that if the milkweed's range expands further from the hibernation/breeding ground then the butterflies' reproductive activity will decline. This would consequently mean that the butterflies would need to migrate longer distances, reducing the time spent at the breeding grounds.'[53]

Rising levels of carbon dioxide in the atmosphere from fossil fuel use, cars, deforestation, wildfires and other sources also pose a threat to the monarchs. A University of Michigan study explains, 'Mounting levels of atmospheric carbon dioxide reduce the medicinal properties of milkweed plants that protect the iconic insects [monarchs] from disease.'[54]

In an opinion piece that appeared in *The Herald Journal*, Rachel Taylor, research associate for Southwest Monarch Study, an organization studying the migration and breeding patterns of monarch butterflies in Southwestern US, wrote, 'Some wonder what the big deal is if we lose the monarchs. To me, not only are they my favorite, but they are our modern-day canary in a coal mine—a warning of what's happening to our environment.'[55]

I'm not fond of the phrase—until 1986, canaries were actually taken down into coal mines in Britain to detect toxic gases, the idea being that if the canary fell ill or died, it was time to get out. They have thankfully been replaced with technology.[56] But Rachel has a point. Many of the factors that impact monarchs' survival affect other species too, and these factors are certainly not restricted to Mexico and the US.

A 2021 article in *Science* revealed, in the forty years prior, over 450 butterfly species in the western US have been on a fast decline—reducing in numbers by an average of 2 per cent each year—due to rising fall temperatures. Some are tearing towards extinction. It is believed the warmer temperatures during this time of year affect the butterflies' hibernation-like state and thus food availability.[57] Across the ocean in Europe, butterfly numbers have also been dropping. In the UK, numbers dropped by half in forty-five years, and 8 per cent of species there have gone extinct. In the Netherlands, numbers dropped to half only since 1990, and 20 per cent of the species there have gone extinct. In Belgium, nearly 30 per cent of butterfly species have gone extinct, and total numbers declined by 30 per cent in just a fifteen-year span. Since 1990, grassland butterfly numbers in Europe have plummeted by nearly 40 per cent. Many other butterfly species on the continent are near threatened. Habitat loss and environmental degradation due to reasons such as clearing land for agriculture, chemical pollution, air pollution like aerial nitrogen build-up and climate change are thought to be the key culprits for this decimation.[58]

Chemical pollution from insecticides such as neonicotinoids is also associated with the decline of bees and insect-feeding birds. The International Union for Conservation of Nature calls neonicotinoid pesticides 'a worldwide threat to biodiversity, ecosystems and ecosystem services'. They are now largely prohibited in the EU, but still in use elsewhere around the world.[59] Key sources of aerial nitrogen accumulation are ammonia from animals farmed for food and nitrogen oxides from vehicle emissions. Nitrogen pollution changes the vegetation and environment butterflies need to survive and thrive.[60]

Scott Black, ecologist and executive director of the Xerces Society, remarked on a study of butterflies telling *National Geographic*, 'It adds to our growing understanding of what's going on with insects and insect decline across the globe.'[61] And indeed, butterfly health is a strong indication. (The Xerces blue butterfly was the first butterfly to go extinct in North America from human actions, thus the organization's name. It's a non-profit that focuses on invertebrate conservation.)[62]

While climate change effects and human meddling cause some insect species numbers to rise, in recent years, there have been alarming reports of insects disappearing from across the globe—the rate appearing to be an average decline of 9 per cent of terrestrial insects each decade according to a recent report in *Science*. This is a conservative figure—less than what has been estimated by other studies—and even so, it signals a loss of over a quarter of the troubled insect populations in three decades.[63]

The worldwide waning of bee populations in particular has been widely reported. An article published by *One Earth* reveals about a quarter less bee species were found in the period between 2006 and

2015 than prior to 1990, and that the number of bee species found in Global Biodiversity Information Facility (GBI) data has dropped since the 1990s.[64] GBIF is a public science database supported by world governments.

The FAO warns, 'The global decline in bee populations poses a serious threat to a wide variety of plants critical to human well-being and livelihoods, and countries should do more to safeguard our key allies in the fight against hunger and malnutrition…' The organization further stresses, 'Bees and other pollinators are declining in abundance in many parts of the world largely due to intensive farming practices, mono-cropping, excessive use of agricultural chemicals and higher temperatures associated with climate change, affecting not only crop yields but also nutrition. If this trend continues, nutritious crops such as fruits, nuts, and many vegetables will be substituted increasingly by staple crops like rice, corn, and potatoes, eventually resulting in an imbalanced diet.'[65]

There is that mention of agricultural chemicals such as pesticides and herbicides again. And indeed, the risk they pose to insects all over the world is so severe, they are worth the emphasis. 'Meat Atlas', the 2021 report by Heinrich-Böll-Stiftung, Friends of the Earth Europe and BUND mentioned in a previous chapter, reveals, 'The worldwide use of pesticides has doubled since 1990, with over 4 million tonnes of active ingredients now applied every year to control weeds, insects and other plant pests.' The report says, 'While applications have stagnated in many parts of the European Union over the last 30 years, they have increased sharply elsewhere in the world.' The authors blame this in large part on 'the rising global demand for meat' and name the five firms that dominate 70 per cent of the world pesticides market as Syngenta, headquartered in Switzerland; Bayer and BASF in Germany; and Corteva and FMC in the US. They explain, 'These companies are grouped into a trade association known as "CropLife International". They do a particularly good business in highly hazardous pesticides for growing feed crops. Applications for soy and maize account for almost half their sales of such pesticides.'[66]

Then there is the lesser highlighted threat of artificial light, which covers about a quarter of the planet.[67] As *The Guardian* notes, 'Artificial light at night can affect every aspect of insects' lives…from luring moths to their deaths around bulbs, to spotlighting insect prey for rats and toads, to obscuring the mating signals of fireflies.'[68] Washington University in St Louis researchers explain the disruption is because many insects 'have evolved to use light levels as cues for courtship, foraging and navigation'. Individuals can easily help address the chaos artificial light causes in insects' lives by simply turning off lights we don't need. Other steps the researchers advise are using motion sensor lights, using fixtures to cover up direct bulbs and light, and to use amber lights (for now we know insects are most attracted to blue and white light, followed by yellow, red and orange lights).[69]

Undeniably, there are numerous compelling reasons to address all of these threats. Bees are popular and take a lot of the credit for being helpful to humans, but as we know, they aren't the only insects who play this important role, or other vital roles in nature. Insects are, in fact, so crucial to ecosystems that the late biologist Edward O. Wilson declared, 'If all mankind were to disappear, the world would regenerate back to the rich state of equilibrium that existed ten thousand years ago. If insects were to vanish, the environment would collapse into chaos.'[70]

Apart from many being pollinators and food for both animals who live in water and those who live on land (it seems bird populations have already taken a hit from fewer insects[71]), insects do many other valuable things. Some release nutrients from various organic matter such as dung, dead plants and animals into the soil—making sure dead matter does not simply collect—helping plants grow. Some predator insects eat other insects who would otherwise damage crops or other plants. Yet other insects help distribute seeds. Some burrow in soil, helping to aerate the ground.

A couple of researchers tried to calculate the monetary value of the work done by insects. They looked at data for 'dung burial, pest control, pollination, and wildlife nutrition' and calculated at least USD 57 billion to be the 'annual value of these ecological services' provided in the US alone.[72]

But it seems insects aren't worthy only because they are useful—increasingly, scientists argue they are intelligent, have consciousness and an ego, and can feel, raising ethical questions about our moral responsibility to them. After all, they do so many clever and even difficult things if we're willing to look: such as identify plants and hunt, communicate and engage in teamwork, travel long distances and navigate flight, steer clear of danger, guard eggs and do lots of other things humans cannot do. However, for scientists to start coming around to these ideas, they had to get over their human egos first.

Dr Antoine Wystrach who studies animal cognition describes what began to change in an article he wrote for *The Conversation*. He says in considering animal intelligence, 'We are inclined to tackle this question using a top-down approach. It seems intuitive to start with our own assumptions about human intelligence, and design experiments that ask whether animals possess similar anthropomorphic abilities.' Rather, he says, we can 'Assume an animal is the simplest it can be, whilst looking for proof of a higher level of intelligence. With such an approach, research in insect intelligence is working bottom-up, with simple (and boring) initial explanations being steadily replaced by increasingly complex (and exciting) explanations.'[73]

Lars Chittka is the founder of the Research Centre for Psychology at Queen Mary, University of London, and leads the institute's Bee

Sensory and Behavioural Ecology Lab. He regards measuring animals' abilities on human parameters 'a bit one-dimensional and ultimately boring'. In speaking about insects, he told environmental website Mongabay, 'Animals' sensory systems expand into many aspects of the environment that are entirely inaccessible to us…'[74] Imagine if we could see in the ultraviolet spectrum like a bee can. What new information about the world would seeing this provide to us?

Several University of Adelaide evolutionary biology experts also argue we need to look at animal intelligence and abilities as 'different kinds' to those of humans altogether as they are based on species' unique environmental needs.[75] Most of us don't need to know which flowers have been recently sapped of pollen—but bumblebees do, and they leave each other messages through transferring positive electrical charges to flowers by flapping their wings. Other bees know which flowers to avoid based on these charges.[76] Likewise, humans would find it pretty impossible to follow a scent trail in any precise manner, but this is what ants do with ease (they can even follow a zigzag trail, no problem).[77] If bumblebees or ants judged humans purely by these bee and ant qualities, they would think we are really inept. Similarly, more and more scientists believe looking at insects only in terms of how similar they are to us makes little sense.

That said, in an article about insect feelings for BBC Future, writer Zaria Gorvett reminds us that in many ways, insects are, in fact, not so different from us.[78] They breathe, have eyes and hearts and brains. They have digestive tracts and reproductive organs, and eat and excrete.

We're 60 per cent genetically identical to fruit flies.[79] This shouldn't come as a huge surprise. Humans and insects stem from a common ancestor[80]—albeit from hundreds of millions of years ago, with the human side going the way of fish and then on land, and the insect side evolving into crustacean-type land or water-dwelling animals.[81]

Gorvett tells us insects have brain regions that do the same kinds of things vertebrate brains do, such as learning and memory. (Biologists have found beetles start using their brains at the larvae stage, despite still being under development![82]) Sure, insects have tiny brains, but over time, powerful computer chips have gotten smaller—we get that size does not necessarily determine capacity. (Or strength for that matter—the horned dung beetle is only 10 millimetres long but can pull the weight comparable to an average-sized man lifting two fully-loaded 18-wheeler trucks.[83]) In fact, in computer chips, smaller can mean more efficient, requiring less power.

Like humans and other vertebrates, according to a study published in *Proceedings of the National Academy of Sciences*, the brains of insects 'also support a capacity for subjective experience'. The researchers call this 'the most basic aspect of consciousness'.[84] A subjective experience meaning a personal, emotional, cognitive experience occurring in an individual insect's mind. The implication being they could be motivated by *feelings*, or a state of mind, like hunger (in a study, flies did better at remembering where to find food when they were deprived of it[85])—rather than in an automaton kind of way.

And why not? They also have the same primary reason for feeling emotions humans and other animals do—to survive. A cockroach in a bathroom will hide behind the toilet, presumably from fear, or move fast up the wall, to avoid being killed. Similarly, a wasp will seemingly be motivated to feed on flowers if it is satisfying.

Lars Chittka told BBC Future, 'Let's say you're a bee that ends up in a spider web, and a spider is swiftly coming towards you across the web. It's not impossible that the escape responses are all triggered without any kind of emotions. But on the other hand, I find it hard to believe that this would happen without some form of fear.'[86]

Today, scientists tell us bumblebees even show 'positive emotion-like states',[87] or in other words—something like *happiness*. The use of words like that makes most scientists nervous—they'd rather stick to clinical terms and phrases like 'positive emotion-like states', since after all, a bee cannot *tell* us she is happy, we have to infer it from her behaviour. Well, a dog or a baby cannot tell us either.

Scientists also tell us that cockroaches, like us and other animals like cows, have rich spatial memories and social lives.[88] They also tell us paper wasps appear to use known relationships to make inferences about unknown relationships (in other words, if A is greater than B, and B is greater than C, then A is greater than C type reasoning),[89] that bees can learn tasks from others and then improve upon them,[90] that bees can learn simple math and perform better when under pressure,[91] that honeybees and wasps can recognize human faces,[92] that ants can adapt tool use,[93] that different fruit flies communicate in different dialects[94] and can learn each other's and much more.

Who knows what else we will learn about these magnificent little beings as we open our minds to them? And as we learn more, what will it mean for how we then treat them for their own sake and ours?

CRYING OVER MILK

My dear late friend the fearless Riyad Wadia is not the only person I know or have heard of who suffered or succumbed to tuberculosis (TB). A former colleague in India struggled with TB recovery. Over the years, TB would come up in conversation with my parents about people they knew growing up in India. My mother suffered some then-unknown condition with a terrible cough when she was young in the 1950s, and the panicked word on the street at that time was that it was TB (it wasn't). But people could be forgiven for making the guess.

That's because even today, India is called the TB capital of the world, accounting for over a quarter of the global 10 million cases per recent figures and a huge number of deaths.[1] TB is, in fact, a top leading global infectious killer, coming in second only to Covid-19 and surpassing HIV and AIDS. But just eight countries make up two-thirds of total cases: India, China, Indonesia, the Philippines, Pakistan, Nigeria, Bangladesh and the Democratic Republic of Congo.[2] What is it about them causing this? (A deep dive into all the reasons would be far longer than one chapter of a book, but here I share a serious contributing factor.) And why, despite TB first being recognized in India in 1912 and the country launching its first National Tuberculosis Control Programme in 1962,[3] is the situation in some ways getting worse?

According to the latest WHO Global Tuberculosis Report, in 2021, India, on its own, accounted for 36 per cent of deaths in HIV-negative people and 32 per cent of combined deaths of HIV-negative and HIV-positive people from TB. That year, 1.6 million people worldwide died from the disease.[4] In 2015, it was reported a TB patient in India died every two minutes.[5]

In late 2022, India's Ministry of Health and Family Welfare reported an 18 per cent decline in TB cases since 2015.[6] Frighteningly, however, the true pervasiveness of TB in India is thought to be greater than official accounts due to reasons including underreporting, lack of thorough surveys, the stigma surrounding TB and HIV and undiagnosed disease.[7] (As mentioned in Chapter 2, since HIV weakens the immune system, people infected by it are more likely to contract TB. India has the world's third largest number of HIV cases, with some 2.3 million people there living with HIV.[8])

India has intentions to turn this trend around. The country has an ambitious plan to eliminate TB there by 2025 through its 'National Strategic Plan for Tuberculosis Elimination 2017–2025'. Yet, Indian researchers studying the prevalence of TB in the country have noted, 'Despite these impressive commitments, due to less-than-optimal service delivery and various challenges, [India] could not make much progress in terms of achieving substantially high cure rates and carries the by-far highest burden of TB and MDR-TB.'[9] Multidrug-resistant TB (MDR-TB) is TB that does not respond to at least two of the most useful anti-TB drugs (isoniazid and rifampicin).[10]

TB is a bacterial infection that typically infects lungs, but can affect the brain, kidneys, stomach, spine, bones and other body parts. From humans, it spreads through droplets in the air such as from when a person speaks, laughs, coughs or sneezes (similar to Covid-19). Symptoms can include fatigue, persistent coughing, coughing up blood, chest pain, weight loss, night sweats, a loss of appetite, fever and chills.

People can either have latent infection without symptoms or active infection, with only the latter being contagious; but latent TB can become active if not treated. People who get infected by someone with drug resistant-TB disease can even develop extensively drug-resistant tuberculosis (XDR-TB).[11] XDR-TB is resistant to even more TB drugs (including any fluoroquinolone and to any of the second-line injectables—amikacin, capreomycin and kanamycin).[12]

Then there is totally drug resistant TB (TDR-TB). It is the mother of all—TB that is resistant to *all* known drugs. (The WHO does not use the term totally drug resistant TB even though it is used in the media and often appears in scientific literature. The WHO considers such cases forms of XDR-TB.[13] Either way, you don't want to contract TB, and you certainly don't want any form of drug-resistant TB.) An estimated 50 to 70 per cent of people infected with XDR-TB die[14] and attempted treatment for it can last for over two years.[15] Medications can be so aggressive, they cause nausea, joint pain, hearing loss and terrible depression. Life-saving efforts can even involve cutting out affected parts of lungs.

People travel, they get on flights, and as we know very well from Covid-19, any infectious disease prevalent anywhere is a threat to people everywhere. A few years ago, the *Scientific American* reported on a patient with 'supercharged tuberculosis' who flew from Mumbai to Chicago, warning 'the deadly disease could become an infamous export' from India. That patient, who was suffering from XDR-TB, drove around visiting relatives in different states before being quarantined. The article warns, the more people with XDR-TB, the higher the chances of wider global spread.[16]

According to research published in *Scientific Reports* a few years ago, 'India accounts for about one-fourth of the global burden of MDR-TB.'[17] Drug-resistant TB can develop when infected people do not adequately complete their prescribed course, when the wrong treatment is provided (such as when a prior check on whether the patient has the drug-resistant form of TB is not conducted), or the drugs are not of good quality.[18] In these instances, the TB can simply become stronger.

There's another factor for drug resistance too—the overuse of drugs.[19] Among other reasons, overuse has occurred when people in India have been misdiagnosed as having TB due to faulty tests and were prescribed drugs. It also happens when chickens there are given drugs humans need.

Today, India is the world's third-largest egg producing country and has the second highest number of egg-laying hens.[20] It is the fifth-largest producer of chickens for meat. This is driven, in part, by the rise of factory farming in the country. According to WattPoultry.com, a resource website for the global poultry industry, 85 per cent of egg production in India now comes from 'commercial farms'[21]—in other words, factory farms versus family-run backyard facilities. In them, birds used for eggs are reared in crowded battery cages in which each chicken is provided no more space than the size of an A4 sheet of paper.

The Federation of Indian Animal Protection Organisations (FIAPO) coalition group is trying to stop the use of battery cages there through a case in the Delhi High Court.[22] FIAPO describes that on farms, battery cages are 'stacked one on top of the other, in row after row.'[23] As stated before, this forces chickens on lower tiers to suffer the falling waste of those above.[24] For treatment like this and the severe confinement, they point out the 'extreme cruelty'[25] housing system violates the Indian Prevention of Cruelty to Animals Act, 1960. This law, as you will recall, prohibits confining animals in a way that prevents reasonable opportunity for movement, but that hasn't stopped battery cages from becoming the dominant housing system for egg-laying hens in the country.

Alokparna Sengupta, Managing Director of Humane Society International (HSI) India, explains 'a 2 to 3-foot pile of litter and faeces'[26] commonly collects under the stacked rows of cages of a huge number of birds. Her group says, 'With up to ten hens per cage and thousands of cages stacked vertically in multiple tiers, facilities stocking 10,000 to 50,000 birds are now common in India.'[27]

Crowding and filth is common on Indian broiler farms too—that is, farms rearing chickens for meat—as the number of birds processed by each facility can be enormous. In fact, just one Indian company, Suguna Foods, kills 400 million chickens in a year.[28]

HSI explains, 'Industrial practices crowd birds from the start; producers may deposit 20,000 to 30,000 day-old broiler chicks atop litter material in a shed, and as the chicks grow, the crowding intensifies.'[29] In India and around the world, the legs of many of these birds, who are bred to be top-heavy for meat, buckle under their own abnormal weight. This results in them spending the majority of time lying in wet faeces on the floor.

All these factors make the birds susceptible to illness. In 2014, India's Centre for Science and Environment (CSE) shared the findings of an exercise to determine the link between the rampant use of antibiotics by the country's poultry sector to try to prevent sickness, for growth and other reasons and antibiotic resistance in humans. Their findings were startling.

They described, '[M]any essential and important antibiotics for humans are being used by the poultry industry. In India, there is growing evidence that resistance to fluoroquinolones such as ciprofloxacin is rapidly increasing. Treating fatal diseases like sepsis, pneumonia and tuberculosis (TB) with fluoroquinolones is becoming tough because microbes that cause these diseases are increasingly becoming resistant to fluoroquinolones.' The organization further reported, 'The CSE study found two fluoroquinolone antibiotics—enrofloxacin and ciprofloxacin—in 28.6 per cent of the chicken samples tested.'

Explaining what this means, the CSE said, 'Large-scale misuse and overuse of antibiotics in chicken is leading to the emergence of antibiotic-resistant bacteria in the chicken itself. These bacteria are then transmitted to humans through food or environment. Additionally, eating small doses of antibiotics through chicken can also lead to development of antibiotic-resistant bacteria in humans.'[30]

A couple of years after that, Ramanan Laxminarayan, director and senior fellow at the Washington DC-based Center for Disease Dynamics, Economics & Policy, told Bloomberg that antibiotics are often used by India's poultry farms in place of adequate sanitation and hygiene. Bloomberg had visited several poultry farms in south India and reported, 'Records shown by the farmers indicated that at least nine antibiotics were in use, five of which are critical for treating everything from pneumonia to lethal bloodstream infections in humans. Among them were products made by Bayer AG, Zoetis Inc. and Cadila Healthcare Ltd.'s Zydus animal health unit, which are prohibited for use in poultry in Canada, the U.S., the European Union and Australia.' The outlet reported, 'Most of the farmers didn't know what an antibiotic was, describing it as just one of the vitamins, medicines and disinfectants they use to keep the birds healthy.'[31]

In 2019, India's Ministry of Health prohibited the 'manufacture, sale and distribution of the drug Colistin and its formulations for food-producing animals, poultry, aqua farming and animal feed supplements as it is likely to involve risk to human beings.'[32] Colistin is a critical last-resort option in human medicine, used for infections where other drugs have failed.[33]

A promising step, but problems with the overuse of antibiotics in the Indian poultry sector persist. In 2020, *Down To Earth* magazine reported that the CSE contacted three key Indian poultry producers as potential customers. They were Komarla Feeds, Skylark Hatcheries and Krishi Nutrition Private Limited. Its authors wrote, 'All the companies accepted that their feeds contain antibiotics or medicines. Animal husbandry officials and academicians in six important poultry-producing states of India—Andhra Pradesh, Haryana, Karnataka, Punjab, Tamil Nadu and Uttar Pradesh—also confirmed that a variety of antibiotics, such as ciprofloxacin, levofloxacin, erythromycin, nalidixic acid, neomycin, kanamycin, avilamycin, apramycin and flavomycin, are administered to poultry through feed for growth promotion, in response to a questionnaire by CSE. Ciprofloxacin and levofloxacin belong to the class of fluoroquinolones used to treat tuberculosis in humans.'[34]

Then, in 2021, *Comparative Immunology, Microbiology & Infectious Diseases* published a study 'regarding the antimicrobial resistance of pathogens in poultry environment in India and its transmission to humans'. The researchers observed, 'The use of antimicrobials in food animal production is not properly regulated in India. So, many clinically important antimicrobials are used indiscriminately.'

The group focused on two poultry farms in a region of Kerala state to collect faecal matter and other samples. They simultaneously collected samples of antibiograms from urinary tract infection (UTI) patients from a nearby hospital. Antibiograms are profiles of how specific microorganisms react to antimicrobial drugs. They determined bacterial infections in the public residing near the poultry farms were caused by similar drug-resistant Escherichia coli (E-coli) as that affecting chickens. Specifically, they found, 'All samples were resistant to ampicillin, amoxicillin, meropenem and tetracycline. Similar resistance pattern in poultry environment and UTI patients was seen for antibiotics such as ampicillin, amoxicillin, amikacin, and ofloxacin.'[35] The conclusion being that the use of antibiotics in nearby chicken production as a growth booster and other treatment made the local community resistant to the same drugs used.

Most recently, in 2023, *The Times of India* reported, 'Doctors are finding it increasingly difficult to treat simple stomach upset cases, which would otherwise heal with antibiotics, due to growing antimicrobial resistance (AMR).' The article quotes experts as blaming 'Liberal antibiotic use in poultry, aquaculture and livestock' for growth promotion and in place of hygiene, and specifically cites resistance to fluoroquinolone and ciprofloxacin.[36]

Consumers are naturally concerned. A couple of years ago, World Animal Protection conducted research in various Asian countries, including India, about what consumers think about chicken meat production. They did this through focus group discussions and found nine out of ten consumers had some concerns about chicken farming, with one in five specifically worried about where meat came from, and how the animals were raised. Among their concerns were hygiene, the spread of diseases and chickens fed with antibiotics. Indian consumers thought there should be stronger government controls.[37]

As far back as 2017, the WHO had appealed for a cessation of the use of antibiotics in healthy animals worldwide. Their plea read, 'WHO is recommending that farmers and the food industry stop using antibiotics routinely to promote growth and prevent disease in healthy animals.' Their aim was 'to help preserve the effectiveness of antibiotics that are important for human medicine by reducing their unnecessary use in animals.' The agency said, 'In some countries, approximately 80% of total consumption of medically important antibiotics is in the animal sector, largely for growth promotion in healthy animals.'[38] Artificially larger, fast-growing animals means more meat per animal and quicker time to slaughter. However, the

WHO can only recommend such steps to governments, not require them of them.

Compounding the issue is the use of antibiotics such as streptomycin and tetracycline against diseases in crops in India. The CSE found various farmers were spraying these drugs on to crops regularly, like pesticides, without adequately understanding their use.[39] Streptomycin is important for the treatment of formerly treated TB patients, multidrug-resistant TB and some cases of TB meningitis (of the brain), while tetracycline is an important antimicrobial used to treat a variety of bacterial infections. Among its many uses are treating sexually transmitted diseases—syphilis, gonorrhoea and chlamydia. In late 2021, the Indian Union Ministry of Agriculture and Farmers Welfare issued a draft order that, if passed, would prohibit the use of streptomycin and tetracycline on crops by the start of 2024.[40]

At least there is some news coverage and public awareness about the misuse of antibiotics and its role in the TB crisis in India. Very little mainstream coverage exists on the role of the Indian dairy industry in TB spread.

As mentioned in a previous chapter, India is the world's largest milk producer and has the world's largest cattle population. In *Transboundary and Emerging Diseases*, researchers share, 'Bovine tuberculosis (bTB) is a chronic disease of cattle that impacts productivity and represents a major public health threat.' Although they say, 'accurate estimates of bTB prevalence are lacking in many countries, including India', the researchers reviewed the data available by 2018 to calculate an estimate. They found, 'there may be an estimated 21.8 million infected cattle in India—a population greater than the total number of dairy cows in the United States.'[41] bTB is primarily caused by Mycobacterium bovis (M. bovis).

It's believed that M. bovis is behind about 10 per cent of all TB cases in people in developing nations. And before it became a requirement to pasteurize milk in many countries, M. bovis was responsible for about a quarter of all childhood TB cases. However, these figures are likely an underestimate. A paper shared by *Wartazoa, Indonesian Bulletin of Animal and Veterinary Sciences*, explains there is a lack of adequate information about how much M.bovis contributes to the global TB crisis because of how similar various TB lesions clinically look, and since the treatment of TB regardless of the causative agent is the same, researchers are not always motivated to figure out the cause.[42]

Even now, looking at the other countries with high TB rates, despite generally poor documentation and assessment of bTB in cattle or TB due to M. bovis in humans, researchers found bTB was widespread in cattle in China;[43] bTB in cattle used for dairy in Indonesia has long been a known issue;[44] a bTB positive herd of cattle was killed in the Philippines a few years ago;[45] numerous slaughterhouse workers and livestock farmers tested positive for M. bovis in Pakistan during a study;[46] bTB is considered endemic in Bangladesh;[47] in Nigeria the proximity of humans to cattle is considered a risk factor for TB and the consumption of raw meat and milk are regarded as major sources of human infection with M. bovis,[48] and in the Republic of Congo, adjacent to the Democratic Republic of Congo, slaughterhouse workers are considered to be at TB risk.[49] In fact, generally in Africa it is recognized that 'bovine tuberculosis occurs throughout the African continent'[50] where the combination of HIV and tuberculosis is of major concern.

There is also M. orygis. A recent *BMC Infectious Diseases* publication reads, 'In South Asia, M. orygis is a causative agent of tuberculosis in cows, rhesus monkeys and humans.'[51] In India, in one study using patients from Christian Medical College in Vellore, M. orygis was found to be the more common agent of TB than M. bovis.[52] Other researchers have raised the possibility that humans can transmit M. orygis to cattle (this had happened in a case in

New Zealand[53]) or that our species and theirs can transmit it to each other.[54]

In countries around the world, the pasteurization of milk does not always happen perfectly. Inadequate pasteurization occurs due to reasons such as faulty equipment, problems with the process or poor sanitization. Unpasteurized milk is also deliberately sold.

According to an estimate from some years ago, 70 per cent of milk in India is sold without pasteurization.[55] Perhaps the figure today is less, but it remains customary for many households to get milk straight from dairies, raw.[56] This milk is usually boiled at home in an attempt to get rid of harmful bacteria.[57] Many Indians (and in fact, people around the world) consider raw milk more natural and thus healthier.[58] As would be clear to you by now, drinking or eating unpasteurized dairy products is a risk factor for being infected with bovine-related TB. So is consuming the meat of a TB-infected animal (and meat too is often improperly cooked). It can also be spread to humans from infected cattle through the air, and then onward from person and person.

At the start of the Covid-19 pandemic, Maneka Gandhi, Member of Parliament in India, wrote an article for the newspaper *Mathrubhumi* warning the public about TB from cattle. She was worried that the pandemic would mean people would pay even less attention to the risk posed by bTB. She expressed, 'Much of [TB] is from drinking milk, eating milk products and eating beef. The bacterium, Mycobacterium bovis, survives 1-8 weeks in cattle faeces, so anyone handling gobar [manure] is at risk. Pasteurization kills the bacteria but is your milk pasteurized? Forget the consumer, when the dairy owner is physically taking out the milk from the animal, he stands a strong risk of getting bTB. When we surveyed the Idgah slaughterhouse, which I shut down 30 years ago, most of the butchers had bTB, getting it from the infected meat. It is as prevalent today among dairy workers and butchers.'[59]

She also wrote much of the milk that ends up in Indian households is from dairies with 'no licence, no parameters, no government controls'. World Animal Protection's 2020 report on the Indian dairy industry reads, 'Up to 50 million dairy animals are suffering every day in dairy farms; with millions kept in illegal local dairies located in our cities (urban dairies) and suburbs (peri-urban dairies). These dairies supply milk to city dwellers who crave for rural fresh milk and believe that this fresh milk is more healthy—when in fact it is not.'[60] A few years ago, FIAPO visited dairies in Delhi and nine high dairy-producing Indian states. It noted, only 14.3 per cent of dairies observed were registered with relevant authorities. FIAPO's report described illegal dairies that exist without official permission, and therefore, without oversight, as the norm in India, rather than the exception.[61]

The Cattle Site exists as a resource for the beef and dairy industries. Its 'Cattle Disease Guide' says, 'Animals are probably more likely to be infected by M. bovis when they are poorly nourished or under stress.'[62] And the disease spreads among cattle primarily the same way it does among humans—through close contact—however, it can also spread through feed or water contaminated with the urine or faeces of an infected animal.[63] It can spread to calves through saliva, colostrum or milk from infected cattle too.[64]

On Indian dairy farms, there are plenty of opportunities for vulnerable animals to experience stress and contract and spread M. bovis. FIAPO reports crowding due to space limitations, particularly when dairies are crammed into city spaces and urban areas—locations that help meet the demand for 'fresh' milk. They also reveal most cows and buffaloes on the farms they visited as suffering from illness or injuries and facing stressful situations—including calves commonly taken away from their mothers immediately after birth so that milk they would otherwise drink could be sold. The physical ailments FIAPO noted included large gaping wounds, tumours and fractures in cattle. The organization found veterinary care lacking and irregular, with most dairy owners permitting the milking of sick animals for milk sale.

FIAPO also observed most cows and buffaloes were kept constantly tied by extremely short ropes. This meant they were unable to escape their own waste and were forced to eat and drink near where they excrete, and made to stand in painful, uncomfortable postures. They documented that most of the farms fed the cattle less than the required minimum per day too. Poor diet and being tied in waste results in animals slipping on hard floors slick with diarrhoea.

More recently, three individuals who were part of an animal welfare fellowship submitted a report of their observations at nine major Delhi-based dairies to the chief secretary and Delhi Pollution Control Committee (DPCC). They reported severe overcrowding, with animals essentially immobile from short ropes and chains, slippery floors, facilities laden with excreta, sick and injured and dead and dying animals—particularly malnourished calves who had died. The report says, 'All the dairy colonies had carcasses of dead calves lying in the middle and corners of the streets with swarms of flies and crows hovering over them.'[65]

The trio had reported the calves were actively deprived of nutrition. Because male calves cannot produce milk, they are often left to starve on Indian farms. PETA India's investigative report on the dairy industry there reads, 'In Mumbai tabelas [dairies], male calves have their feet tied so they cannot try to go over to their mothers for milk and their mouths tied shut with ropes so they cannot cry out when they are hungry (this is done so the residents of buildings near the tabelas do not come to investigate why they hear the babies' cries). These babies are then left to die a slow, agonising death in a corner.'[66] Many male calves in India are also abandoned on the street or are sent to slaughter, even though it is illegal in India to butcher animals under the age of three months old in India. (In other countries, too, male calves are often immediately shot[67] or confined to a crate so narrow they cannot turn around for veal.)

Antibiotics are fed to cattle for the same reasons they are fed to chickens and other animals reared for food—for treatment, as a growth promoter, or to try to prevent disease in filthy conditions—contributing to the drug-resistance crisis. According to a booklet by ReAct, an international independent network raising awareness about antibiotic resistance, 'Presence of antimicrobial residues in milk has been reported from different parts of India, indicating wide antimicrobial use in food animal production in India. One of the most common clinical issues encountered in the dairy farms is mastitis, and milk from cows and buffaloes affected by the disease [has] been shown to contain bacteria with a wide spectrum of resistance against commonly used antibiotics. In some cases, multiple drug resistant bacteria have been seen to co-infect animals suffering from mastitis.'[68] Similar to what the CSE explained, the organization shares that resistant bacteria can affect humans through improperly cooked food and that bacteria and antibiotic residues from factory farming spread to the environment, such as through manure. Antimicrobial-resistant bacteria can also be transferred to humans from animals reared for food through direct contact with animals.[69]

An article published a couple of years ago in *Antimicrobial Resistance & Infection Control* reports, '[S]everal [antimicrobial] resistant bacteria have been isolated in milk sampled within India.' ESBL (extended spectrum beta-lactamase)-producing bacteria is resistant to many antibiotics, making it difficult to treat. The authors reported 'ESBL producing E. coli' and 'ESBL producing K. pneumonia' in bovine milk collected from various parts of India. The study authors said 'most of the ESBL producers from bovine milk' also harboured 'fluoroquinolone resistance gene(s)'.

Fluoroquinolones, you will recall, are used to treat TB. They are also used to treat a huge variety of other bacterial infections. The authors also list studies reporting evidence of resistance to a huge variety of other drugs by scientists studying bacteria in Indian milk samples. One study reported vancomycin resistant S. aureus (VRSA) 'for the first time in bovine and goat milk'.[70] Vancomycin is used to treat a variety of conditions such as endocarditis (which can destroy heart valves), meningitis (which can cause death), osteomyelitis (painful swelling of bone marrow) and numerous others when caused by bacterial infection.[71]

So TB is a dairy-linked public health crisis, but what about breast cancer? Dr Michael Greger, who was also mentioned in a previous chapter, is a physician, bestselling author and speaker on nutrition, food safety and public health issues. In an article titled, 'Should You Be Concerned about Bovine Leukemia Virus in Milk?' he writes, 'Decades ago, concern was raised that the milk of dairy cows frequently contains a leukemia-causing virus—more specifically, bovine leukemia virus (BLV), the leading cancer killer among dairy cattle. Most U.S. dairy herds are infected with the cancer virus.'[72] Actually, BLV infects cattle all over the world.

He explains this question has long been studied, and it has been determined humans can be infected with BLV, but the necessary tests were not sensitive enough years ago to examine whether the virus contributes to human disease—but times have changed. Scientists worked to determine whether BLV found in human breast tissue are cancer-causing. (In one study, 44 per cent out of 219 samples of human breast tissue tested positive for BLV.) They decided to look at breast tissue from cancer patients collected by the US-based Cooperative Human Tissue Network. They found, 'Presence of BLV-DNA in breast tissues was strongly associated with diagnosed and histologically confirmed breast cancer … As many as 37% of breast cancer cases may be attributable to BLV exposure.'[73]

The Washington DC-based Physicians Committee for Responsible Medicine (PCRM) want us to know drinking bovine milk is linked to poor health in other ways, too. The doctors' group warns milk and other dairy products can be a 'top source of saturated fat' in the diet, 'contributing to heart disease, type 2 diabetes, and Alzheimer's disease'. They further warn, 'Studies have also linked dairy to an increased risk of breast, ovarian, and prostate cancers.'[74]

You may be thinking that may be so, but what about bone health? Dr Amy Joy Lanou, professor of health and wellness and the executive director of the North Carolina Center of Health and Wellness for the University of North Carolina Asheville published a response to that in *The American Journal of Clinical Nutrition*. It reads, 'Osteoporotic bone fracture rates are highest in countries that consume the most dairy, calcium, and animal protein. Most studies of fracture risk provide little or no evidence that milk or other dairy products benefit bone. Accumulating evidence shows that consuming milk or dairy products may contribute to the risk of prostate and ovarian cancers, autoimmune diseases, and some childhood ailments. Because milk is not necessary for humans after weaning and the nutrients it contains are readily available in foods without animal protein, saturated fat, and cholesterol, vegetarians may have healthier outcomes for chronic disease if they limit or avoid milk and other dairy products. Bones are better served by attending to calcium balance and focusing efforts on increasing fruit and vegetable intakes, limiting animal protein, exercising regularly, getting adequate sunshine or supplemental vitamin D, and getting ≈500 mg Ca/d from plant sources.'[75]

India's dairy industry causes grief in other ways too—the country has over five million stray cows and buffaloes, most of whom are males or other dairy industry rejects. Strays also include dairy animals allowed to roam in search for food.[76] These animals suffer tremendously from things such as car accidents, being attacked with acid and weapons by farmers trying to protect crops and from ingesting huge amounts of plastic and other harmful waste from garbage dumps. In one incident, Indian veterinarians tried to save the life of a pregnant cow by pulling 71 kg of plastic, nails and other ingested waste out of her stomach.[77] Despite their efforts, the cow and her baby died. There are numerous other stories of veterinarians removing kilos of garbage from a few lucky Indian animals' stomachs.

As you can surmise from what happens to many male calves, not all Indian cows and buffaloes end up on the roads—many end up at slaughterhouses. A very small percentage of Indians eat beef[78] and cow slaughter is banned in many states, but there are thought to be thousands of unlicensed (and thus illegal, unregulated) slaughterhouses in India,[79] and buffalo meat is legally exported. Although the export of cow beef is illegal, some export samples tested have been found to be cow beef.[80] India is also the sixth largest supplier of leather in the world[81]—working to meet the demands of its largest buyers: primarily the US and numerous European nations[82]—while gravely harming the health and well-being of many of its citizens.

SKIN IN THE GAME

At COP26—the United Nations Climate Change Conference attended by world leaders—famed British fashion designer Stella McCartney appealed to delegates and members of the public to sign a pledge to end the use of animal fur and leather.[1] In an unusual move, the designer, known never to use fur and leather in her own designs, is inviting, even begging for, more regulation of her own industry for the sake of animals and the planet. From the event, she told *Forbes* magazine, 'I'm here today because I'm begging for policy to be put in place for the fashion industry.'[2]

Nearly ninety companies are listed as signatories to the Fashion Industry Charter for Climate Action. This includes numerous huge, recognizable names including Stella McCartney herself, French luxury group Kering (owner of high-end brands including Gucci, Yves Saint Laurent, Bottega Veneta, Balenciaga, Alexander McQueen and more), Inditex (owner of Zara, Bershka and more), H&M (the second largest global clothing retailer after Inditex[3]), Target Corporation, Nike and more. The charter is a mission developed by fashion stakeholders with UN Climate Change for signatories to work to 'drive the fashion industry to net-zero greenhouse gas emissions no later than 2050 in line with keeping global warming below 1.5 degrees'.[4] But there is no legal requirement for brands to take part or to stick to any promises.[5]

Stella says this is a problem. In an interview with *CNBC*, she explained, 'We have no policy. We have no restrictions in fashion. If you look at the automobile industry, they've got hard hitting timelines they have to achieve … We have nothing like that, we need some kind of policy in fashion … just to encourage us to do the right thing.'[6]

The UN knows the use of such initiatives for greenwashing is a major issue. During COP27, held a year after COP26, a UN high-level expert group issued a report called, 'Integrity Matters: Net Zero Commitments by Businesses, Financial Institutions, Cities and Regions'. It reads, '[M]any corporations, cities, states and regions have made voluntary commitments to reach net zero. This is commendable, but in the absence of regulation, too many of these pledges are not aligned with the science, do not contain enough detail to be credible, and use the terms "net zero" or "net zero aligned" (as well as many other similar terms) inconsistently. Deceptive or misleading net zero claims by non-state actors not only erode confidence in net zero pledges overall, they undermine sovereign state commitments and understate the work required to achieve global net zero.'[7]

These concerns are serious. The UN reveals, '[T]he fashion industry is widely believed to be the second most polluting industry in the world.' The agency says, 'According to UNCTAD [United Nations Conference on Trade and Development], some 93 billion cubic metres of water—enough to meet the needs of five million people—is used by the fashion industry annually and that around half a million tonnes of microfibre, which is the equivalent of 3 million barrels of oil, is now being dumped into the ocean every year. As for carbon emissions, the industry is responsible for more than all international flights and maritime shipping combined.'[8]

Numerous factors have resulted in the fashion industry achieving this notorious distinction. Among them, the 'fast fashion' model where consumers are encouraged to buy and cast off ever-changing cheap fashions; retailers overproducing stock; unsold stock not reused or recycled; and the use of unsustainable materials. A key goal of the Fashion Industry Charter for Climate Action is, 'Source 100% of priority materials that are both preferred and low climate impact by 2030.'[9]

Considering their environmental toll, Stella's focus on animal-derived materials at COP26 makes sense. A few years ago, a reputed *Pulse of the Fashion Industry* report by Global Fashion Agenda, Boston Consulting Group and Sustainable Apparel Coalition (SAC) ranked cow leather as having the worst 'cradle to gate environmental impact index per kg of material' with silk coming in second most problematic. Wool also ranked in the top five worst offending materials.[10] Later, Higg Materials Sustainability Index (Higg MSI), a resource that was produced by SAC for comparing the environmental impact of different fashion materials, listed silk, alpaca wool, leather and (sheep) wool as among the most environmentally destructive materials in fashion (in slightly varied order in different years).[11,12,13] Higg MSI says up to 80 per cent of a brand's environmental footprint depends on its choice of raw materials.[14]

Unsurprisingly, powerful animal material industry bodies have worked relentlessly to condemn and refute these rankings and the SAC has been forced to temporarily suspend and review its programme.[15] These are the same industry bodies that misleadingly (as I will explain) use words such as 'natural' and 'by-product' to try to appease consumers' concerns. But these rankings are hardly the only sources for information on the damaging environmental impacts of leather, wool and other animal derived materials and such impacts are not the only concerns—animal welfare is among them. Take for instance the documented observations of 117 wool operations on four continents by PETA. The group says, 'Shearers are usually paid by volume, not by the hour, which encourages fast work without regard for the welfare of the sheep.'[16]

Their investigative videos reveal cruelties like sheep shearers in Australia, the world's largest wool producer,[17] punching sheep in the face and beating and jabbing them in the head with metal clippers and a hammer to knock them down; a shearer in the US bending and twisting dozens of sheep's necks and forelimbs and even breaking one's neck; and in Argentina workers shearing off parts of lambs' ears and slicing off their tails. In Chile, shearers lacerated sheep bloody, and in the UK, they stomped and stood on the heads and necks of panicked sheep, punched them in the face and slammed their heads to the floor to pin them down.[18]

In any case, leather and wool would be better described as co-products or subsidies of the meat industry rather than mere 'by-products' when we consider their value. The global leather goods market size is estimated to reach over USD 405 billion by 2030,[19] while the global wool market value is estimated to reach USD 48 billion by the end of 2029.[20] That is, these are major industries in and of themselves. So much so that Material Innovation Initiative, a non-profit that works to advance the development of sustainable non-animal materials, reports, 'It's commonly but mistakenly believed that animal-derived materials are "by-products" of the meat industry. However, leather is a significant profit-driver for industrial animal agriculture as the second most valuable product from the cow, and in the case of silk, down, wool, and exotic skins [of wild species], the materials are the most profitable products.'[21]

As co-products, leather and wool production directly supports the environmental problems linked to meat production. Among them, land use and degradation, colossal water use, deforestation, methane emissions from ruminant animals such as cattle and sheep, waste from farms polluting waterways and the resulting risk of all this to wild species.

The International Wool Textile Organisation admits, 'For wool garments, greasy wool production on sheep farms contributes most to greenhouse gas emissions (climate change impact) producing in the order of 50% of the total emissions. The dominant greenhouse gas is methane…'[22] They mean it contributes most to greenhouse gas emissions out of wool garments' life cycle, that is raw materials to shipping. Greasy wool simply means untreated wool. You will remember from Chapter 4 that methane is twenty-five times more potent as a greenhouse gas than carbon dioxide at trapping heat in the atmosphere.

Scientists from New Zealand's AgResearch and China's Zhejiang Sci-Tech University have raised concerns about detergents, wetting agents and emulsifiers used for scouring wool, too, stating, 'Some of the detergents and auxiliaries used in scouring are eco-toxic and some of them are endocrine disruptors.'[23] That means they can have a negative effect on the endocrine systems (which regulate numerous bodily functions through the release of hormones) of living beings. They have also highlighted that wool is often chemically treated for certain properties (to make it stain-resistant, shrink-resistant etc.).

Meanwhile, the Council of Fashion Designers of America says methane emissions and eutrophication (water pollution that can lead to algae blooms) due to animal waste are among the concerns raised about alpaca wool production.[24] PETA's undercover investigation in Peru, the world's top alpaca wool producer, exposed workers yanking alpacas around by their tails, slamming even pregnant alpacas to tables and pulling their legs with ropes so hard to restrain them that the workers were 'nearly wrenching their legs out of their sockets', and shearing them bloody.[25] And their investigation of the mohair industry in South Africa shows shearers cutting broad swathes of skin off some goats and then crudely sewing up the most gaping wounds without any pain relief.[26]

Silk production is considered energy-intensive with farms kept at controlled temperatures as well as water-intensive, and chemical pesticides and fertilizers are sometimes used for the mulberry trees silkworms eat. Then there are environmental issues regarding the chemicals used for cleaning and other parts of silk production and dyes.[27]

The confinement of around one hundred million animals[28] on fur factory farms each year also contributes to similar environmental problems as leather and wool for similar reasons. According to the Fur Free Alliance, an international coalition of over fifty animal protection organizations, 'Just as animal agriculture, the keeping of thousands of animals on fur farms has a severe ecological footprint, as it requires land, water, feed, energy and other resources.'[29] These days, however, public opinion polls from around the world demonstrate tremendous unease over the use of animals for fur,[30] and the global fur industry, while still robust—valued at USD 22 billion worldwide a couple of years ago[31]—is nowadays usually described as in freefall, plummeting nearly 60 per cent from its value at USD 40 billion in 2015.[32]

Awareness over the fur trade's impact on the environment has been increasing despite its attempts at touting itself as 'sustainable'. Raül Romeva i Rueda is a politician who was a Green Member of the European Parliament (MEP) from Spain. Several years ago, he presented concerns to the European Commission citing the findings of a 2011 report titled 'The environmental impact of mink fur production' by independent research and consultancy CE Delft. It focused on Dutch mink farms because of the Netherlands' rank as the world's third-largest mink-pelt-producing country then.

The report concluded, 'Fur production is analysed on 18 environmental impacts, among which impact to climate change, eutrophication, particulate matter formation, ozone depletion, toxicity, land occupation and fossil depletion. On 17 of the 18 environmental impacts studied, 1 kg of mink fur scores worse than 1 kg of other textiles. Only in the case of water depletion does fur have a lower score, but the water used to produce the chicken feed (grains, etc.) was not included in the mink life cycle…' The report says mink feed 'consists of chicken and fish offal, supplemented with wheat flour and additives' and that 'feed conversion is highly inefficient: to produce 1 kg of mink fur requires 563 kg of feed.'[33]

Romeva i Rueda raised, 'Regarding the ecological cost of fur garments, a simple linear scale determines that these animal products have a greater impact than synthetic and natural alternatives, such as polyester and cotton. The CE Delft researchers and international organisations warn of the highly toxic chemicals used to treat pelts and to stop them rotting in the days following the death of minks, in this case, and of other species. Some of these chemicals have been identified by United States health authorities as carcinogenic.'[34]

Leather, regardless of the species it is from—cow, crocodile or someone else—is also treated so that it doesn't simply rot off a person's feet. A paper in the *Indian Journal of Occupational and Environmental Medicine* reads, 'Work in leather tanning involves exposure to a wide range of chemicals. Some of these are carcinogens or suspected carcinogens.' Like chromium. And that, 'The exposures within the leather tanning industry [to chromium and other chemicals] have been suggested by some investigators to result in the development of a variety of specific cancers including lung, bladder, kidney, pancreatic oral cavity, nasal and soft tissue sarcoma and skin along with dermatitis, ulcers, perforation of the nasal septum, respiratory illnesses.'[35] The paper goes on to list studies of cancers found in tannery workers from various countries. Most—90 per cent—of the world's leather is tanned using chromium.[36] (For the rest, non-profit group Alliance for International Reforestation says vegetable-tanned leather is not eco-friendly either, as it uses tree bark and can, therefore, contribute to deforestation and climate change.)[37]

By 2007, 60 per cent of the world's leather was produced in developing nations.[38] In 2002, a journalist for India's *Down To Earth* environmental magazine had noted a reason for this shift. He wrote, 'Due to strict enforcement of environmental norms in industrialised nations during the past few decades, tanning operations gradually shifted to developing countries like India. The leather industry boomed here since green laws had no teeth.'[39]

While the leather industry boom lined the pockets of executives (Indian tannery workers receive a poverty wage), the precious income sources of many others died. That same year, India's *Frontline* magazine reported on how tannery pollution had put more than 36,056 farmers in various districts of Tamil Nadu state out of work by damaging more than 17,170 hectares of farmland—'soaked as they were for decades in tannery effluents' as the author described. These figures are a grave underestimate because only some farmers and farmland were counted by the Loss of Ecology Authority then, set up by the Supreme Court, not those in all the devastated districts of the state.[40]

The farmers were hoping for compensation from the leather industry following a case filed by the Vellore Citizens Welfare Forum in the top court. In reality, all affected persons were left 'bitterly disappointed' as the *Frontline* author describes. Even many years later, the compensation agreed had yet to be fully paid, and the farmland remained destroyed.[41]

Vellore Citizens Welfare Forum had raised that tannery effluents were being dumped into the Palar river. Their petition read, 'It is stated that the tanneries are discharging untreated effluent into agricultural fields to, road-Sides [sic], Water ways [sic] and open lands. The untreated effluent is finally discharged in river Palar which is the main source of water supply to the residents of the area. According to the petitioner the entire surface and sub-soil water of river Palar has been polluted resulting in non availability Potable [sic] water to the residents of the area.' The petition alleged, 'tanneries use about 170 types of chemicals in the chrome tanning processes'.[42]

Decades later, the fight for a clean Palar river continues. In February 2022, *The Hindu* reported, 'The water is practically sludge, contaminated with untreated effluents from leather tanneries in Ranipet, Arcot and Walajah. Voters in these neighbourhoods seek an end to indiscriminate discharge of pollutants into the river.'[43]

In another part of India, tannery pollution has helped make the Ganges one of the most polluted rivers in the world. Water from the Ganges is used for irrigation, bathing and drinking[44] for hundreds of millions of people. Considered a holy river by Hindus, hundreds of thousands of people immerse themselves in it too during certain ceremonies.

In 2021, when there were reportedly 250 tanneries around Kanpur and Unnao districts, which the Ganges separates, *The Free Press Journal* reported, 'Earlier, plans were made to shift tanneries to the outskirts of Kanpur on the recommendation of the NGT but no headway has been made in this regard.'[45] NGT stands for National Green Tribunal. It was created under India's National Green Tribunal Act, 2010, to consider environmental court cases. Out of these tanneries, ninety-four were ordered shut in 2021 by the Uttar Pradesh State Pollution Control Board for relentless pollution despite having received warnings. In November of that year, in response to contaminated groundwater, the discharge of chromium into the river and untreated waste affecting the health of citizens as it has done for decades—the NGT finally assembled a five-member committee to address tannery pollution of the Ganges.[46] As of 2023, there are still hundreds of tanneries on the banks of the Ganges.[47]

Laxer labour welfare controls and low wages in developing nations are also a draw for the tanning industry. Common Objective (CO), a fashion industry business network, reports, 'Tannery workers—including children as young as 10 in some countries—risk severe side-effects from exposure to these toxic substances. Acute effects include irritation to the mouth, airways and eyes; skin reactions; digestive problems, kidney or liver damage; long-term cancer and reproductive problems.'[48]

Child Labour: Action-Research-Innovation in South and South-Eastern Asia (CLARISSA) studied the use of child labour by the leather industry in Bangladesh in 2020. They found children working in leather production ranged from seven to seventeen years old, and that they were involved in 'every stage of the leather industry supply chain'—cattle rearing, animal slaughter, hides collection, tanning, waste disposal, manufacturing and everything in between—using knives, hazardous machines and dangerous chemicals.

The report describes a case study of Forkan, a thirteen-year-old boy, who is addicted to sniffing the glue he uses to stick shoe soles to uppers, taking periodic whiffs of it from a plastic bag. And of teenagers Firoz and Miraz, who got so severely burned when a barrel of hydrochloric acid they were carrying fell open that they were each hospitalized for a month. They then had to pay back loans towards their treatment.

Children told researchers they were often made to work all day and night, in the direct sun, amidst noise and toxic stench, and that being tired put them at risk of further injury from accidents. Many said they were routinely shouted at, threatened and even physically abused by their employers.

CLARISSA's report reads, 'Some [of the children] also reported mental health problems, such as poor memory (which can lead to reduced wages). Common ailments experienced by the children in this study were fevers, colds, coughs, headaches, etc. Almost one fifth said they had experienced coughing and headaches in the last 12 months. Other common health problems reported included diarrhoea, asthma, shortness of breath, vomiting, typhoid and jaundice. Some of the children complained of problems with their eyesight or earache. Some reported problems like dizziness, stomach pain, heart problems, toothache, weakness, throat pain, kidney stones, chikungunya and shoulder pain. One of the children had had surgery and another had been pregnant in the last 12 months. Some of the children reported accidents such as cuts or burns.'[49]

The occupational hazards are so severe, some years ago, the WHO revealed 90 per cent of tannery workers in the tanning region of Bangladesh die before their fiftieth birthday.[50] According to a report by Bangladesh's Society for Environment and Human Development (SEHD), 'About half a million residents of the Bangladesh capital, Dhaka, are at risk of serious illness due to chemical pollution from tanneries near their homes…'[51]

The world's topmost leather producers, however, are China and Brazil.[52] China produces about a third of the world's greenhouse gasses[53] that cause climate change, making it the world's worst contributor of these gasses.[54] While this is largely thanks to industries such as coal and steel, China Dialogue, a non-profit organization focused on China's environmental challenges, says China is also the world's largest source of agricultural greenhouse gases, which have a carbon footprint equal to all of China's cars, planes and boats. And that more than a quarter of emissions from Chinese farms come from ruminant animals like those turned into gloves and shoes such as cows, sheep and goats.[55]

As mentioned in Chapter 4, leather production is devastating the Amazon. Stand.earth, a supply chain research firm, released a report in late 2021 highlighting a probability of leather products from various well-known brands being linked to cattle ranching in this rainforest.[56] The firm analysed hundreds of thousands of rows of customs data obtained from various sources and cross-referenced this with other information. Their primary research focused on identifying leather exported by JBS from Brazil, but they looked at other top Brazilian exporters too. JBS is the world's largest leather processor,[57] handling about ten million cow skins a year.[58]

Stand.earth says, 'Countless studies and investigations have consistently demonstrated that JBS, the largest beef/leather company in Brazil, is the largest contributor to Amazon rainforest destruction.' And that, 'All companies sourcing directly from JBS or indirectly from JBS via leather processors are therefore linked to deforestation of the Amazon rainforest.' They go on to state, 'Furthermore, these studies also show that while JBS is the largest leather exporter and the most implicated in deforestation, this problem is endemic of the entire Brazilian leather industry—not just JBS.'

In their ongoing investigations, Stand.earth found over 400 unique supply chain connections between Brazilian leather companies and leather processors and manufacturers in countries such as China, Italy, India, Vietnam, the US and elsewhere, as well as to global shoe and fashion brands. That means, a shoe assembled in Italy, for instance, could be made of Brazilian leather. At the time of their report, Stand.earth had found connections to over 100 brands. The firm says, 'Each individual connection is not absolute proof that any one brand uses deforestation leather, it demonstrates that many brands are at very high risk of driving the destruction of the Amazon rainforest.'

Brands deemed at the time to have the highest risk of contribution to deforestation in the Amazon included Gap, Zara, adidas, Clarks, Marks & Spencer, Vans, Polo Ralph Lauren, Skechers, Nike and many others that are equally well-known.[59] Numerous other brands were found to have a risk, although a lower one, of contributing to Amazon destruction.

Stand.earth explained this meant numerous companies are potentially breaching their own policies against contributing to deforestation. The firm also said some brands pointed to Leather Working Group (LWG), but it reports LWG's work in this area is insufficient, stating, 'While the LWG claims that it will address deforestation in the future, they currently only rate tanneries on their ability to trace leather back to slaughterhouses, not back to farms, nor do they provide any information on whether or not the slaughterhouses are linked to deforestation.' LWG describes itself as 'a global multi-stakeholder community committed to building a sustainable future with responsible leather'.[60]

Out of all the world's animal protection groups, PETA has perhaps most extensively documented and exposed the treatment of animals for the widest variety of animal-derived materials. This includes an exposé of the treatment of cattle by JBS. In 2016, the group released video footage from Repórter Brasil of several cattle ranches in Brazil supplying JBS. The footage shows cows and calves being manhandled, painfully hot-iron branded on the face and beaten and electroshocked to move them down a chute. It also shows cows with untreated, bloody, festering wounds. PETA linked car brands to JBS for leather at that time, including General Motors, Volkswagen, Toyota, BMW, Audi, Mercedes-Benz, Jaguar, Land Rover, Hyundai, Ford, Mazda and numerous others.[61] The group says it takes two to nine cow skins for the interior of a car.

In 1999, PETA joined hands with journalist Manfred Karreman[62] to document the treatment of animals in India for leather. It was their first of what would be many times highlighting what happens to animals for leather there. The investigative crew documented cattle fastened into trucks by ropes threaded through their noses, with their necks twisted into awkward positions for lack of space. These vehicles careened down potholed roads at breakneck speed causing the ropes to often snap and the animals' noses to rip and bleed. By the time they arrived at slaughterhouses, many live cattle would be trapped under the dead, and many would be pulled or pushed off the trucks with broken bones, broken horns or other serious injuries. Since then, nothing has changed in how animals are transported to be killed in the country. For example, two decades later, PETA India visited the market adjacent to Mumbai's Deonar slaughterhouse posing as meat buyers. They filmed bodies of buffaloes dead from transport being moved through the market premises by a bulldozer and a shed full of the corpses of buffaloes, goats and sheep.[63]

In India and Bangladesh,[64] as the group and Karreman have documented, cows, buffaloes, goats and other animals used for leather are typically killed by being cast to the ground, bound and then having their throats slit, while they are still conscious in full view of other frightened animals. In India, the Prevention of Cruelty to Animals (Slaughterhouse) Rules, 2001, had vaguely asked that slaughterhouses, 'as soon as possible', create an area for stunning—a procedure that is supposed to render the animal unconscious before being bled out and is thus considered more humane. More than two decades on, that hasn't happened in most facilities,[65] and in numerous countries, including China, stunning prior to slaughter is not required.[66]

PETA Asia investigators have extensively documented what happens to animals for fashion in China. China is among the largest fur-producing nations and 90 per cent of the world's angora wool is produced there. Angora wool is the hair of Angora rabbits. One

PETA video shows workers in China stretching Angora rabbits across a bench and yanking out their fur by the fistfuls as they scream, actually *scream*, in pain—an ordeal they endure every three months until they are killed in a few years. Those who are sheared are also tied down and sharp tools are taken to their bodies as they writhe and struggle to escape.[67]

Another PETA Asia video shows howling dogs being brought into a blood-drenched room full of dog corpses and dog pelts, and other dogs having their throats slit. Once inside, they are bludgeoned repeatedly with a wooden pole. PETA says these animals are turned into leather gloves, belts, jacket collar trim and other products to be sold to unsuspecting consumers around the world.[68]

A report about China's fur trade by ACTAsia reads, 'China has three sources of fur supply: farming, wild trapping and theft of pet or stray cats and dogs.' The report also states, 'There is very little legislation around fur farming that is enforceable by law in China. There are no penalties for businesses that do not follow suggested standards outlined by legislation.'[69] In another report specific to China's dog and cat fur trade, the group warns, 'All market traders interviewed confirmed that pelts are exported outside of China as well as used within China … As the inhumane slaughter of dogs and cats is viewed as unacceptable in western countries, the Asian fur industry attempts to conceal the truth by intentionally mislabelling fur exports. With few exceptions, produce from dog and cat fur is not labelled as such. In the West, dog fur is often sold as "Asian wolf", while cat fur is often labelled as "rabbit fur".'[70]

In describing an investigation by Swiss Animal Protection/ EAST International, PETA explains what essentially no legislative protection means for foxes, minks, cats and other fur-bearing animals in China. They describe, 'Before they are skinned, animals are yanked from their cages, thrown to the ground, and bludgeoned … [M]any animals are still alive and struggling desperately when workers flip them onto their backs or hang them up by their legs or tails to skin them. When they begin to cut the skin and fur from an animal's leg, the free limbs kick and writhe. Workers stomp on the necks and heads of animals who struggle too hard to allow a clean cut. When the fur is finally peeled off over the animals' heads, their hairless, bloody bodies are thrown on to a pile of those who have gone before them. Some are still alive, breathing in ragged gasps and blinking slowly. Some of the animals' hearts are still beating five to 10 minutes after they are skinned.'[71]

PETA investigations have repeatedly shown even in countries with stronger animal protection standards, cruelty to animals for fashion is rife. PETA UK features a video from a few years ago on its website depicting the treatment of animals for fur in Denmark, Finland, France, Italy, the Netherlands, Norway, Poland, Sweden and the US—countries that were producing fur products permitted to use the International Fur Trade Federation's 'Origin Assured' label. This tag is supposed to guarantee a level of humane treatment. The video shows animals, often with open wounds, in wire cages.

PETA UK warns, 'In "high-welfare" countries, animals on fur farms endure neglect, starvation, and thirst and often have untreated, bloody wounds. Many go insane as a result of their confinement, and some are driven to self-mutilation and cannibalism. Dead animals are left to rot, often in cages alongside their desperate family members. At the end of this ordeal, of course, the animals are killed, usually in the most gruesome ways—including, in many cases, via anal or vaginal electrocution.'[72]

In 2020, fur farms started posing another ethical problem: Covid-19 among mink farmers and mink that ultimately spread the disease across hundreds of farms in Europe. Humans are able to infect mink and the mink are able to infect humans and each other.[73] This resulted in Denmark hurriedly killing seventeen million mink and gasses from the animals' bodies during decomposition causing some carcasses to rise out of mass graves.[74] The country placed a temporary ban on mink breeding and farming, but as of the start of 2023, expressed plans to import 10,000 mink from various countries for fur farms.[75] In contrast, the Netherlands moved up its timeline for a mink fur farming ban by a few years.[76] Denmark and the Netherlands, along with China, were the biggest mink fur producers.[77]

Today, as concern over animal welfare, environmental problems and zoonotic disease grows, many other countries have full, partial, planned or proposed bans on fur farming. These include Latvia, Malta, Italy, France, Estonia, Ireland, Slovakia, Norway, Belgium, Luxembourg, Czech Republic, Austria, Bosnia and Herzegovina, Croatia, Slovenia, the UK and numerous others. Israel has even banned the retail sale of fur.[78]

Conservationists warn it's not only mink we need to worry about. They say the international trade in 'exotic' skins of wild animals such as pythons, alligators, stingrays and crocodiles is also a zoonotic disease risk. These animals are either farmed or caught from the wild. Drawing a comparison to the commonly believed wildlife meat market origin of Covid-19, Dr Lynn Johnson, founder of Nature Needs More, told *The Independent*, 'Any industry that involves humans handling—not just consumption of—exotic animals poses a risk of animal-to-human transmission for a newly evolved virus.'[79]

Likely unsurprising to you by now, PETA has extensively researched exotic skin production. They recount crocodiles and alligators being reared in fetid, crowded tanks and report cruelties: 'Snakes are commonly nailed to trees and their bodies are cut open from one end to the other. Their mutilated bodies are then discarded, but because of these animals' slow metabolism, it can take hours for the snakes to die. Lizards are often decapitated, and some writhe in agony as the skin is ripped from their bodies … The [alligators] are shot or crudely bludgeoned with hammers. Workers sometimes use a mallet and chisel to sever crocodiles' spinal cords—which paralyzes, but does not kill, the animals.'[80]

The group also warns the demand for exotic skins keeps poachers in business, threatening pythons and other species in nature. Indeed, based on what researchers from City University of New York (CUNY) told *National Geographic*, the outlet reported, 'Famous luxury fashion brands—Ralph Lauren, Gucci, Michael Kors, and dozens of others—had more than 5,600 items made from illegal wildlife products seized by the United States Fish and Wildlife Service at U.S. ports of entry from 2003 through 2013…' LVMH claimed the seizures were 'generally related to paperwork and labelling processes', while Ralph Lauren called the researchers' findings 'misleading and flawed' and other companies failed to comment.[81]

Regardless, the production of wild animal skins, like other animal-derived materials in fashion, comes with significant consequences including potential harm to human life, as does the use of wild animals for experimentation.

TESTING 123

On a snowy day in January 2022, a dump truck and pickup hauling a trailer collided near Danville in Pennsylvania, US, resulting in numerous crates containing long-tailed macaque monkeys being flung out across an icy highway.[1] One hundred of these animals were being driven to a quarantine facility, ultimately destined to be victims of laboratory experiments. Some of the crates burst open as they hit the ground and several panicked monkeys made a daring escape, scampering across the slippery highway, miraculously evading speeding cars and ascending nearby trees. The monkeys were from Mauritius, unequipped to bear the cold, which was set to drop to sub-zero temperatures by night.

Michele Fallon, commuter and mother of three witnessed the crash and pulled over to help. She checked on a dazed driver and a hurt passenger and told them medical help was on the way. Meanwhile, another person walked up to the crash site and informed Michele that the crates contained cats and that a cat had run away. She decided to investigate.

Each crate was covered partially by green cloth. It was not possible to clearly see the animals inside. Faeces and urine were spread across the ground. Michele stepped in faeces as she walked around and approached a crate with a tuft of brown fur peeking out. The animal inside started making a strange sound. Michele moved closer and slid the cloth aside. That's when she saw the crash victims were monkeys, not cats. The initial sight of the monkey startled Michele and she scared the monkey too, who hissed at her, covering her face in misty droplets of saliva. Finally, noticing her near the crate, the driver told her to back away, warning the monkeys had not been quarantined yet.[2,3]

State troopers, firefighters, the Pennsylvania Game Commission and the CDC, all embarked on a frantic search for the monkeys who had fled. High-tech equipment such as a helicopter, powerful lights and thermal cameras were employed. Three of these monkeys were killed as soon as they were found. They were likely shot as a gunshot could be heard in a video from the incident.[4] Ultimately, all the monkeys were accounted for, but even months later, there was no information publicly available on where the remaining dozens ultimately ended up.[5]

The police had cautioned locals not to approach or to try to catch the monkeys themselves, as cute as they may be with their round eyes, Mohawk-like crests and whiskers. A primatologist working with PETA US, Dr Lisa Jones-Engel, also issued a quick public statement warning area residents that, 'The four who got away are undoubtedly terrified and likely injured, and they may be harbouring viruses that are transmissible to humans. There is no way to ensure that monkeys are virus-free, and state veterinary and other records show that monkeys in laboratories in the U.S. have been found with tuberculosis, Chagas disease, cholera, and MRSA.'[6]

Indeed, several days after Michele's encounter with the crated long-tailed macaque (also called crab-eating macaques or cynomolgus monkeys), she developed a cough and pink eye and checked herself into the emergency room. There, she began rabies treatment out of caution and was given anti-viral drugs. Later, she vomited too.

While it was unclear whether Michele's condition was related to meeting the monkey, Barry Ciccocioppo, director of communications at the Pennsylvania Department of Health, told *The New York Times*, 'We take any report of exposure to these nonhuman primates very seriously.' The CDC also advised anyone who had been close to the monkeys without wearing protective equipment to keep an eye out for fever, cough, vomiting or other signs of illness.[7]

Perhaps by now you're thinking if coming into contact with these monkeys was considered so potentially dangerous, how could this have been allowed to happen? Shouldn't better precautions have been taken to stop monkey encounters with the public? Or maybe you're concerned about how the monkeys were handled. Weren't they at risk of freezing to death? PETA US' Dr Alka Chandna from their Laboratory Investigations Cases division had similar questions. She filed a complaint with the US Department of Agriculture urging federal authorities to investigate.

In her complaint, she wrote, 'We believe the handling and treatment of monkeys before, during, and after the collision may constitute violations of the federal Animal Welfare Act (AWA) and the Animal Welfare Regulations (AWRs).' She noted the monkeys had been brought to New York's John F. Kennedy (JFK) International Airport by Kenya Airways on a flight that would have taken no less than nineteen hours, following which they were loaded on to a truck for a seventeen-hour journey to a facility in Missouri state.

She noted there was no indication from reports that the monkeys—at least several of whom were almost certainly injured—were evaluated or provided with immediate veterinary care. She also wrote that the crates did not appear to have hooks or other measures to allow them to be secured in place during transport, that ventilation was likely impacted depending on which side the crates landed, that the monkeys were exposed to the bitter cold for hours or even over a day until the escapees and a replacement carrier were found and that three monkeys were apparently shot. Animals who are shot often die of slow and painful blood loss instead of the rapid unconsciousness the AWA definition of 'euthanasia' requires. She also wrote that the monkeys' health had not been assessed before passers-by were allowed to be around and peer into their crates.[8]

PETA US contacted Kenya Airways' CEO Allan Kilavuka and Chairperson Michael Joseph urging the company to consider the fear, pain and suffering these monkeys endured and to issue a policy against transporting monkeys to laboratories again. Within twenty-four hours, Joseph responded stating, '[T]he current contract for the transport of the Macaques (captive-bred for export) will not be renewed when it expires at the end of February.'[9]

By law, in the US, monkeys used for experiments are to be examined by a veterinarian within ten days of shipment between laboratories or breeding facilities.[10] In April 2022, PETA US reported it had examined documents and 'discovered that a rogues' gallery of monkey tormentors—including Charles River Laboratories, Labcorp Drug Development, Orient BioResource Center, and PreLabs—had violated this law at least 56 times in the previous 17 months alone.'[11] The group further reported, 'That amounts to at least 1,881 monkeys who hadn't been examined within the required time frame but were trucked to and from multiple states … In one particularly egregious violation, the National Institutes of Health examined monkeys to be shipped to Boston and then let an astounding 230 days—more than 7 months—pass before shipping them.'[12]

PETA US is not just being alarmist. You remember the HIV, Ebola and other disease links to primates from Chapter 2. We didn't always know of these links—scientists had to discover them, and there could be other risks, too, that we do not yet know of.

Take, for example, monkeypox. Today, who hasn't heard of monkeypox? On 7 May 2022, it was announced a person who had travelled to the UK from Nigeria had contracted monkeypox. A week later, two other people unrelated to this case in the UK were diagnosed with it.[13] Unfortunate, but it's only a handful of cases, there's no need for alarm—or so most people thought. By less than a week after that, the WHO warned of outbreaks in twelve countries and ninety-two cases worldwide.[14] As of July 2023, the figures reached 88,122 confirmed cases and 148 deaths in 112 countries.[15]

Monkeypox was only first discovered in 1958 through long-tailed macaques sick with it in a laboratory in Denmark. The monkeys became noticeably ill nearly two months after they had been shipped to the facility from Singapore. Luckily humans did not contract the disease then, but since 1970, that has changed. Prior to the 2022–23 outbreak, the disease showed up primarily in people in central and western African countries. However, since people travel, sometimes so does monkeypox.[16] Since 1958, there have also been numerous monkeypox outbreaks in captive monkey populations in laboratories and zoos in countries around the world.[17]

Humans can catch monkeypox from bites or scratches, from preparing the meat of or eating the improperly cooked meat of infected animals.[18] Humans can also catch monkeypox from each other. The virus enters our body through close contact with infected scabs and blisters, such as during sex, our respiratory tract and even indirect contact with bodily fluids or lesion matter of an infected person (like from bedding or a towel).[19] The disease causes round, hard, fluid-filled lesions all over the body and patients may suffer fever, swollen lymph nodes, other distressing symptoms and even death.[20]

The year 1958 was over sixty years ago, but we do not have to look that far back for concerning examples of how the use of animals for experiments creates disease risk for humans. Just over a decade ago, a titi monkey at the California National Primate Research Center in Davis contracted pneumonia. In a short matter of time, twenty-three monkeys became ill and nineteen of them died. Several people with links to the laboratory had been ill around the same time too.

It turned out the monkeys were suffering a unique adenovirus that had never been seen before. Researchers called it titi monkey adenovirus (TMAdV). However, with an over 80 per cent death rate in the monkeys who contracted it, the researchers surmised this species was unlikely to be the original disease host. It was initially theorized a laboratory worker may have infected the monkeys or that the monkeys were infected by a rhesus macaque at the same facility, who was found to have TMAdV antibodies. They guessed this may have been from sharing laboratory equipment between animals.

A laboratory worker and her family member had antibodies that matched those of the titi monkeys, but no other humans in the community were found with them, making it unlikely that the disease originated in humans. Thankfully, no humans got very sick, but it was the first known incident of an animal adenovirus infecting people.[21,22] Adenoviruses cause a variety of illnesses in humans such as pneumonia, acute bronchitis, acute gastroenteritis, sometimes neurologic disease and other ailments.[23]

Although TMAdV was not life-threatening to the humans who contracted it, it was a reminder and a warning of what could happen in a laboratory—virus and disease transfer between species, including of the kind never seen before. Just as many experts consider SARS to have been a warning shot for Covid-19.

That laboratory workers can get sick from the animals they handle is not new information. Princeton University lists numerous viruses, bacteria and parasites that can cause problems in humans from monkeys as a warning for laboratory workers. They include Herpes B, which has a 70 per cent mortality if not urgently treated. The university warns, 'All macaques are assumed to be capable of shedding Herpes B virus, even if they have no symptoms of the disease.' People have gotten infected by being bitten or scratched by a monkey, or through tissues or fluids on broken skin.[24] Some years ago, a laboratory worker died from being infected through a monkey's bodily fluid splashing in her eye. There has also been a case of human-to-human transmission.[25]

Herpes B infections in humans are not very common, and the TMAdV infections were dismissed as not too serious and were even celebrated as a learning experience about the disease, but there are some lessons we may end up wanting to do without. After all, with some diseases, such as Ebola, it only takes the first patient to quickly snowball towards disaster.

In 1989, Americans made a lucky escape from that kind of lesson. That year, a shipment of monkeys arrived at a company that was called Hazelton Research Products in Reston, Virginia, near Washington DC, from the Philippines. Some of the primates soon started acting strange and died. The researchers initially thought they could be dealing with a haemorrhagic fever outbreak.[26] Investigators from the Army Medical Research Institute of Infectious Diseases were called in and discovered at least one monkey was infected with Ebola and deemed others suspected cases. All were soon killed.

Ebola, with its rapid spreading capabilities and 50 to 90 per cent mortality rate in people, is ranked as among the deadliest viruses in human history. These monkeys had also flown via JFK and health officials in New York had to be notified about the risk to anyone who had handled them along the way. Hazelton Research Products imported the monkeys to test cosmetics and drugs.[27]

State and federal officials scrambled to make an emergency plan and to try to determine if any of the laboratory workers who were near them were sick. At that time, there had never been any cases of Ebola in the US before. Later it was revealed that neither the Army Medical Research Institute of Infectious Diseases nor the CDC had suitable experience in containing a disease outbreak at a private facility. The two agencies split duties to try to cover ground. In recounting the incident years later, Dr C.J. Peters, who worked for the US Army, told CBS News, 'There was a little shopping center nearby … There was plenty of opportunity for trouble.'[28]

Initial test results indicated they were dealing with the Zaire strain of Ebola, which kills 90 per cent of people who contract it. Bad news, because four workers who had interacted with the monkeys tested positive for it. Oddly, none of them developed symptoms. So what was going on? Thankfully for Americans (and indeed, perhaps the world), it turned out the strain of Ebola it actually was, which had not been seen before, is one of the only two ebolaviruses that does not cause symptoms in humans. It was named Reston virus (RESTV).[29]

The whole episode was so frightening, and the potential damage that could have been done to humanity so vast, that it inspired author Richard Preston to write *The Hot Zone*, a book on viruses that tells the tale of what could have happened if it was an Ebola version deadly to humans. Preston described Ebola as a disease that 'does in ten days what it takes AIDS ten years to accomplish'. Referencing Ebola's ability to jump species with ease and the damage most strains can do to humans, he wrote, 'It did not know boundaries. It did not know what humans are; or perhaps you could say that it knew only too well what humans are: it knew that humans are meat.'[30]

If only the American researchers had known how potentially deadly using primates in a laboratory could be, if only there had ever been some warning, they could have done something differently. Well, there had been a warning—just over twenty years before. In 1967, Germans and Yugoslavians in an area that is now Serbia had already experienced what it means to face a disease that treats humans like meat.

In August of that year, laboratory workers—and soon other medical personnel and their families—in Marburg and Frankfurt, Germany, and in Belgrade, Yugoslavia, became violently ill, at the same time. Gavi—the Vaccine Alliance, an organization that focuses on vaccine accessibility and availability for people around the world—describes patients in these cities as, '…began showing symptoms of an infectious disease—a high fever, chills, muscle ache, and vomiting.' And that, 'The patients worsened over the next few days, until they began bleeding from every orifice in their body, including needle puncture wounds.'[31] Seven of them died.

Those who were first infected had been handling African green monkeys imported from Uganda, or their body parts, for experiments.[32] The monkeys and the experimenters had been infected by a virus that shares a family with the six species of Ebola virus—the only other members we know about of the filovirus family. This is how what is now called Marburg virus was first discovered.

Since then, most outbreaks of Marburg virus disease have been in Africa, but there have also been cases elsewhere, such as in Europe and the United States.[33] People can be infected from each other, but also seemingly from fruit bats who appear to be the reservoir host, from hunting and handling monkeys and other animals for meat, and even from pigs.[34,35]

But surely, we must have *finally* learned our lesson about the dangers of meddling with monkeys? Apparently not. In December 2022, upon reviewing documents from the CDC and a case report published that month by persons affiliated with this agency, Texas government authorities and the Nonhuman Primate Quarantine Facility in that state—PETA warned that 'highly pathogenic agents—including one classified as a bioterrorism agent—regularly enter the U.S. in shipments of monkeys imported for laboratory experiments'.[36] The papers show six cases of Burkholderia pseudomallei from macaques in Cambodia imported into the US, with one being euthanized, another identified during quarantine, and four others found months after they were released from quarantine.[37] The macaque who had been euthanized had flown to the US with 359 other macaques. The CDC lists 'Melioidosis (Burkholderia pseudomallei)' as a potential bioterrorism agent.[38]

The case report states, 'Melioidosis, a potentially fatal infectious disease of humans and animals, including nonhuman primates (NHPs), is caused by the high-consequence pathogen Burkholderia (B) pseudomallei. This environmental bacterium is found in the soil and water of tropical regions, such as Southeast Asia, where melioidosis is endemic. The global movement of humans and animals can introduce B. pseudomallei into nonendemic regions of the United States, where environmental conditions could allow establishment of the organism. Approximately 60% of NHPs imported into the United States originate in countries considered endemic for melioidosis.' It also notes quarantine does not stop the spread of B. pseudomallei as, '[A]nimals infected with B. pseudomallei may appear healthy for months to years before showing signs of illness, during which time they can shed the organism into the environment.'[39]

PETA alleges the CDC hid information about the dangers of importing these monkeys from the American public. The group says, 'The same day that the CDC turned over the damning documents to PETA, the agency distributed a news release alerting the public to the presence of the bioterrorism agent Burkholderia pseudomallei in the soil and water of the Mississippi Delta region. Astonishingly, CDC officials said publicly that they had no idea how the bacterium got there. But the agency clearly knew of one possible source: monkeys infected with the agent imported into the U.S. for use in experiments, including as recently as 2021.'[40]

Depending on whether a person gets treatment, between about 40 to 90 per cent of melioidosis patients die.[41]

PETA says the documents also 'show that the CDC knew that imported monkeys, stressed and traumatized during a grueling international journey, were arriving infected with tuberculosis and other "unknown/indetermined" viruses that cause diarrhea so violent that it sheds the lining of the gut.' And that 'The documents reveal that between 2019 and 2021, hundreds of monkeys who were imported into the U.S. and underwent quarantine exhibited gastrointestinal diseases and "[i]llness that may be of public health concern such as clinical signs consistent with filovirus [Ebola-like viruses] infection, confirmed Shigella and Campylobacter infection and malaria".'[42] It would be reasonable to conclude these problems are not only being imported into the US, but also potentially wherever primates are used for laboratory experiments.

Today, long-tailed macaques and rhesus macaques are among the species of monkeys most commonly used in laboratories.[43] They are native to many parts of Asia. They are social, intelligent animals and it should not surprise us that clever long-tailed macaques kept numerous agencies using advanced equipment on a manhunt for over a day despite being in an unfamiliar environment in Pennsylvania. Jayshree Mazumder is a scientist with the Indian Council of Medical Research who studies their behaviour. She says long-tailed macaques are so smart, they learn by trial and error and are quick to change to better tools if what they are using doesn't work as well.[44]

This is significant, because there was a time scientists thought only humans repurposed objects and made tools.[45] Many scientists have also been quick to dismiss animal intelligence as mere 'instinct', by which they mean behaviour that is ingrained and fixed, rather than adaptable and learned—but this is also changing. University College London (UCL) scientists found that wild long-tailed macaques living on two different Thai islands, 15 km apart, who could have never met, used the same stone tools differently despite living in the same kind of environment, with the same access to food and stones. Their conclusion—the macaques' behaviour did not seem inherent—that it was *learned*.

Remarking on this, Dr Tomos Proffitt of the UCL Institute of Archaeology said, 'We observed differences among macaques on two different islands, in relation to tool selection and the degree of tool re-use when foraging for marine prey. The theory is that if the environmental factors are the same—the only reasonable conclusion is that one island has developed its own tool-using culture either through genetics or through passing down through a learning mechanism. While the other group exhibits a tool use culture which is more ephemeral and ad hoc.'[46] These archaeology researchers are fascinated by what observing the wild macaques' stone tool use might help us understand about similar tool use by early humans.

Macaques' smarts can also be compared to those of humans in other ways. Dario Maestripieri is a professor of Comparative Human Development at the University of Chicago and an expert in primate behaviour. He explains rhesus macaques can be incredibly cunning and manipulative, as well as cooperative, for political manoeuvring in their societies. The quest for social power also results in what Maestripieri describes as 'revolutions', where lower-ranking monkey families organize to overthrow the higher-ranking one.[47]

Like humans, monkeys strive for social status or respond to each other in the ways they do because they have *feelings* and are complex individuals. They display different behaviours when experiencing different emotions such as jealousy, contentment, being frightened or sad. For instance, titi monkeys arch their backs when they are in a situation that scientists know from observing the species' behaviour would be causing jealousy, and swoosh their tails.[48] Monkeys form strong friendships and also have enemies. They nurture their babies and get stressed out from social problems, the same way we do. In fact, they can even suffer from high blood pressure and ulcers from such situations and exhibit signs of depression—such as when they fall from a social rank. Mother monkeys who have lost their babies can have difficulty recovering from the shock, often carrying around the baby's body for days.[49]

They take care of strangers too. At Ifrane National Park in Morocco, a young Barbary macaque was hurt in a road accident and became separated from his group. Another group came across him, and despite having never met him before, adopted him and helped him get better. The young monkey stayed with the new group for four months even after recovering, eventually finding his way back to his own.[50] In contrast, in a laboratory setting, we humans do not tend to show monkeys much empathy.

Monkeys are used for a variety of experiments—toxicity testing of drugs, disease and reproduction research, vaccine testing and more.[51] There have been recent restrictions on wildlife trade from China affecting monkey exports from there due to Covid-19.[52] But in an article from a few years ago titled 'The Case for Phasing Out Experiments on Primates', Dr Andrew N. Rowan, former chair of the Department of Environmental Studies at Tufts University School of Veterinary Medicine, along with Kathleen M. Conlee, vice president for animal research issues at the Humane Society of the United States, explained, 'Each year, thousands [of monkeys] are captured from the wild, mostly in Asia and Mauritius, and transported to other countries. For example, China sets up breeding colonies, and the infants are sold to various countries, including the United States and European countries. The animals experience considerable stress, such as days of transport in small crates and restrictions on food and water intake. Studies show that it takes months for their physiological systems to return to baseline levels, and then they face the trauma of research, including infection with virulent diseases, social isolation, food and water deprivation, withdrawal from drugs, and repeated surgeries. Providing for the welfare of primates in a laboratory setting is very challenging.'[53] Conlee used to work at a primate breeding and research facility.

Over decades, PETA has publicized undercover video footage and photographs taken from various laboratories revealing that drugging, poisoning, surgeries and other experiment requirements aside, the laboratory environment alone causes monkeys immense suffering. This group's vast documentation shows social, intelligent monkeys all alone in barren metal cages, without even so much as a soft blanket to sleep on.

At Wisconsin National Primate Research Center in the US, a PETA investigator who worked there undercover for six months documented Noah, a macaque who spent that entire time pacing a small steel cage in a windowless room. He had apparently been at the facility for nearly twenty-two years. Another monkey there, Cornelius, who was also typically kept alone in a cage, would spend his time hunched over, as if he had lost the will to live. Other monkeys there, Charlie and Princess, would pull out their own hair. A bald Princess was still used for breeding, with all her babies pried away from her one by one. When traumatized animals were finally put together, they often injured themselves or attacked their cage-mates. One monkey had picked at his own leg creating a gaping wound down to the muscle.[54]

In another video revealing the findings taken over eleven months at a US facility run by Covance[55] (now called Labcorp Drug Development), PETA showed what it describes as 'lab-induced insanity', a 'psychosis' caused by a 'lack of socialization and enrichment': monkeys whirling, pacing and screaming as laboratory workers listened to loud rock music.[56]

This isn't just how US laboratories house monkeys. In India, some years ago, PETA India released undercover video footage exposing the prestigious All India Institute of Medical Sciences (AIIMS) medical school for keeping dozens of monkeys alone in rusty wire cages for up to nearly two decades. In the video, distressed monkeys can be seen endlessly circling, pacing and screaming when approached.[57,58,59,60,61] As a result of PETA India's efforts, AIIMS agreed to permit six monkeys to be rescued and shifted others to group housing with access to small extra space for movement.[62] Today, monkeys are not mentioned on the AIIMS Central Animal Facility website as laboratory animals they maintain at all, while other species are, and PETA India is working to get clarity on what this means.[63]

Astonishingly, despite knowing monkeys are social animals and already being able to see, in laboratory after laboratory, over decades, how barren, isolated laboratory environments affect them, institutes linked to the University of Massachusetts Amherst were paid millions of dollars by the US government to confine monkeys alone in metal cages. The purpose? To study how being caged in laboratories affects monkeys. Their findings? What they undoubtedly already knew—that these profoundly lonely monkeys who have little space to move and nothing to do become severely disturbed: that they circle, rock, pace and shake their cages. They self-harm including by tearing their own fur out and painfully press their own thumbs into the corner of their eye sockets (referred to as 'eye-poke') out of frustration and to try to relieve mental distress. The US government has never acted on the findings to improve the way monkeys there are treated and housed in laboratories.[64] These experiments took place recently, over thirty years, but similar studies were conducted as far back as the 1960s.

Then, University of Wisconsin–Madison psychologist Harry Harlow conducted experiments on rhesus macaques that would be hard not to describe as sadistic. In one experiment, he put monkeys alone into an inverted pyramid-shaped contraption, which he called 'the pit of despair', for weeks at a time to induce depression. Seemingly, it worked—most monkeys would eventually sit hunched over at the bottom of the device, hugging themselves.[65] Harlow also described isolated monkeys as 'profoundly disturbed, given to staring blankly and rocking in place for long periods, circling their cages repetitively, and mutilating themselves'.[66] It was noted those who were caged the longest could never recover from their experience. Melinda Novak, who led the University of Massachusetts Amherst caged monkeys study, was a student of Harry Harlow.[67]

If experimenters can attempt to apply what happens to animals in a laboratory to human beings, we should be able to do the same in reverse. In 1951, McGill University researchers paid male graduate students to stay alone in a sensory deprived environment for six weeks with only a bed. Toilet breaks were allowed, but otherwise they wore goggles, earphones and gloves to limit what they could hear, see and touch. None of the students lasted more than a week in the experiment and reported experiencing bizarre hallucinations and an inability to think.[68] Yet, more than seventy years on, we continue to deprive monkeys of all that is natural and important to them in laboratory environments, and then yank them out of their cages to torment them some more.

Many people think of this torment as a necessary evil—horrible to have to do, but a necessity, for the advancement of science. But Dr Jarrod Bailey, a geneticist who spent years in research and now works as the director of science for Animal Free Research UK, argues that stress in animals can affect experimental data. He writes, 'Recurrent acute and/or chronic stress can affect all vertebrate species, and can have serious consequences. It is increasingly and widely appreciated that laboratory animals experience significant and repeated stress, which is unavoidable and is caused by many aspects of laboratory life, such as captivity, transport, noise, handling, restraint and other procedures, as well as the experimental procedures applied to them. Such stress is difficult to mitigate … Psychological damage can be reflected in stereotypical behaviours, including repetitive pacing and circling, and even self-harm. Physical consequences include adverse effects on immune function, inflammatory responses, metabolism, and disease susceptibility and progression. Further, some of these effects are epigenetic, and are therefore potentially transgenerational: the biology of animals whose parents/grandparents were wild-caught and/or have experienced chronic stress in laboratories could be altered, as compared to free-living individuals.' Dr Bailey observes that the effect of stress on experimental outcomes 'may not be recognised sufficiently among those who use animals in experiments'.[69]

And increasingly, progressive scientists and governments are examining whether animal experiments should be relegated to the history books. Many scientists are even questioning whether animal experiments ever worked in the first place, if they lead researchers down wrong and expensive paths and if the use of animals in laboratories is simply an old habit. It is a lucrative habit that keeps many people in business—from researchers who receive grants from governments and other sources, to laboratory equipment providers, veterinarians and other workers, feed and medicine providers, animal transporters and so on.

Scientists who question animal use in research point out the vast physiological differences between humans and animals means experiment outcomes in them cannot reliably predict how a drug or chemical will react in a human body. In a 2015 paper titled 'The Flaws and Human Harms of Animal Experimentation', neurologist and preventive medicine/public health specialist Dr Aysha Akhtar, warns, 'Humans are harmed because of misleading animal testing results. Imprecise results from animal experiments may result in clinical trials of biologically faulty or even harmful substances, thereby exposing patients to unnecessary risk and wasting scarce research resources. Animal toxicity studies are poor predictors of toxic effects of drugs in humans…[H]umans have been significantly harmed because investigators were misled by the safety and efficacy profile of a new drug based on animal experiments. Clinical trial volunteers are thus provided with raised hopes and a false sense of security because of a misguided confidence in efficacy and safety testing using animals. An equal if indirect source of human suffering is the opportunity cost of abandoning promising drugs because of misleading animal tests.'[70]

In fact, as far back as 2004, the *British Medical Journal* published an article titled 'Where is the evidence that animal research benefits humans?' Its authors argued, 'Clinicians and the public often consider it axiomatic that animal research has contributed to the treatment of human disease, yet little evidence is available to support this view. Few methods exist for evaluating the clinical relevance or importance of basic animal research, and so its clinical (as distinct from scientific) contribution remains uncertain. Anecdotal evidence or unsupported claims are often used as justification—for example, statements that the need for animal research is "self-evident" or that "Animal experimentation is a valuable research method which has proved itself over time." Such statements are an inadequate form of evidence for such a controversial area of research.'[71] Some, like cardiologist Dr Rachel Hajar, point out that animal experiments have been conducted since the time of Aristotle (384–322 BC),[72] but now increasingly, scientists believe scientific methods have to modernize and evolve as our understanding of the human body and technology advances.

Indeed, it seems even for Covid-19 vaccines, progress or even moving on to human clinical trials was not reliant on animal experiments. In November 2020, after Pfizer announced that clinical data shows that its Covid-19 vaccine, produced with German company BioNTech, is 90 per cent effective at preventing infection, PETA scientist Jeffrey Brown noted, 'Pfizer and BioNTech didn't wait for lengthy tests on monkeys and mice but did the majority of the animal tests *at the same time* that the vaccine was being tested on humans.'[73]

And while there are signs this deadline may have been too ambitious, Martijn van Dam, then state secretary of economic affairs of the Netherlands, stated in 2016 that he wanted the Netherlands to become a frontrunner in innovation without the use of laboratory animals by 2025.[74] Meanwhile, in September 2021, the European parliament passed a resolution 'to accelerate the transition to innovation without the use of animals in research, regulatory testing and education.'[75] And the US Environmental Protection Agency has committed that it will stop conducting or funding studies on mammals at least by 2035.[76]

This is because concerns over cruelty to animals combined with the scientific community progressively recognizing the need for human-relevant techniques rather than those based on animal models are leading to the development of sophisticated non-animal tools for testing and research. These include tissue-on-a-chip models—silicon chips using human cells that mimic human organs' and organ systems' structure and function—used for things like disease modelling and drug testing. They also include a high-throughput screening robot that can test more chemicals in one day than have been tested over decades using animals. There are also in silico, or rather computer-based methods, to study disease progression and drug metabolism and distribution by simulating human biology. Or micro-dosing, where a miniscule amount of a drug is administered in controlled human trials.[77] These are just some examples. Due to such advancements, in 2022, a law passed allowing the US Food and Drug Administration to consider non-animal drug testing methods instead of animal tests.[78]

However, there is still a long way to go before we live in a world without animal experiments as old lucrative habits die hard. Despite this progress and growing public opposition to the use of primates and other animals for research, there are still so many monkeys in laboratories—especially in the US, Japan, China and the European Union[79]—that for the first time, long-tailed macaques have been listed as 'endangered' with key threats to them including being captured for research and human consumption. Video footage by Action for Primates shows how this is done—they are carried with their hands tied behind their backs, shoved head-first into sacks, hit and crammed into wooden crates to then be shipped to laboratories around the world.[80]

The late George Bernard Shaw, winner of the Nobel Prize for Literature in 1925, is famously quoted as having expressed, 'Atrocities are not less atrocities when they occur in laboratories and are called medical research.'[81] Many would say the same could be said about animals who are cruelly treated in a sanctioned manner in a ring.

THE DEADLY GAMES

In Suzanne Collins' novel *The Hunger Games*, a cruel government, the Capitol, punishes citizens and keeps them under control by choosing two tributes, a boy and a girl, between the ages of twelve and eighteen, to fight to the death in an arena for their district on the day of reaping. The winner lives and their district is rewarded with food. The book featured on *The New York Times'* bestseller list for over 260 weeks because of its impressive plot and character development, which left readers gripped and intrigued as to how things will turn out for Katniss. Katniss is the novel's narrator, who is pitted to fight against Peeta, the son of a baker who once saved her from starvation. Readers are also enthralled by the sheer ruthlessness of such a game, so brutal it can only happen in fiction—at least in the modern day—and at least for humans.

There was a time this wasn't true—in ancient Rome, slaves, criminals and prisoners of war were turned into gladiators to fight against each other, often to the death, or to fight wild animals in public spectacles called venationes. Lions, bears, bulls, hippopotamuses, panthers and other animals were used in venationes, with up to 11,000 animals killed in an enormous bloodbath at a single event.[1] Sometimes hungry animals were released on to a helpless human tethered to a stake.[2]

Despite the obvious psychological pressure of the extreme risk to themselves, gladiators were expected to put on a show—and so they had to trap and injure their opponent, not kill them outright. The bloodthirsty crowd needed to be satisfied with the performance, or else there were severe consequences, as putting up a good fight meant that you might live. That's because when one gladiator managed to corner another for death, the loser could signal the crowd, hoping for mercy.[3] The winner would then look to the crowd for instruction on what to do. The crowd would respond by either waving handkerchiefs, which meant the defeated gladiator lived to see another day, or by turning their thumbs downward, meaning it was game over for him. A pleased crowd may opt to spare the loser's life, but more often than not, they chose murder,[4] justified, we can guess, by gladiators being considered rejects of society. After all, criminals would often be pushed into the arena unarmed.

Movie depictions of gladiators make them seem brave and heroic, and good gladiators did become famous and winners were rewarded with a palm branch (like a trophy), money, perhaps even sex or occasionally freedom. Some even volunteered themselves into the profession. But many had to be forced into the arena with whips and hot irons.[5]

The Hunger Games is the first of a trilogy in which Katniss 'follows the same arc from slave to gladiator to rebel,' as explained by the author, like the story of Spartacus.[6] Spartacus was a gladiator who had served in the Roman army but at some point was captured and made a slave. He and dozens of other gladiators managed to run away from a gladiatorial training school. Other escaped slaves joined their group, and eventually Spartacus led an impressive revolt.[7]

Animals pushed into rings, however, have no chance of gaining anything because surviving another day simply means another opportunity of being subjected to cruelty. Just as reluctant gladiators were driven into arenas, reluctant bulls are still goaded into them for jallikattu in the Indian state of Tamil Nadu.

During jallikattu, held in various rural villages across the state, men clamour to hang on to a bull's hump, head and horns as he wildly flings about, trying to flee. In the past, the object of the spectacle was to stay on to untie a bag of gold coins on the bull's horns. Nowadays, participants can win refrigerators, motorbikes and cars for 'taming' bulls.

The frenzied thrashing to try to throw men off gives the fearful bull the appearance of ferocity, just as a bull speared with decorated banderillas and incited to charge a matador's cape in a bullfight seems angry, rather than hurt and scared. The supposed fierceness of the bulls is the thrill—it makes the participants look valiant, rather than like bullies.

The bulls are unleashed on to the players from the vaadi vaasal, a barricaded entrance. From it, they can see a mob of participants waiting to pounce and an enormous, roaring crowd, often of hundreds or thousands of spectators. There are jallikattu events with arena seats, but otherwise spectators mix with the players from the sidelines or crowd behind barricades.

The bulls, as prey animals, have an inherent nervousness, always alert to potential danger. They are naturally afraid of the crowd and try to back up out of the vaadi vaasal, but there is no escape. Handlers force them forward by yanking on ropes threaded through their nostrils until they rip and bleed. They twist and snap their tailbones, jab them with nail-tipped sticks and prod them with metal sickles. Ultimately, the bull relents from pain and flies out of the only exit, making it seem as if he's so raging, he simply cannot wait to attack.

All of this mistreatment makes the bull so upset, he races helter-skelter when he manages to escape the hangers-on, only to be met by groups of more men trying to do the same. They beat the bull along the way or yank his tail. And many get in the way and get speared in the chest or stomach by a bull running at full speed. The bolting bull also often slams into barricades or attempts to jump over them, breaking his bones or dying.[8]

Following efforts by PETA India and others in the Indian Supreme Court, jallikattu was temporarily prohibited in 2014, but then allowed again by the state in 2017—a decision PETA India and other animal protection groups are working to overturn. According to a collation of media reports, since 2017 and at the time of writing, at least 33 bulls and over 105 men (and children) have died due to jallikattu and thousands more participants and spectators have been injured.

Jallikattu supporters hail those who die as 'warriors', but the real battle comes afterwards—for the wives, children and elderly parents who are left behind, often without their sole or main breadwinner. The game is not a friend to women in other ways too—in one video from just a few years ago, a jallikattu announcer says a twenty-one-year-old woman will be handed over to the winner as a prize.[9] After a huge hue and cry, organizers denied that was ever a real plan, but there is reason to believe it was the true intention. After all, historically, women were given to winners to marry.[10]

In ancient times, gladiator battles, chariot races and other Roman games were sponsored by the emperor. Without the entertainment, citizens would have too much time to focus on their poverty and joblessness and could plan a revolution.[11]

Similarly, allowing jallikattu again in 2017 could have been a ploy to distract the rural Tamil population. Newspaper reports and investigations by reputed organizations such as the People's Union of Civil Liberties (PUCL) and the Tamil Nadu Federation of Women Farmers' Rights reveal hundreds of Tamil farmers committed suicide or died of heart attacks in December 2016 and January 2017 alone, having suffered the effects of drought, climate change and economic loss. The Indian National Human Rights Commission says over 100 farmers killed themselves only in December 2016.[12] Many Tamil farmers travelled to Delhi, the nation's capital, in the earlier part of 2017 to draw attention to their plight, protesting while gruesomely holding the skulls of other farmers who had committed suicide, making sure they would not be ignored.[13]

Suddenly, with the public focus shifted to overturning what was by that point a three-year ban on jallikattu by the Supreme Court, the state government gave the farmers something else to be upset about. The ban on jallikattu was spun as an affront to state pride, and tens of thousands of people, rural and urban, poured on to the streets there to demand that the spectacle be allowed again on cultural grounds. The protests provided an opportunity for various other grievances with the government to also be aired,[14] and the state government responded through the passage of a law permitting jallikattu again, essentially saying to hell with the Supreme Court. The local public rejoiced and state government authorities were hailed as heroes, but other problems raised like water scarcity remained.

Like gladiators were, and bulls used for jallikattu, certain breeds of dogs such as pit bulls are goaded into combat in dogfighting rings around the world. The history of this goes back to sixteenth- and seventeenth-century England, where cruelty was a popular form of entertainment. Then, a variety of animals such as dogs, bears, bulls—even chimpanzees—were pitted against each other in front of raucous spectators excited by the violence, blood and gore. The events included dogfights, cockfights, other bizarre acts such as whipping blind bears and unleashing dogs on different animals like rats and badgers.

In one kind of show, a chimpanzee would enter tied to horse. Dogs would be released to lunge at and rip him to shreds. One Italian merchant described it as, '...the horse galloping along, kicking up the ground and champing at the bit, with the monkey holding very tightly to the saddle, and crying out frequently when he is bitten by the dogs'.

During bull-baiting, a helpless male cow was chained in place as dogs were set upon him to tear into his flesh. Just as certain people today get a thrill out of watching a bull 'win' against a man during jallikattu by trampling over him, back then people would cheer as bulls hurled the dogs into the air with their horns.

The most attended shows of all were bear-baiting. They were so popular that in the 1500s, venues were built specifically for them. During these events, a bear would be dragged into a ring and chained to the wall or a stake by the leg or neck. A pack of dogs would then be set upon the bear. The excitement was in seeing the terrified bear growl, bite, claw and writhe in attempt to defend himself as he was attacked. The fight ended when the bear either killed dogs or just before the bear suffered lethal injuries—so the expensive animal could be used again in other fights.

Although blood-sports were all the rage in England back then, they also had their fair share of critics, and the voices of these opponents ultimately won (at least largely so). The decriers included people upset for the animals and worried about the effect the games were having on society. Clergymen cautioned they encouraged other vices, such as boozing and debauchery, gambling and prostitution. Finally, around the 1700s, popular public attitudes there began shifting towards concern for animals.[15] After hundreds of years of animals being tortured in rings, at last, in 1835, most forms of forcing animals to fight, such as cockfighting, bear-baiting and badger-baiting (for which dogs are incited to draw badgers out of their burrows for attack) were outlawed in the UK.[16] However, even today, certain illegal activities like the terrorizing, hunting and killing of badgers still occur there.[17]

Today, bear-baiting still takes place in rural Pakistan. There, even before the bears are pulled into the ring, their canine teeth are smashed out, claws yanked out and muzzles pierced with rope. This is all so that human handlers can more easily control them.[18]

The breeds of dogs used for such gruesome displays in England were typically bulldogs or mastiffs. In fact, bulldogs are called bulldogs because of their use in bull and bear-baiting events.[19] Today, pit bulls and various mastiffs are among the breeds of dogs used for dogfighting, a blood-sport that is still prevalent in India, Pakistan, Latin America, the US and elsewhere despite being illegal in most countries around the world.[20] Pit bulls, also called American Pit Bull Terrier or Pit Bull Terrier, come from bulldogs and terriers and were created by breeders to display aggression towards other dogs and to be determined fighters.[21]

Dogs used in dogfights are trained to attack each other from puppyhood. In India, pit bulls and other dogs are also trained through practice fights with stray dogs, who are no match for them, as well as leopards, wild boars, Asian palm civets, foxes and other wild animals, in violation of the country's Wildlife Protection Act, 1972.[22]

During dogfights, which can last up to two hours, dogs are incited to charge at each other and to rip into each other's faces, throats, torsos and legs. Common injuries include severe bruising, deep puncture wounds and broken bones. The bloody ordeal often leaves the animals too exhausted to go on or to even defend themselves. Some dogs die in the ring, whereas many others do so afterwards due to exhaustion and injuries. Death results from blood loss, shock, dehydration, exhaustion or infection hours or even days after a fight.[23]

As dogfighting is typically illegal, injured dogs do not usually see a veterinarian. Instead, dogfighters tend to wounds themselves or not at all. The UK Royal Society for the Prevention of Cruelty to Animals, the world's oldest animal welfare charity, which has existed since

1824, says this can be in the form of crude surgeries with staple guns or super glue to seal wounds. The group also says despite dogfighting being illegal there for over 185 years, it received over 9,000 reports of organized dogfighting in the UK between 2015 and 2020.[24]

Losing dogs and those who refuse to fight are abandoned or killed. This can be through any manner of brutal methods, like siccing other dogs on them; beating them to death; shooting or drowning them.[25] Some years ago, one of America's most notorious dogfighters, Harry Hargrove, was sentenced to a federal prison for five years for dogfighting. Among the devices found on his property were jumper cables used to electrocute dogs to death. During the trial, the US Attorney's Office described electrocuted dog carcasses found there in a garbage pit. There were also treadmills on which dogs spent hours to build stamina and spring poles—a hanging rope on a spring that dogs can pull and hang from—for stronger jaw strength. When not being trained or in a fight, the dogs would spend their days chained to the ground.[26]

Just as clergymen warned hundreds of years ago that the English blood-sports were linked to other societal problems, dogfighting is referred to as a 'cluster' crime—one that happens alongside others. Apart from dogfights being a form of gambling, Humane Society International (HSI) says, 'Illegal firearms, other weapons and drugs are commonly found at dogfights. Homicides and child pornography and abuse are not uncommon in dogfighting.'[27]

In fact, while investigating one American man, Juan Verdin, for dogfighting, authorities found images and videos of children, even an infant, forced into sexual acts with each other or adults in his possession. The police also seized around 150 dogs during raids, USD 10,000 in cash and more than sixty guns of various types from Verdin.[28]

In another case, also from the US, two men and a woman associated with a dogfighting ring and a marijuana business were murdered. Officers found sixty-four pit bulls used for fighting, money as well as marijuana plants worth USD 95,000 along with the bodies at a residence.[29]

When responding to a domestic violence issue in the US state of Florida, the police stumbled on a dogfighting match. There, being a spectator at a dogfight is also a crime.[30] Meanwhile, in the US state of Georgia, two people were arrested for their involvement in dogfighting and dealing cocaine.[31] In Guyana, a thirty-year-old auto-salesman and father-of-three died from about fifteen stab wounds after an argument broke out over which dog won in a fight. He was apparently just a spectator.[32] In Scotland, a man involved with wildlife crime left dogs disfigured after inciting them to fight badgers and foxes. Police found seriously wounded dogs, numerous guns and more than 140 bullets at his home.[33]

HSI warns, 'Because dogfighting yields such large profits for participants, minor fines are not a sufficient deterrent. Dogfighters merely absorb them as part of the cost of doing business.'[34] In the US, it is reported USD 50,000–60,000 may be at stake at each fight, but it can go up to USD 1 million.[35] Compare that to fines for dogfighting, which vary there from state to state. They can be as low as USD 100.[36] Meanwhile, in India, where gambling and dogfighting also go hand in hand, under the country's Prevention of Cruelty to Animals Act, 1960, a fine can be as low as Rs 10 (about 12 cents US).[37]

Around the world, most dog breeders and pet stores sell dogs to anyone willing to buy them, whether for a dogfight, to live on the end of a chain as a guard or attack dog or as a loved companion. This combined with pit bull enthusiasts working hard to try to convince people it's always the owners, not the pit bulls, who are the problem if they bite, means the trade in pit bulls—including to dogfighters—continues.

And they do often bite, according to DogsBite.org, a non-profit founded by Colleen Lynn, a victim of a pit bull attack. The website says, '[S]he was attacked for approximately 5-seconds by a leashed pit bull while jogging in her former Seattle neighborhood. She was hospitalized for two days at Harborview Medical Center after undergoing surgery to repair a severe bone fracture.' The non-profit explains, 'In the 16-year period of 2005 through 2020, canines killed 568 Americans. Pit bulls contributed to 67% (380) of these deaths.'[38] In a story about two American siblings who got mauled to death by the family's pit bull—a five-month-old boy and his two-year-old sister—a *Daily Mail* reporter remarked, 'The reason that pit bulls are so dangerous is a combination of their volatile temperament and their incredibly strong jaws.'[39]

There are many people who argue this is not so, that pit bulls are not genetically predisposed to attack. The American Society for the Prevention of Cruelty to Animals (ASPCA) explains it like this, 'Dog breeds are characterized by certain physical and behavioral traits. Each breed was developed to perform a specific job, whether that job is hunting rabbits, retrieving downed birds, herding livestock or sitting on people's laps. When developing a breed, breeders selected only those dogs that performed their job best to produce the next generation.'

Many people think of dog breeds as naturally existing, but they are man-made, descended from grey wolves and domesticated by us starting around 130,000 years ago.[40] The ASPCA elaborates, 'Today's pit bull is a descendant of the original English bull-baiting dog—a dog that was bred to bite and hold bulls, bears and other large animals around the face and head. When baiting large animals was outlawed in the 1800s, people turned instead to fighting their dogs against each other. These larger, slower bull-baiting dogs were crossed with smaller, quicker terriers to produce a more agile and athletic dog for fighting other dogs.'[41]

Often purchased for their tough image, PETA says pit bulls are the most abused and neglected dog breed in the world. They are also the most abandoned at US shelters and are the most euthanized for a lack of enough homes.[42] Similarly, they are the most commonly abandoned dog breed in India too.[43]

The group is in favour of legislation that makes it mandatory to spay and neuter pit bulls. They explain, 'Pit bulls are abused specifically because of their breed. That's why they need breed-specific measures to protect them.' They further clarify, 'In fact, PETA advocates for a ban on breeding *all* dogs, including pit bulls as breeding *any* dogs should be illegal as long as millions must be euthanized in animal shelters every year. But more than any other breed, pit bulls are in crisis and need help *right now*.'[44] PETA has a point. The dog and cat abandonment crisis is at catastrophe levels worldwide. According to ASPCA, 'Approximately 6.3 million companion animals enter U.S. animal shelters nationwide every year. Of those, approximately 3.1 million are dogs and 3.2 million are cats.'[45] That's just in one country. And many of these animals are euthanized for a lack of enough good homes.

Animals in zoos are often killed too—and I don't mean only the sick ones. A few years ago, the Copenhagen Zoo caused a furore by making public its intention to kill Marius, a healthy male giraffe, because he was deemed to have the wrong genes for their breeding programme. Thousands of people from around the world begged the zoo not to kill young Marius, who could have lived for decades more, and to find an alternative solution. They signed an online petition, made appeals via the press and expressed their pleas on social media.

Yet, to their horror, despite captive wildlife facilities in Britain, Sweden and the Netherlands offering to welcome Marius to save his life, the Copenhagen Zoo lured Marius with rye bread—a food that he loved—and shot him dead with a bolt gun to the head at only eighteen months old. The zoo maintained that he was born too genetically close to other giraffes in the European captive breeding programme, but some argued he could have simply been castrated instead. The Copenhagen Zoo said letting him live would have meant taking the place that could have been filled by another giraffe with the 'right' genes, but why they didn't just hand him over to one of the places that offered to take him in is a mystery.

To add insult to injury, the zoo invited visitors, including children, to watch a three-hour-long butchering of Marius whose body parts were then fed to the zoo's lions as a macabre educational exercise. Bengt Holst, the scientific director of the zoo then, told the press that the zoo routinely kills 'surplus' animals because of space.

This was a revelation to most, and it resulted in a flurry of news reports on how zoos function. In an article titled 'How many healthy animals do zoos put down?', after talking to then executive director of European Association of Zoos and Aquaria (EAZA), Dr Lesley Dickie, the BBC reported that European zoos kill between 3,000 and 5,000 healthy animals every year, and perhaps even more.[46]

Holst was quoted by *National Geographic* as explaining, 'When breeding success increases it is sometimes necessary to euthanize. We see this as a positive sign and as insurance that we in the future will have a healthy giraffe population in European zoos.' Note that he did not say 'in the wild', but rather 'in European zoos'.[47] Today, wild giraffe populations in Africa are plummeting, but improving their numbers or helping them in any way is not even the goal. Moreover, the reticulated giraffe (Giraffa camelopardalis reticulata), Marius' species, was not endangered in the wild then.[48]

A recent Born Free Foundation report titled 'Conservation or Collection' reads, 'The prospects of reintroducing captive-born individuals to the wild are remote. A 2000 study found that just seven of 54 projects were successful where captive-born animals were reintroduced to the wild. A more recent study found only 13% of carnivore reintroduction projects were successful when the animals were captive born.'[49]

As such, in the guise of conservation, apparently European zoos are breeding giraffes and other animals only to keep in European zoos, but then kill them by the thousands each year due to a lack of space. You might be thinking, why breed the animals at all when the zoos clearly have more than enough of them, and when the idea is not to try to introduce them into the wild?

Virginia Morell asked herself the same question and wrote in *National Geographic*, 'For answers, you need look no further than the Copenhagen Zoo's Facebook page, where it celebrates the birth of a baby giraffe (possibly Marius) in 2012. Humans, science has shown, are drawn to babies of all kinds; we love the big eyes, the floppy limbs, the fluff and fuzz of infants. Baby leopards, baby pandas, baby elephants ... baby giraffes. They all draw huge, paying crowds to zoos.' In other words, babies are good for zoo business.

She goes on to state, 'Genetics and the carefully planned breeding program aside, it's hard not to suspect that the real reason Marius had to die was simply that he was past his human-appealing prime.'[50]

PETA points out, 'Most animals confined in zoos are not endangered, nor are they being prepared for release into natural habitats.'[51] And Born Free reports that in the UK, '73% of species kept in leading charitable zoos aren't threatened with extinction.'[52] Meanwhile, wildlife protection charity Zoocheck warns, '[A]lmost all zoos and captive wild animal display businesses claim they are focused on animal welfare. They also claim they play a vital role in the conservation of wildlife and in public conservation education. Unfortunately these claims don't usually stand up to scrutiny and are often exaggerated, untrue and/or unproven.'[53]

So what are zoos today really for? In the eighteenth and nineteenth centuries, private collections of animals called menageries were a way for the wealthy to display their power, and those were eventually opened to the public, largely for entertainment. Even today, it can be said zoos are about exerting power for amusement. They imprison animals, often denying them their natural behaviours and climactic and other environments important to their well-being, just so a bored couple can have something to do on a Sunday.

According to Zoocheck, 'Wild animals in captivity, even in the largest zoos, often suffer physically, psychologically and socially from lack of space, under-stimulation, inappropriate environmental conditions, antiquated or abusive management practices and other issues.'[54] As such, many animals in zoos display abnormal repetitive behaviour such as pacing, circling, swaying and head-bobbing. Many also constantly engage in bar-biting or excessively groom and lick themselves. This obsessive behaviour is called 'zoochosis' and animals behaving this way are described as 'zoochotic'—terms first coined by Bill Travers, co-founder of Born Free.[55]

The imprisonment of humans in zoos also had a detrimental effect on their mental health. Yes, you read that right—up until as recently as the 1950s there were human zoos that kept so-called 'primitive' people from Africa, Asia and the Americas on display for other people, usually Westerners, to gawk at. Sometimes they were kept in enclosures alongside animals.

For instance, one photo from 1931 shows German zoologist Professor Lutz Heck with an elephant and a family who appear to be from the Indian subcontinent. He had brought them to the Berlin Zoo in 1931. Another example is Ota Benga who was snatched from Congo and exhibited in New York's Bronx Zoo in 1906 with apes. Ota attracted tens of thousands to the zoo who laughed and jeered at him.[56]

African American clergymen were the first to protest Ota being kept like this and demanded his release, but William Temple Hornaday, the zoo's founding director, said the show must go on for science. He said, 'I am giving the exhibition purely as an ethnological exhibit'. *The New York Times* heard about the clergymen's complaints but could not fathom them.

And so, they published an editorial that read, 'We do not quite understand all the emotion which others are expressing in the matter ... Ota Benga, according to our information, is a normal specimen of his race or tribe, with a brain as much developed as are those of its other members. Whether they are held to be illustrations of arrested development, and really closer to the anthropoid apes than the other African savages, or whether they are viewed as the degenerate descendants of ordinary negroes, they are of equal interest to the student of ethnology, and can be studied with profit.' The editorial argued Ota could not possibly be suffering or feel humiliation in the zoo because he cannot possibly be intelligent. Many people make similar arguments about animals today—that even though we would obviously suffer on display in a cage, animals do not, which zoochosis shows us is not true.

For periods of time, Ota would be let out of his prison to walk around the zoo under the close watch of rangers. However, he began to lash out in self-defence when visitors to the zoo pursued, poked and prodded him. Zookeepers would then have the job of trying to put him back into the animal enclosure, but Ota started to fight back and was soon regarded as a problem.

In the meantime, the voices of the African American community and other objections began appearing in the press, even in *The New York Times*. Ultimately, and quietly, Ota was freed and sent to the Howard Coloured Orphan Asylum and eventually to the Lynchburg Theological Seminary and College in Virginia. By this point, he could speak a little English and befriended some local children. Later they would describe that they would often hear him sing a song he learned in this college: 'I believe I'll go home / Lordy, won't you help me.'

But over time, Ota began to retreat into himself and sit for long periods isolated and alone. And one night, when everyone in the town was asleep, Ota managed to get his hands on a gun and shot himself through the heart.[57]

Cruelty to animals and abuse of humans often goes hand in hand. For instance, numerous trafficked Nepali women and children who were beaten and sexually assaulted have been rescued from Indian circus bosses.[58] Today, India and numerous countries around the world have various prohibitions against the use of different species of animals in circuses because an increasing number of people realize beatings and other punishment is how the animals are also forced to perform. And now, law enforcement officials recognize that cruelty to animals can be a warning sign that violence towards humans will follow.

CREATING A MONSTER

American serial killer Jeffrey Dahmer was fascinated by animals as a child. When he was only five years old, his mother wrote that Jeffrey 'has a great interest in insects and animal life'.

This isn't unusual—most kids are intrigued by animals. Everyone knows this. Cartoons are full of animal characters, many toys come in the shape of animals and many parents welcome a dog into their home to provide their child company.

But Dahmer's fascination with animals was different—he was mesmerized by them dead. This interest was first observed by his father, Lionel. Lionel noted a very young Jeffrey became excited while watching him drag out bones of rodents who had died under their house.[1] Dahmer enjoyed the sound the bones made when they ricocheted off of each other in a bucket.[2]

Still, not that unusual probably. Little Jeffrey was likely just glad to be doing something with his father and simply enjoying the moment, even if it was just a usually off-putting part of home care. Besides, who isn't captivated by nature, especially when seeing something for the first time, and particularly when just a child.

Fairly understandably then, Lionel interpreted Jeffrey's interest in animals as an interest in science. After all, Lionel was a scientist himself—a chemist. It only made sense that his son would be interested in science too.

Dahmer started picking up animals of all sorts of species from everywhere, often dead. This included rats, mice, snakes, rabbits, toads, turtles, crabs and more. He would like to feel their bones. The bones part is kind of weird, but still arguably science-y, yes?

A school-age Dahmer thought some tadpoles he collected in a jar would be a nice gift for a teacher. She thanked him and put them on a ledge but later gave them to another child. When Dahmer found out, he killed them with motor oil. Yikes! Well, boys will be boys, right? Or at least, that's how a lot of people dismiss such actions.

When Dahmer was ten, his father gave him a chemistry set, which sparked his interest about various compounds and what they are used for. One evening, after dinner, Dahmer asked his father what would happen if chicken bones were put in bleach. Lionel was excited by his son's scientific curiosity and showed him.

By the time he was a teenager, Dahmer was conducting experiments with animals' bodies. For instance, he plunged insects into formaldehyde. He would gather the bodies of animals who died on the road or from the woods near his family home. He would dissect these animals, which included dogs, cats, opossums, foxes, raccoons and more. He would skin them and clean their bones using chemicals and tools.[3] And he would put their body parts in jars. Lionel still considered all of this *legitimate* activity, after all, kids are often made to dissect animals in school. (*Made to*, often *forced to*, because many are sickened by it.)

But Dahmer not only *liked* dissecting, he would take it a step further by collecting the animals' skulls, and at times impaling them on small crosses around his yard. When he was fifteen, he impaled a dog's head on a stick in the woods near his parents' home and nailed the skinned and gutted body to a tree. One neighbour who stumbled upon it said it looked like the site of cult worship. It terrified him.[4]

Dahmer was particularly interested in what happens *inside* animals' bodies—was *aroused* by it.[5] He even presented this while fishing, another 'legitimate' activity in terms of how most people see it, by slitting and chopping the fish just to look inside.[6]

Just weeks after he graduated high school, Dahmer killed his first victim. He was an eighteen-year-old hitchhiker, Steven Hicks, who Dahmer had invited into his parents' home for drinks. After all, the two boys would have been around the same age then. Why not, Steven must have thought. But when Steven made it clear he wanted to leave, Dahmer stopped him—forever. He bludgeoned the teenager with a barbell and then strangled him to death.[7] He then had sex with the body,[8] before dismembering it and smashing up the bones with a sledgehammer, strewing them in the woods. He was used to doing that—casting off bodies and body parts nearby. After all, those impaled animal heads in his yard marked animal graves.

Dahmer would go on to kill and violate seventeen men[9] that we know of, many of them African American and other persons of colour. According to a US Federal Bureau of Investigation (FBI) file, Dahmer would try to meet his victims in bars with gay clientele and was obsessed with dominating and controlling them.[10]

Similar to the way he practised on animals' bodies, Dahmer would conduct experiments on his human victims. He would try to create zombie lovers by drilling holes into their skulls and pouring hydrochloric acid into their heads. Unsurprisingly, his victims would die. And similar to how Dahmer preserved and kept certain body parts of squirrels[11] and other animals, he would keep body parts of his victims as mementos. This would include their skulls, genitals, hands or other body parts. To do this, he would cut them open using a large hunting knife, boil the flesh off the bones and dispose of the flesh and body parts he didn't want to keep by dissolving them in hydrochloric muriatic acid. He sometimes ate his victims' body parts too, such as their hearts and livers.[12]

Had Dahmer's parents recognized their son's macabre interest in dead animals, the animal heads dotted around his yard, the Satanic-like dog display, his desire to cut up animals and so on as red flags and gotten their son psychological help rather than *encourage* his behaviour, would things have turned out differently? In reading the FBI file on Dahmer, when special agents asked him if there was anything people in his life such as co-workers may have noticed as a warning sign, he said that he kept things well-compartmentalized and hidden.[13] This would have made Dahmer's extreme fascination with animals' bodies likely the most visible clue into what he would ultimately do with humans.

Considering how a person behaves with animals as an indication of how they might act with people is not far-fetched when we consider certain facts including that almost half, 45 per cent, of mass school shooters have a recorded history of cruelty to animals.[14] This becomes even more alarming when we take into account that not all cases of cruelty to animals are documented—likely most are not. And even when noticed by somebody, are often not taken seriously.

School shooting and other mass killing tragedies occur with alarming frequency in the US where many people can buy a gun in less than an hour (as compared to it taking months in some countries).[15] Numerous mass shooters there have used AR-15-style rifles, available at places like sporting goods stores, designed to kill a lot of people at once. These weapons of mass destruction really have no other purpose, although gun advocates in the US claim they use them for hunting animals, target practice and shooting competitions.[16] Even so, why these excuses and activities have so far justified these kinds of firearms being available in America despite their mass shooting crisis and the laxity of US gun laws is a whole other book.

Cruelty to animals appears so frequently in the histories of school shooters and other mass gunmen (and it is usually men for a variety of theorized reasons) that *Time* recently published an article titled, 'We Need to Talk About Animal Cruelty and Mass Shooters'. In it, Marc Levin, chief policy counsel for the non-profit Council on Criminal Justice, writes, 'Amid arguments over whether the recent massacres in Uvalde, Texas and Buffalo, New York should lead policymakers to focus more on gun control or mental illness, there is an elephant in the room. One trait the alleged perpetrators in both cases share in common is a propensity for animal cruelty.'[17]

What Marc is referring to is a racist attack at a grocery store in a predominantly African American neighbourhood in Buffalo, New York that left ten people dead and others wounded on 14 May 2022,[18] and the massacre of nineteen children and two adults just ten days later at Robb Elementary School in Uvalde County, Texas.[19]

Eighteen-year-old Payton Gendron, the Buffalo shooter, once publicly described torturing and beheading a cat on the social platform Discord. He chased the stray cat around his garage while stabbing the animal with a knife. He then described using the cat's tail to smash the animal onto concrete and taking around twenty attempts to cut off the cat's head.[20] Salvador Ramos, who was also eighteen at the time of his crime, formerly studied at Robb Elementary School. Peers later described him as someone who would attack animals. One high school classmate told *Daily Beast*, 'He would try and call people names and start fights. I remember there was one time we saw him beating a little dog senseless.'[21]

One of the deadliest mass shootings at a place of learning in US history took place at Columbine High School in Colorado. Fifteen students, including the perpetrators, teenagers Eric Harris and Dylan Klebold, lost their lives in the massacre. The boys entered the school armed with semiautomatic rifles, pistols and explosives, and the bloodbath only stopped when they took their own lives.[22] Both boys had bragged about mutilating animals previous to this tragedy.[23]

Also among the top deadly US school shootings is the one that took place at Marjory Stoneman Douglas High School in Florida. Following it, *NY Daily News* published an article titled, 'Nikolas Cruz may have never killed if society took more action on link between animal abuse and mass murderers'. That's because before Nikolas Cruz, who was nineteen at the time, opened fire at this high school, he spent time hurting animals. He would shoot squirrels and chickens with a pellet gun, kill toads and more. People knew this. He shared his pursuits on social media.[24]

These examples are from the US because while some school shootings have happened in other countries, it is largely an American phenomenon.[25] There are numerous factors and theories for why this is so including the easy availability of dangerous weapons there, copycat crimes, kids who want to become famous and more.[26] But the link between harming animals and hurting humans is not unique to the US.

As a result of various published studies and in-depth media coverage of crimes, there is a growing awareness in the US and elsewhere that cruelty to animals and violence to humans can be linked, and so, increasingly, authorities and others are taking note of it—although, still more so in hindsight than as an acted-upon warning. Nevertheless, an article that appears on the US FBI Law Enforcement Bulletin website reads, 'Historically, animal cruelty has been considered an isolated issue, but recent research shows a well-documented link that it is a predictive or co-occurring crime with violence against humans (including intimate partners, children, and elders) and is associated with other types of violent offenses. Increased awareness of this linkage and a collaborative approach to these investigations strengthens the identification and reduction of such crimes.'[27]

Apart from Jeffrey Dahmer, numerous other serial killers and violent criminals from all over the world started out by abusing animals first. They include Ian Brady, who along with Myra Hindley, murdered five children and sexually assaulted four in and near Manchester, England, in the 1960s. Ian had bragged about killing his cat as a child. He is said to have burned a different cat alive and to have engaged in abuses like stoning dogs and decapitating rabbits. They also include Robert Thompson and Jon Venables, who, when they were just children themselves, sadistically tormented to death James Bulger, a two-year-old child they snatched from a shopping centre in Merseyside, England. This included dropping the toddler on his head, throwing paint in his eye and hurling bricks at him. They also kicked him, put batteries in his mouth and ultimately dropped a 10 kg iron bar on his head. They then laid his body across the railway tracks to fool anyone who found him into thinking his death was an accident. Their play previous to this murder included using air rifles to shoot pigeons and, lo and behold, tying rabbits to railway lines to be crushed.[28]

Then there was Steven Barker, who as a child had skinned frogs before breaking their legs and tortured guinea pigs.[29] Later in life, he would go on to rape a two-year-old girl and torture Peter Connelly in London. Peter was a baby who died after suffering a series of horrific injuries inflicted on him by Barker, his mother Tracey and Barker's brother Jason Owen. By the time he died, Peter had a broken back and ribs. The many abuses Peter endured included being choked repeatedly until blue and having a Rottweiler incited to hurt him.[30]

American serial killer Ted Bundy, who ultimately confessed to twenty-eight murders but may be responsible for up to hundreds,[31] first mutilated dogs and cats.[32] John Wayne Gacy, another American serial killer, alarmingly worked as a clown at children's parties before anyone knew who he really was. He killed thirty-three boys and young men in the 1970s. He is reported to have set turkeys alight with balloons filled with gasoline as a youngster.[33] Rapist Albert DeSalvo is now regarded as likely being the notorious Boston Strangler. A DNA test linked him to the last victim of the unknown serial killer.[34] He would put cats and dogs into crates and then use them as target practice.[35]

In India, a law student known simply as Jisha was raped and murdered. She was found with her intestines spilling out and wounds all over her body. Following public outrage and extensive research, the police identified Jisha's neighbour, Ameerul Islam, as the culprit. According to police, as she resisted rape, he bashed her with sharp objects.[36] While being questioned for this crime, Ameerul confessed he had sexually assaulted animals too. Going by what he said, authorities found a goat with matching injuries.[37]

Meanwhile, Koose Muniswamy Veerappan, an Indian bandit, poacher and smuggler who was killed by the Tamil Nadu State Special Task Force in 2004, may have killed some 2,000 elephants and was wanted for the murders of 120 people.[38] Most of his victims were police and forest officials and persons he thought were snitching to authorities about his crimes. And before killing a woman to eat her flesh, Japanese cannibal Issei Sagawa had sexually abused his dog.[39]

The examples are endless. Does this mean every kid who kicks a dog is going to turn into a serial killer? Or that cruelty to animals is the only contributing factor to violent behaviour toward humans? Of course not. However, data shows that cruelty to animals is a major red flag, especially for domestic abuse, and that cases of cruelty to animals should be taken far more seriously than they usually are.

A paper published in *Forensic Research & Criminology International Journal* explains, 'There have been consistent research findings to suggest a strong link between animal cruelty and violence towards people including domestic abuse and child abuse … Animal abusers are more likely to engage in criminal behavior and to be diagnosed as having Antisocial Personality Disorder. Those who engage in animal cruelty were 3 times more likely to commit other crimes, including murder, rape, robbery, assault, harassment, threats, and drug/substance abuse. The major motivations for engaging in animal cruelty include anger, fun, control, fear, dislike, revenge, imitation, and sexual pleasure.'[40]

Being bullied and abused oneself is also a motivating factor for animal abuse. A child who is taking their issues out on animals may be having serious trouble that needs addressing at home. A paper on school shooters in *Homicide Studies* shares the idea that 'sadistic violence committed by serial killers results from the humiliation and internalized shame certain individuals experience during their childhood.' And that, 'To compensate, they develop a generalized malevolence whereby they inflict pain and suffering onto others.' The authors elaborate, 'School shooters, too, often experience humiliation and shame because they have been severely bullied for prolonged periods. Whether for mass or serial killers, the drive to harm animals may be a quest to exert power and dominance over another being, albeit a non-human animal.'[41]

Cruelty to animals can also happen simultaneous to human abuse rather than as a progression, can follow harm to a human or be committed to hurt a person. The article on the FBI Law Enforcement Bulletin website describes how domestic abusers often target animals beloved by the victims stating, 'Unfortunately, the abuser often exploits this bond to manipulate, control, and punish victims. To create fear and control, the abuser may threaten, hurt, or kill the animal. Cruelty to the animal may be used to convince the victim to return to a violent relationship, keep the victim isolated, financially control the victim, or coerce the victim into staying. Further, the offender may physically harm the animal to psychologically punish the victim or to remind the victim that the abuser can assert physical force to maintain dominance and control. Often, the abused partner will choose to stay in the violent situation out of concern for the pet's safety.'[42]

Researchers from Teesside University looked at Eastern European communities with large stray dog populations—where such animals were normally attacked, roughly rounded up and poisoned or killed in some other cruel way—and found a link to domestic violence. Malcolm Plant, one of the researchers, said the public handling of stray dogs in some Eastern European communities had normalized aggression towards them in the eyes of children. This made the animals soft targets and perpetuated aggression towards them in society.

They found, 'In rural areas where violence against animals is seen as more socially acceptable, adolescent males were more likely to abuse animals and had higher exposure to domestic violence.' They warn, 'violence breeds violence, with individuals who have been exposed to domestic abuse having also committed cruelty against animals.' They say, adolescent males 'either showed displaced aggression against the stray animals or progressed to commit violence against family members…' They called it a 'societal cycle of abuse'.[43]

But what about *sanctioned* cruelty to animals? If witnessing cruelty to or harming a dog can progress to harm to humans, what about witnessing cruelty to or harming a pig? What about a rat? Or a monkey?

Imagine for a moment what it would be like to work in a slaughterhouse. Being a slaughterhouse worker is regarded as one of the most violent, dangerous, physically and emotionally taxing professions. It is also low paid and generally condemned by society as a shameful, reprehensible job. Workers typically include members of the most vulnerable populations, such as illegal immigrants, who cannot stand up for their rights, as they are kept mum out of fear of loss of their jobs if they complain.[44]

In some countries, such as Brazil, there have been reports of slave labour in this sector.[45] (Similarly, Thailand's seafood sector is notorious for human trafficking, slavery and even murder. A United Nations Inter-Agency Project on Human Trafficking report exposes that nearly 60 per cent of trafficked migrants working on Thai fishing vessels have seen a worker get murdered.[46])

Human Rights Watch says workers in slaughter environments 'are regularly exposed to industrial equipment, stressful repetitive motions, sharp-edged hooks, knives, and band saws, heavy bags and boxes, and unpredictable animals, among uncountable other hazards.' And that, 'Moving machine parts can cause traumatic injuries by crushing, amputating, burning, and slicing. The tools of the trade—knives, hooks, scissors, and saws, among others—can cut, stab, and infect. The cumulative trauma of repeating the same, forceful motions, tens of thousands of times each day can cause severe and disabling injuries.'[47] While the group's report is focused on the US slaughter industry, these descriptions apply across the board for mechanized slaughter everywhere.

Workers showed Human Rights Watch that they have missing body parts, scars, swollen joints and other injuries. Many cried while describing their stress and working conditions. Meanwhile, an Oxfam report on poultry production also reveals how workers who have to handle knives and other sharp machinery report losing fingers and suffering stabs and lacerations. They talk of slippery floors and falling. Of respiratory difficulties from chemicals and toxins, dust and the birds' feathers and animal waste.[48] In numerous countries, such as Kenya[49] and India, workers often do not even wear any protective clothing. Many times, they don't even wear shoes.

While a teenager in Romania may witness dog catchers violently rounding up dogs, it is unlikely to be something he sees every day. But in a slaughterhouse, on top of facing the other insufferable conditions, a worker who was born with feelings, just like you and me, has to play some role in handling, killing, dismembering, disembowelling, skinning and packaging up to thousands of animals every single day. If harming a few dogs or rabbits can help desensitize a person to violent crime, or act as practise for it, what might all of this do?

The world's butchers and slaughterhouse workers process over 92 billion animals[50] through the meat processing system each year (and that's not counting the huge numbers of fish who are also killed). In other words, they are expected to handle over eleven times the number of animals than there are humans on Earth each year. This makes the line speed so demanding that in some slaughterhouses, the employee tasked with stunning animals with a bolt gun prior to slaughter handles one cow every twelve seconds.[51] (In many slaughterhouses around the world, including in India, animals are not stunned prior to slaughter and feel every inch of the knife going across their throat or into their chest.)

One worker told Human Rights Watch, 'We've already gone from the line of exhaustion to the line of pain … When we're dead and buried, our bones will keep hurting.'[52] Their hearts may keep hurting too. One former slaughterhouse worker wrote for the BBC, 'At night, my mind would taunt me with nightmares, replaying some of the horrors I'd witnessed throughout the day.' And that even after leaving the profession, 'When I close my eyes and try to sleep, I still sometimes see hundreds of pairs of eyeballs staring back at me.'[53] It is now recognized that slaughterhouse work can lead to disorders such as post-traumatic stress disorder (PTSD) and perpetration-induced traumatic stress (PITS). The latter is from hurting someone else, rather than being a victim.

Researchers studying the psychological impact of slaughterhouse work found workers reporting 'suffering from trauma, intense shock, paranoia, anxiety, guilt and shame'. Slaughterhouse workers in South Africa described feeling agonized particularly after their first kill. They also found high rates of depression, psychosis, anxiety, aggression and feelings of low self-worth in slaughterhouse workers, especially those dealing directly with animals. And they found an association between slaughterhouse work and crimes against humans such as sexual offenses like rape.[54] One study used the FBI's Uniform Crime Report and US census data to consider the impact on crime as industries set up in a new location. They found an increase in overall crime when slaughterhouses came to town.[55]

In November 2022, a UK court heard how two former slaughterhouse workers allegedly stabbed two men, one of them dozens of times, disembowelled the other and then put their slashed and mutilated bodies on gory display in a house.[56] Canadian serial killer Robert Pickton was a pig farmer who bragged about feeding his human victims to pigs, many of them vulnerable sex workers and drug users picked up in a red-light district. He also used a meat rendering plant, where dead animals are ground up into gruel, to hide evidence. He was charged with dozens of murders.[57]

Was the most famous serial killer of all, Jack the Ripper, a slaughterman? Dr Andrew Knight, professor of animal welfare and ethics at the University of Winchester, and Dr Katherine Watson, historian at the School of History, Philosophy and Culture at Oxford Brookes University, think it highly likely. In a paper published in the journal *Animals*, the research pair note, 'The identity of Jack the Ripper remains one of the greatest unsolved crime mysteries in history. Jack was notorious both for the brutality of his murders and also for his habit of stealing organs from his victims. His speed and skill in doing so, in conditions of poor light and haste, fueled theories he was a surgeon. However, re-examination of a mortuary sketch from one of his victims has revealed several key aspects that strongly suggest he had no professional surgical training. Instead, the technique used was more consistent with that of a slaughterhouse worker.'[58]

Countless investigations by animal protection groups show upset factory farm and slaughterhouse workers taking out their frustrations on the animals who already have to suffer the cruelties inherent in the system. There have been reports of slaughterhouse workers kicking animals like footballs, electrocuting them, beating them with metal pipes and other weapons and even ripping them apart alive. Gail Eisnitz, author of *Slaughterhouse: The Shocking Story of Greed, Neglect, And Inhumane Treatment Inside the U.S. Meat Industry*, quoted a slaughterhouse worker as saying, 'Down in the blood pit they say that the smell of blood makes you aggressive. And it does. You get an attitude that if that hog kicks at me, I'm going to get even. You're already going to kill the hog, but that's not enough. It has to suffer.'[59] It's that 'cycle of abuse' the Teesside University researchers talked about.

PETA set out to find out if there is a link between experimenting on animals and crimes against humans. On a webpage called 'Sex, Violence, and Vivisection: Are Some Animal Experimenters Psychopaths?', the group describes the many cases they found and says, 'When animal experimenters cut up, burn, torment, and deliberately sicken animals, they're almost never subject to punishment since that cruelty is being done under the guise of research.'

The examples they cite include that of Tracy McIntosh, the former director of the University of Pennsylvania's Head Injury Clinical Research Laboratory. There, he bashed in the heads of cats and other animals and inflicted severe brain injuries on them. PETA exposed this laboratory in 1984 through a video shot by the experimenters themselves to document their own work. In it, they caused severe head injuries to primates, including those inadequately anesthetized, while mocking them. As part of one experiment, McIntosh would fold back the scalps of anesthetized rats and then use a pressurized pulse that essentially scrambled their brain tissue.

Just short of twenty years after PETA's expose, McIntosh was arrested for the rape of a veterinary student. The victim accused him of giving her Nembutal, a drug that was used in his laboratory to kill rats, and raping her there. She also accused the University of Pennsylvania of covering up his 'history of acts of sexual harassment'.

He brought millions in funding to the university, with the US' National Institutes of Health (NIH) granting him almost USD 18 million for his experiments and programme expenses. McIntosh received a jail sentence, and in 2007, he and the university came to a confidential settlement with the victim.

Another example is that of University of Pittsburgh's Robert Ferrante who is serving a life sentence for poisoning and murdering his wife, Dr Autumn Klein, with cyanide he had sent to his laboratory. He conducted Huntington's disease experiments on mice. He would drug these animals and then put them on a spinning rod. When the mice could not right themselves within a certain time frame and with prodding, they would be killed. He also conducted experiments concerning amyotrophic lateral sclerosis (ALS), which involved suspending mice by their tails to check for motor deficits.

Yet another example is the case of Wyndham Lathem, who was an associate professor at Northwestern University. There, he infected mice with the bubonic plague. In July 2017, Lathem and a man called Andrew Warren were charged with the murder of twenty-six-year-old Trenton Cornell-Duranleau. Evidently, Lathem and Warren hatched a plan online where they talked about their fantasies of killing other people and themselves over months. The victim was killed from being stabbed dozens of times. Wyndham Lathem and Andrew Warren were sentenced to decades in prison.

In total, PETA describes the cases of seventeen animal experimenters on its web page.[60] Their findings are disturbing, and it is worth reading all the stories.

So what do we do about all of this? Bradley Miller, president of the Humane Farming Association, which campaigns against factory farming, is widely quoted to have said: 'Teaching a child not to step on a caterpillar is as valuable to the child as it is to the caterpillar.'[61] Our answer seems to lie there.

HOW TO HEAL FROM BITES

I could use this final chapter to suggest what governments and industries should do to be more at peace with nature for all of our sakes. How it is imperative that they recognize and demonstrate through their policies and decisions that humans, other animals and the environment are interdependent. I could rail against the powers that be for endorsing damaging systems and policies. But governments and industries are made up of individuals, and so these steps focus on you and me.

1. Respect the Golden Rule

Do you remember when we were kids and the teacher would write the Golden Rule on the blackboard? I went to school in the US and teachers always wrote it there.

It read, 'Do unto others as you would have them do unto you.' It is a concept from Biblical literature and exists to remind Christians to treat their neighbours with kindness.[1] Of course, this basic ethical principle is espoused by people of all religions, as well as those with none. It is so fundamental today to human ethos that it reads almost like common sense, even though we are all guilty of sometimes forgetting it.

Well, flora and fauna are our neighbours, and just as it is useful to have happy human neighbours, it is beneficial for our own welfare, as I hope you will by now agree, to live in harmony with animals and our planet.

There is another form. It reads, 'Do not do to others what you would not like done to yourselves.'

People often ask me how I define what counts as good animal welfare. You may have heard about the widely accepted 'Five Freedoms' for animals, which are also recognized by the World Organisation for Animal Health (WOAH). WOAH is an intergovernmental organization focusing on global animal health with 182 member countries.

The five freedoms for animals are:

1. Freedom from hunger, malnutrition and thirst
2. Freedom from fear and distress
3. Freedom from heat stress or physical discomfort
4. Freedom from pain, injury and disease
5. Freedom to express normal patterns of behaviour

WOAH uses these as guiding principles to frame their recommendations for terrestrial animals (sorry, fish) such as those used for food.[2] However, battery cage and other factory farming systems like breeding for rapid growth and less food intake mean even these basics are commonly ignored.

I have a different view than WOAH for what should constitute good animal welfare. It goes back to the Golden Rule and simply asking ourselves if we would like an action done to ourselves. Would we want to be confined to a cage? Would we want to have our throats slit? Would we want to be used as a test tube? And so on. By asking ourselves these kinds of questions, I believe, more often than not, we can determine the most humane course of action.

I like to think Ms Boone, my first-grade teacher, would be proud.

2. Consume Like You Care

If the content of this book has inspired you to live vegan, or to live more vegan than what you may do now, there's good news—it's easier than ever to do, and you'd be in great company too.

According to a report by data and analytics firm GlobalData, which works with 4,000 of the largest companies, 70 per cent of the world population is either going meat-free or reducing meat consumption.[3] Due to the demand this presents, packaged vegan foods like 'meat', 'eggs' and 'milk' made from plants rather than animals are increasingly available in stores and restaurants around the world. In fact, in 2021, consumer market research firm Rakuten Insight Global reported 81 per cent of people worldwide have tried plant milk, 44 per cent have tried plant-based 'meat' and 25 per cent have tried vegan 'egg' options.[4]

That said, there is no requirement to buy packaged vegan foods to eat vegan. If you live near a grocery store, chances are you have an abundance of fruits, vegetables, grains, pulses, nuts and seeds to choose from. If you prefer to include more locally grown produce to reduce your contribution to transport emissions, there are plenty of edible, nutritious plants that grow even in colder climates.

If you could use support, Vegan Outreach has a mentorship programme with 1,200 mentors in 750 cities in 44 countries to help participants eat vegan.[5] Washington-DC-based Physicians Committee for Responsible Medicine (PCRM) runs a vegan kickstart programme via an app.[6] Their 'Plant-Based Nutrition FAQ', which can be found on PCRM.org, is a must-read for those new to eating vegan as it answers the most common health-related questions. In India, Sanctuary for Health and Reconnection to Animals and Nature (SHARAN) offers a variety of health programmes for motivation to eat vegan. There are also countless vegan recipes on the internet, including websites to try, like my favourites Bosh.TV and VeganRicha.com, and many vegan cookbooks. You will easily find recipes to create your own vegan milk from oats, hazelnuts or other plants; vegan eggs from tofu, mung beans or chickpea flour; and vegan meats from mushrooms, wheat gluten and more, should you desire.

PETA operates a global database called Beauty Without Bunnies accessible from crueltyfree.peta.org. It lists cosmetics, personal care and household product brands (like cleaners) that do and do not test on animals and marks vegan companies. The group also runs a 'How to Wear Vegan' webpage via PETA.org that helps consumers better interpret clothing and accessories labels to determine which are made of vegan materials.

Then there is the growing popularity of second-hand clothing and online and offline shops that cater to this interest. Both people looking for something unique and those interested in reducing their impact on the planet enjoy used items. Many people opt to choose only vegan items from pre-worn suppliers too considering any use of animal-derived clothing as normalizing and perpetuating their use. This is especially so as much recycled clothing is actually nearly brand new. I'm one of those people.

PETA also runs a webpage called 'How to Be a Compassionate Traveler',[7] which provides tips such as avoiding facilities that use captive animals for entertainment, avoiding spectacles like bullfights and saying no to animal rides explaining how the animals are often in pain and in bad shape. The group is working in places like Petra, Jordan, to transition tourism-focused communities reliant on horses or other animals to eco-friendly mechanized transport. For those considering an animal sanctuary visit, PETA recommends, 'The Global Federation of Animal Sanctuaries (GFAS) has rigorous standards of sanctuary management and animal care. GFAS-accredited animal sanctuaries never breed animals or use them in commercial activities. Some of the member sanctuaries provide educational tours, but not all of them do, so if you're interested in visiting one with tours, please check before you go.'[8]

3. Be a Whistle-blower

If you have been to the US anytime recently, you are likely familiar with the simple slogan, 'If You See Something, Say Something®'. It is a US Department of Homeland Security campaign to encourage Americans to report suspicious activity, especially anything that might be linked to terrorism.[9] (How xenophobia and racism sour this advice and concerns about Big Brother are for another book.)

However, 'If You See Something, Say Something®' is undoubtedly catchy and should be applied to other things, such as crimes and other wrongdoing against animals. After all, if you do not speak up, who will? As you know from the previous chapter, the consequences of turning a blind eye to cruelty to animals can be severe for all.

Safia Rubaii saw something and said something.[10] In 1992, she contacted PCRM as a medical student. With their support, she sued her school, the University of Colorado, for forcing her to take part in 'dog lab'—trainings in which dogs were used to teach students basic physiology and pharmacology. After the lessons were over, the dogs were killed. Rubaii wanted to be allowed to use a humane alternative instead—but back then, this was a novel concept.

And so, Rubaii initially suffered a setback. The judge ruled against her, but she persevered. She appealed the judge's decision and ultimately won her case. Rubaii's action set a lot of things in motion, not only at the University of Colorado but in medical schools everywhere. In 1995, Harvard Medical School dropped the use of dogs and rats for physiology courses. The University of Colorado finally ended its dog labs in 2003.[11]

Today, thanks in large part to the work PCRM continued, all US and Canadian medical schools and paediatrics residencies use simulators and other non-animal, human-focused training methods instead of animals.[12]

PETA has donated 122 simulators called TraumaMan to Advanced Trauma Life Support programmes in twenty-two countries. The group estimates this spares the lives of more than 2,000 animals a year, while providing surgeons with modern training.[13] In India, following work by PETA India and others, the use of animals to train undergraduate medical students is now not allowed.[14]

Whistle-blowers have exposed many other cruelties and been instrumental in bringing about major changes. One whistle-blower dying of cancer was encouraged by his wife to send photographs to PETA revealing how Ringling Bros. Circus was training baby elephants by tying them in place, beating and jabbing them.[15] In 2017, this famous American circus closed its doors, and recently announced that it will reopen but with animal-free acts.[16] PETA had protested the use of animals by this circus for decades.

People who report cruelty to animals are so powerful that many animal protection organizations actively send out appeals for whistle-blowers, assuring them protection and anonymity. The Animal Legal Defense Fund is a US-based organization that files lawsuits to protect animals from harm and provides free legal support to prosecutors, among taking other legal-focused action for animals. The group has set up a website, ReportAnimalAg.com, to encourage factory farm and slaughterhouse workers to report concerning practices.

PETA India reports the more members of public who have been reporting crimes against animals through their encouragement, the easier it has become to get police to take these crimes seriously.

4. Inspire Children to be Solutionaries

Zoe Weil is the co-founder and president of the Institute for Humane Education (IHE). She says, 'How can we create a just, healthy, and humane world? What is the path to developing sustainable energy, food, transportation, production, construction, and other systems? What's the best strategy to end poverty and ensure that everyone has equal rights? How can we slow the rate of extinction and restore ecosystems? How can we learn to resolve conflicts without violence and treat other people and non-human animals with respect and compassion? The answer to all these questions lies with one underlying system—schooling. To create a more sustainable, equitable, and peaceful world, we must reimagine education and prepare a generation to be solutionaries—young people with the knowledge, tools, and motivation to create a better future.'[17]

Weil argues that if we change our concept of school from being about learning the basics like reading and math to get jobs, to being a far richer experience—that is to prepare the next generation to make decisions that are better for people, animals and the environment—we will be more suitably placed to tackle, reduce and prevent the world's problems. The idea is not to replace the essentials like science, history and so on, but to teach them through the process of considering real-world troubles and scenarios. She calls it turning young people into 'dedicated solutionaries'.

Solutionaries, according to IHE, are solution-driven individuals who are able to identify when a practice is cruel, environmentally damaging or unfair and who work to turn it around to something that is nurturing for the well-being of humans, animals and the environment. Solutionaries, they say, also live in a way that causes the least harm.

Weil acknowledges that some people worry information about the world's woes is too heavy for children. Some even think burdening young people like this with difficulties caused by previous generations is unfair. However, she considers it unfair to leave children in the dark about what's really going on. She has a point that doing so leads to young people ultimately facing these issues, unprepared. As such, many youngsters end up making decisions that worsen crises as adults.[18]

If this makes sense to you, there are many humane education resources available for free download or mailing provided by different non-profit organizations that you can introduce to teachers or professors, or use them yourself if you are in a guiding capacity with young people. It would be important to go through the materials to ensure they align with what you want to relay. Specific to animals, PETA's TeachKind webpage is a good resource. It reads, 'We are former classroom teachers, here to help schools, educators, and parents promote compassion for animals through free lessons, virtual classroom presentations, materials, advice, online resources, and more.'[19] The materials are designed to build empathy for animals in young people of all ages. PETA entities also offer free humane education programmes for kids aged eight to twelve called 'Share the World' or 'Compassionate Citizen', in different countries.

5. Be a Workplace Solutionary

Perhaps you are a politician or run a clothing shop. Maybe you are a professor or a journalist. You may be a cleaner or work in the IT sector. Or you could be a lawyer or a social media influencer. It could be you are a rock star or a homemaker. Whatever you do, there will be ways to incorporate helping animals into your job in small and big ways.

For instance, you might ask your head of maintenance to use only non-animal tested soaps in bathroom dispensers or revise your stock to selling only animal-friendly products. You may ensure the business turns its lights off at night to protect insects from light pollution or get together with your colleagues to plant a pesticide-free community vegetable garden or one with plants that invite bees, butterflies and other insects on company property.

You might introduce vegan foods to your workmates by taking in delicious treats, or advocate for plant milk to be made available for teas and coffees. Perhaps you will influence the staff canteen to go vegan, meat-free or to at least include vegan options. Sodexo Ireland is a workplace food caterer. They report demand for vegan foods is on the up and up from its corporate clients there. Vegan meals they offer include lentil celeriac chestnut pie, potato mixed bean chilli, tofu summer tart, Southern Indian vegan chickpea curry, vegan mushroom burger, vegan chicken nuggets and aubergine masala.[20] Who wouldn't get into the cafeteria queue for that?

If you have a public platform, you could use it to encourage your readers, followers or fans to think about animal protection issues. You could do this by writing an article on the pitfalls of animal testing, sharing videos about leather production—such as those found on PETA entity YouTube pages—by giving a talk on climate change or simply wearing a slogan T-shirt urging people to be kind.

You might speak to the person in charge of corporate social responsibility to consider supporting an ambulance for an animal protection charity or to meet some other need or ask human resources to start payroll giving—where employees can opt to help charities of their choice each month through a portion of their paycheques that they decide.

The possibilities for incorporating actions for animals into what you do are truly endless. You could offer your artistic, legal or other services pro-bono to help make an advertisement against animal circuses or to fight a court case about dogfighting. You can gather your teammates to volunteer at an animal shelter or pick up plastic waste from the beach that birds and other sea animals otherwise choke on, ingest and get entangled in. When lawyer and concerned citizen Afroz Shah gathered volunteers, he transformed a beach full of trash to one that is pristine in Mumbai, leading to recognition by the United Nations.[21]

As a homemaker, you have the power to raise kind kids, make eco-friendly decisions regarding the running of your home, and to help be a model family in your community.

6. Grow the Vegan Economy

Perhaps this book has inspired you to start a business to help animals. Others who have done that show there's plenty of money to be made from doing good for the world.

If you are a food technologist, chef or anyone else interested in getting into the vegan food products space, I recommend looking up the Good Food Institute (GFI) as a first step. They call themselves, 'a nonprofit think tank and international network of organizations working to accelerate alternative protein innovation'. They do everything from working to influence government policies surrounding food to working with academics, entrepreneurs and industry leaders to advance alternative proteins. They even offer a Startup Manual to help you get your idea off the ground.

'Alternative proteins' means meats made from plants and slaughter-free meat made in a laboratory—cultivated from animal cells. GFI says alternative proteins 'slash emissions by up to 92 percent—especially when produced with renewable energy'.[22] There are also scientists working on creating milk from cells instead of cows.[23]

If you're more of a fashion entrepreneur, check out Material Innovation Initiative (MII). It's like GFI, but for people who are interested in improving materials used in the fashion, automotive, and home goods industries. The group describes itself as 'a think tank focused on research, knowledge-sharing, and fostering connections to fast-track the development of environmentally preferable and animal-free materials'.[24]

Today, animal-free materials include leather made from plants, instead of animals. For instance, Phool is an Indian company that makes vegan leather out of flowers discarded by temples.[25] There's also leather made from mushrooms, cactus, pineapple leaves, apples and more. Many vegan leathers are made from the leftover waste from the food industry.

PETA recently announced a USD 1 million prize to anyone who can create 'a vegan wool material that is visually, texturally, and functionally akin to or better than sheep's wool'.[26] Maybe that award can go to you.

Perhaps you are scientifically inclined. If so, check out the Center for Contemporary Sciences co-founded by Dr Aysha Akhtar, a double Board-certified neurologist and preventive medicine/public health specialist mentioned earlier in the book, for ideas and ways to get involved. The purpose of the Center is 'to unlock the power of science to find solutions that improve the health and wellbeing of humans, animals and the planet'. Specifically, the group works to 'advance innovative technologies that disrupt the status quo and that can solve our most pressing health issues'. It also works to educate stakeholders, and on advocacy to influence policies related to their key goals: improving medical research, tackling the rise in pandemics and antibiotic resistance and addressing climate change and environmental destruction.[27]

If you're a student with an idea, PETA is awarding prizes of USD 1,000 to USD 10,000 'to students who come up with a game-changing idea for an invention that the student can develop into a specific action plan or design to replace animal use'. The initiative is called a 'Future Without Speciesism Cash Award'.[28]

7. Put Your Money Where Your Conscience Is

Whether you dabble in shares or are a venture capitalist, you influence what happens in the world with your money for better or for worse. By being a conscientious investor, you can help make the world a better place.

'Meat Atlas', the 2021 report by Heinrich-Böll-Stiftung, Friends of the Earth Europe and BUND, mentioned earlier in this book, highlights this point. The report says, 'Some meat giants, such as Cargill, are wholly privately owned. Others are at least partially listed on the stock exchanges. Financial firms are major investors, underwriters and lenders to the sector. Over 2,500 investment banks, private banks and pension funds from around the world invested a total of 478 billion US dollars in meat and dairy companies from 2015–2020, according to Feedback, a non-governmental organization. The biggest investors include Black Rock, Capital Group, Vanguard and the Norwegian government pension fund.'[29] Apart from meat, firms could be backing the fur trade, arms, tobacco, other industries that worsen climate change or any number of violent or damaging practices you may not agree with.

Depending on where you live, you may be able to opt to use a financial services provider that is ethically conscious. Ethical Consumer is a British non-profit research organization that puts out a magazine and runs a website aimed at helping consumers make more well-informed and principled decisions. On ethicalconsumer.org, the group has a money guide about ethical banking, pensions, savings accounts, investments and insurance. It would be a good starting point for ideas on what to look for, even if you do not live in the UK. And if you live in a country where you lack choice for financial service providers that are sufficiently ethically driven, perhaps this is a gap in the market you would be able to fill.

If you are interested in impact investing or funding vegan or other animal and Earth-friendly companies, take a look at the work of the FAIRR Initiative and GlassWall Syndicate. The FAIRR

Initiative says its 'mission is to build a global network of investors who are aware of the issues linked to intensive animal production and seek to minimise the risks within the broader food system'. It exists to 'help investors to exercise their influence as responsible stewards of capital while safeguarding the long-term value of their investment portfolios'.[30] Meanwhile, GlassWall Syndicate 'is a large group of venture capitalists, foundations, trusts, non-profits, and individual investors who share a similar investment thesis and want to accelerate mainstream adoption of products and services that will make a difference in the lives of animals, people and that are better for the planet'.[31]

You may also want to explore Vegpreneur, which calls itself 'a media brand and global community for founders and investors building sustainable, vegan, plant-based, animal-free, cruelty-free, earth-friendly, and impact businesses in food/beverage, fashion, climate tech, beauty, wellness, and agtech'.[32] And check out what firms like Veg Capital and Stray Dog Capital are up to. With most investor focus on vegan food in comparison to other animal issues, perhaps you will consider using your investment to advance vegan fashion or to solve another problem animals face.

Of course, as with any investment, you could lose money, and have to be careful and mindful. The guidance in this chapter should not be taken as financial advice or endorsement.

8. Beware of Greenwashing and Humane-washing

You read a little about greenwashing in Chapter 8. Greenpeace defines greenwashing as 'a PR tactic used to make a company or product appear environmentally friendly, without meaningfully reducing its environmental impact'.[33] A company could also be engaging in humane-washing by portraying itself as doing something significant to help animals, workers and so on, while not really doing anything substantial. Greenpeace says, 'Greenwashing aims to boost a company's public image or make more sales by convincing us that buying from them aligns with our values'; humane-washing is the same.

Greenpeace lists ways to spot greenwashing on its website, which can also be applied to humane-washing.

1. Token gestures—like if a restaurant uses paper straws to save sea animals from plastic pollution, while serving up fish caught through hugely damaging fishing practices.
2. Vague claims or misleading labels—such as a shampoo bottle that reads 'no animal testing' but where in truth it is only the finished product, rather than also the ingredients, that are not animal-tested. In contrast, by visiting PETA's online Beauty Without Bunnies database, you can read what criteria the organization applies to the companies it lists.
3. A lack of evidence—like when clothing company Patagonia, with the mission 'cause no unnecessary harm', was busted by PETA for using a 'sustainable' wool supplier from Argentina where workers were actually kicking, stomping on, mutilating and stabbing sheep.[34] Patagonia stopped using this supplier after the exposé but was busted again for using an American supplier that violated its own standards.[35] Patagonia stopped listing that farm as a supplier too, but now PETA is urging the company to drop all wool.
4. Use of buzzwords or images—like using pictures of happy cows in a field to sell milk when the animals used are raised on a factory farm.
5. Carbon offsetting—especially where offset actions like tree planting are used as a substitute for the company taking steps that would genuinely cut its own emissions. You've likely seen this if you've purchased a flight ticket, where the customer is offered a chance to pay to 'offset' their flight.

6. Superfluous claims—the example Greenpeace gives here is when a company marks something as vegan when it is already inherently vegan and no extra effort has been made by the company to help the environment.

Greenpeace explains greenwashing is dangerous because it is merely feel-good, distracting and ineffective. The same goes for humane-washing. The group recommends challenging companies, holding them to account and asking them through social media and other ways what they are *really* doing for the environment, animals and people.

9. Become an Activist

If you take on any of the suggestions in this chapter, you will already be an activist. However, other ways to get involved would be to get active with an animal or environmental protection campaigning group or to gather like-minded individuals to form a community group to identify and problem-solve local or national issues. You can also be a big voice for animals and the environment online on your own.

PETA and many other animal and environmental protection groups offer news on critical issues and ideas on ways to help on their websites, so checking those out will always be a great place to start. This usually includes petitions and other online appeals you can sign to government officials or corporations. Such organizations also usually provide videos and other content that can be shared online via their social media pages and sometimes free informative leaflets too that you can distribute (although some people prefer the online route over concern for trees).

They also usually provide volunteer opportunities. The best way to learn about those is simply to get in touch to relay your interest. If it is a protest-focused group, they would always need people to come out to demonstrations to show that the issue has support, that people care. If you can volunteer a safe, loving home for rescued animals, even temporarily, animal protection groups are certain to want to hear about that too.

You can find an animal protection group close to you through the directory at worldanimal.net. You are also likely to find groups working on matters of concern to you through internet searches about the issues you would like to address. Not all animal protection and environmental groups are the same—they differ in everything from philosophy, size, effectiveness and more—so it would be important to read their mission statements and content to determine which group or groups you would like to help.

Some of the progress that has happened at the local level around the world thanks to people who decided to bring about change include various US towns prohibiting the chaining of dogs;[36] bullfighting being banned in numerous places;[37] and the celebration of Thursdays as Veggie Day in Ghent, Belgium—through which more than ninety restaurants and twenty hotels offer meat-free menus.[38] You, too, can make a difference in your community and country!

10. Support the Third Sector

The third sector includes non-governmental and non-profit organizations, like charities, volunteer groups, cooperatives and the like.

If the work of such a group inspires you, you can often become a member by donating a small amount, which usually comes with some benefits such as being kept updated on their activities. You can also opt to give bigger gifts. This can be done by donating funds for the organization to decide how to use or you can ask them about their specific needs and donate toward projects that move you. You can also leave support to organizations in your will.

Most likely, you live where you can claim a deduction on your taxes if you give to a legally registered charity. If you would rather support the work of grassroots individuals who are not officially formed or registered, then of course you would not benefit from this, but you may decide to support them anyway for other reasons.

Different countries have different ways to look up the legal status of charities. For instance, the Indian government runs a database called NGO Darpan, the UK government has a charity register, and in the US, you can look them up through the Internal Revenue Service (IRS).

Established non-profit organizations should have annual reports available online or on request that you can review to scrutinize how the money they receive is spent, usually have external financial auditors especially if of a certain size, and have compliances to meet to the government. Charity annual reports are typically divided into programme, administrative and fundraising expenses. Programme are those expenses directly related to advancing the mission of the organization. A good organization would be willing to thoroughly answer your questions.

Third-sector organizations cannot do any of the work they do without financial support.

~

I started this book with words of Joaquin Phoenix, and I'll end it with words from him too. After all, he's one of my most favourite actors. He said, 'When we look at the world through another animal's eyes, we see that inside we're all the same—and that we all deserve to live free from suffering.'[39]

ACKNOWLEDGEMENTS

For planting the first seed of thought that animals matter, no matter how big, small, cute or crawly—my late grandmother, Sarlaben. For teaching me to live with empathy, my parents. For challenging me to think about the consequences of food choices way back when we were teenagers, Natalie Hawkins. For being an ear, Megha Joshipura, and being a laugh, Neil Joshipura. For taking me under her wing and continuing to be my mentor, Ingrid Newkirk, founder of PETA entities worldwide. For inspiring me to write my first book, Soum Paul, and then Debasri Rakshit. For keeping me on track, Siddhesh Inamdar and then Swati Chopra of HarperCollins India. For opening doors, my agent, Kanishka Gupta. For recognizing the value of my books, HarperCollins India. For being heroes and working tirelessly toward making the world a better place, PETA entity, Animal Rahat and Petra Veterinary Clinic staff and volunteers and too many effective activists and groups to name. For helping us see the truth and to connect the dots, all of the investigators, authors, scientists, researchers, filmmakers, journalists and others I reference in this book. For being supportive and providing much needed breaks, all of my wonderful friends. For being forever in my heart, Tim and Mil and the late Mehboob.

NOTES

Introduction

1. *The Guardian*. Joaquin Phoenix's Oscars speech in full: 'We feel entitled to artificially inseminate a cow and steal her baby'. 10 February 2020; https://www.theguardian.com/film/2020/feb/10/joaquin-phoenixs-oscars-speech-in-full
2. World Health Organization. 'WHO Director-General's opening remarks at the media briefing on COVID-19 - 11 March 2020'. 11 March 2020; https://www.who.int/director-general/speeches/detail/who-director-general-s-opening-remarks-at-the-media-briefing-on-covid-19---11-march-2020
3. Doucleff, Michaeleen. 'What does the science say about the origin of the SARS-CoV-2 pandemic?'. NPR. 28 February 2023; https://www.npr.org/sections/goatsandsoda/2023/02/28/1160162845/what-does-the-science-say-about-the-origin-of-the-sars-cov-2-pandemic
4. Mullin, Larry. 'The WHO is hunting for the coronavirus's origins. Here are the new details'. *National Geographic*. 6 November 2020; https://www.nationalgeographic.com/science/article/world-health-

organization-china-search-covid-origins-what-to-expect?loggedin=true&rnd=1674307068250

5. Kunzmann, Kevin. 'WHO, China Report Suggests COVID-19 Passed From Bats to Humans Through Another Animal'. Contagion Live. 29 March 2021; https://www.contagionlive.com/view/who-china-report-covid-19-passed-bats-humans-animal
6. Gale, Jason, and Corinne Gretler. 'Contentious Hunt for Covid's Origin Points to China Animal Trade. Bloomberg. 20 March 2021; https://www.bloomberg.com/news/articles/2021-03-20/contentious-hunt-for-covid-s-origin-points-to-china-animal-trade#xj4y7vzkg
7. Li, Wenhui. et al. 'Animal Origins of the Severe Acute Respiratory Syndrome Coronavirus: Insight from ACE2-S-Protein Interactions.' *Journal of Virology*, 4211–19. 2006.
8. Maxmen, Amy. 'Scientists struggle to probe COVID's origins amid sparse data from China'. *Nature*. 17 March 2022; https://www.nature.com/articles/d41586-022-00732-0
9. Chan, Paul K.S. 'Outbreak of Avian Influenza A(H5N1) Virus Infection in Hong Kong in 1997'. *Clinical Infectious Diseases*, vol. 34, issue Supplement_2, pp. S58–S64. May 2002; https://doi.org/10.1086/338820
10. Li, FCK, et al. 'Finding the real case-fatality rate of H5N1 avian influenza'. *Journal of Epidemiology & Community Health*, vol. 62, issue no. 6, pp. 55559. June 2008.
11. PETA. 'Ingrid Newkirk Tackles Speciesism in Cross-Country Tour'. 26 March 2018; https://www.peta.org/blog/ingrid-newkirk-tackles-speciesism-in-cross-country-tour/
12. Freeman, Simon. '£5 trillion: how much the Covid-19 pandemic cost the global economy in 2020'. *Evening Standard*. 24 December 2020; https://www.standard.co.uk/business/economy/how-much-has-the-pandemic-cost-the-world-s-economy-b473369.html
13. University of Cambridge Judge Business School. 19 May 2020; https://www.jbs.cam.ac.uk/insight/2020/economic-impact/
14. Carrington, Damian. 'Most "meat" in 2040 will not come from dead animals, says report'. *The Guardian*. 12 June 2019; https://www.theguardian.com/environment/2019/jun/12/most-meat-in-2040-will-not-come-from-slaughtered-animals-report

15. Greenfield, Patrick. 'Ban wildlife markets to avert pandemics, says UN biodiversity chief'. *The Guardian*. 6 April 2020; https://www.theguardian.com/world/2020/apr/06/ban-live-animal-markets-pandemics-un-biodiversity-chief-age-of-extinction
16. Calarco, Matthew. n.d. 'On the Separation of Human and Animal'. Stanford University Press blog; https://stanfordpress.typepad.com/blog/2015/09/on-the-separation-of-human-and-animal.html#:~:text=In%20Aristotle's%20schema%2C%20plants%20have,%2C%20and%20other%20similar%20traits)
17. Aristotle. *Politics*. 350 B.C.E.; http://classics.mit.edu/Aristotle/politics.1.one.html
18. Calarco, Matthew. n.d. 'On the Separation of Human and Animal'. Stanford University Press blog; https://stanfordpress.typepad.com/blog/2015/09/on-the-separation-of-human-and-animal.html#:~:text=In%20Aristotle's%20schema%2C%20plants%20have,%2C%20and%20other%20similar%20traits)
19. Sartwell, Crispin. 'Humans Are Animals. Let's Get Over It'. *The New York Times*. 23 February 2021; https://www.nytimes.com/2021/02/23/opinion/humans-animals-philosophy.html
20. Martin Luther King, Jr. 'Letter from a Birmingham Jail [King, Jr.]'. 16 April 1963; https://www.africa.upenn.edu/Articles_Gen/Letter_Birmingham.html
21. BBC. 'Ahimsa'. 11 September 2009; https://www.bbc.co.uk/religion/religions/jainism/living/ahimsa_1.shtml#:~:text=Jains%20believe%20that%20violence%20in,bad%20as%20doing%20harm%20yourself
22. Ibid.
23. Kilvert, Nick. 'Bumblebees can create mental imagery, a "building block of consciousness", study suggests'. ABC News. 23 February 2020; https://www.abc.net.au/news/science/2020-02-21/bumblebee-objects-across-senses/11981304
24. Saniotis, Dr Arthur, Professor Maciej Henneberg and David Ellis. 'Humans Are Not Smarter Than Animals, Just Different'. The University of Adelaide. 5 December 2013; https://www.adelaide.edu.au/news/news67182.html#:~:text=%22For%20millennia%2C%20all%20kinds%20of,University's%20School%20of%20Medical%20Sciences

25. Callaway, Ewen. 'How Gibbons Got Their Swing'. *Scientific American*. 11 September 2014; https://www.scientificamerican.com/article/how-gibbons-got-their-swing/#:~:text=They%20also%20may%20explain%20why,than%2055%20kilometers%20an%20hour
26. Australian Government, Department of Climate Change, Energy, the Environment and Water. n.d. 'Whales, dolphins and sound'; https://www.dcceew.gov.au/environment/marine/marine-species/cetaceans/whale-dolphins-sound#:~:text=humans%20to%20hear.-,Echolocation,or%20sinuses%20in%20the%20head
27. Allen, Victoria. 'Listening to elephants stamp their feet and use low-pitched rumbles to warn others of danger may help scientists catch POACHERS'. MailOnline. 7 May 2018; https://www.dailymail.co.uk/sciencetech/article-5700101/Elephants-talk-stamping-feet-warn-friends-relatives-danger.html
28. Saniotis, Dr Arthur. et al. 'Humans Are Not Smarter Than Animals, Just Different'. The University of Adelaide. 5 December 2013; https://www.adelaide.edu.au/news/news67182.html#:~:text=%22For%20millennia%2C%20all%20kinds%20of,University's%20School%20of%20Medical%20Sciences
29. Hopkin, M. 'Homing pigeons reveal true magnetism'. *Nature*. 2004; https://doi.org/10.1038/news041122-7
30. Saniotis, Dr Arthur. et al. 'Humans Are Not Smarter Than Animals, Just Different'. The University of Adelaide. 5 December 2013; https://www.adelaide.edu.au/news/news67182.html#:~:text=%22For%20millennia%2C%20all%20kinds%20of,University's%20School%20of%20Medical%20Sciences
31. BBC. 'Despite what you might think, chickens are not stupid'. 2017; http://www.bbc.com/earth/story/20170110-despite-what-you-might-think-chickens-are-not-stupid
32. Griffiths, Sarah. 'Fish have feelings too: Expert claims creatures experience pain in the same way humans do - and should be treated better'. MailOnline. 19 June 2014; https://www.dailymail.co.uk/sciencetech/article-2662297/Fish-feelings-Expert-claims-creatures-experience-pain-way-humans-better-treated.html

33. Chalmers, Matthew. 'Do Fish Feel Pain? The Science Behind Fish Sentience'. Sentient Media. 16 April 2021; https://sentientmedia.org/do-fish-feel-pain/
34. Cressey, Daniel. 'Experiments reveal that crabs and lobsters feel pain.' *Nature*. 7 August 2013; https://blogs.nature.com/news/2013/08/experiments-reveal-that-crabs-and-lobsters-feel-pain.html
35. Griffiths, Sarah. 'Fish have feelings too: Expert claims creatures experience pain in the same way humans do - and should be treated better'. MailOnline. 19 June 2014; https://www.dailymail.co.uk/sciencetech/article-2662297/Fish-feelings-Expert-claims-creatures-experience-pain-way-humans-better-treated.html
36. University of Houston. 'Do animals think rationally? Researcher suggests rational decision-making doesn't require language'. ScienceDaily. 1 November 2017; www.sciencedaily.com/releases/2017/11/171101151206.htm
37. Aridi, Rasha. 'Four-Month-Old Ravens Rival Adult Great Apes in a Battle of the Brains'. *Smithsonian*. 15 December 2020; https://www.smithsonianmag.com/smart-news/four-month-old-ravens-rival-adult-great-apes-battle-brains-180976547/
38. Bekoff, Marc. 'Animal Emotions: Exploring Passionate Natures: Current interdisciplinary research provides compelling evidence that many animals experience such emotions as joy, fear, love, despair, and grief—we are not alone'. *BioScience*, vol. 50, issue 10, pp. 861–70. October 2000; https://doi.org/10.1641/0006-3568(2000)050[0861:AEEPN]2.0.CO;2
39. University of Tennessee. 'Fish just want to have fun, according to a new study that finds even fish "play"'. ScienceDaily. 20 October 2014; www.sciencedaily.com/releases/2014/10/141020121406.htm
40. Cassella, Carly. 'Octopuses Not Only Feel Pain Physically, But Emotionally Too, First Study Finds'. ScienceAlert. 5 March 2021; https://www.sciencealert.com/scientists-identify-the-first-strong-evidence-that-octopuses-likely-feel-pain.
41. Singer, Peter, and Jim Mason. *Eating: What We Eat and Why It Matters*. p. 58. 2006. London: Arrow Books, Random House.

42. Parker, Laura. 'Rare Video Shows Elephants "Mourning" Matriarch's Death'. *National Geographic*. 31 August 2016; https://www.nationalgeographic.com/animals/article/elephants-mourning-video-animal-grief?loggedin=true&rnd=1674420871522
43. Tennehouse, Erica. 'First-Ever Video May Show Pig-Like Animals Mourning Their Dead'. *National Geographic*. 13 December 2017; https://www.nationalgeographic.com/animals/article/animals-grieving-peccaries-death-mourning
44. BBC. 'World's oldest bird hatches chick at age 70'. 6 March 2021; https://www.bbc.co.uk/newsround/56283082#:~:text=The%20world's%20oldest%20known%20bird,chick%20will%20be%20her%2040th.
45. Vinke, Dr Claudia. 'Can animals fall in love just as humans can?'. Utrecht University. 11 February 2016; https://www.uu.nl/en/news/can-animals-fall-in-love-just-as-humans-can
46. Nowak, Claire. '11 Monogamous Animals That Mate For Life (It's Not Just Penguins)'. *Reader's Digest*. 22 July 2021; https://www.rd.com/list/animals-mate-for-life/
47. Ghose, Tia. 'Animals Are Moral Creatures, Scientist Argues'. Live Science. 15 November 2012; https://www.livescience.com/24802-animals-have-morals-book.html
48. ABC News. 'Gorilla Carries 3-Year-Old Boy to Safety in 1996 Incident'. 19 August 1996; https://www.youtube.com/watch?v=puFCuMac0Vk.
49. The Associated Press. 'Parrot gets award for warning about choking tot'. NBC News. 24 March 2009; https://www.nbcnews.com/id/wbna29858577
50. Robertson, Lindsey. '6 Endearing Tales Of Animals Rescuing Animals'. The Dodo. 21 August 2014; https://www.thedodo.com/6-endearing-tales-of-animals-r-683603429.html
51. Ghose, Tia. 'Animals Are Moral Creatures, Scientist Argues'. Live Science. 15 November 2012; https://www.livescience.com/24802-animals-have-morals-book.html
52. Moodley, Kiran. 'Do animals have morals and show empathy?'. *The Independent*. 23 December 2014; https://www.independent.co.uk/news/world/do-animals-have-morals-and-show-empathy-9940632.html

53. On Demand News. 'Heroic monkey: Monkey saves "dying" friend at train station in India'. 21 December 2014; https://www.youtube.com/watch?v=DVWPbd1UykY
54. Ghose, Tia. 'Animals Are Moral Creatures, Scientist Argues'. Live Science. 15 November 2012; https://www.livescience.com/24802-animals-have-morals-book.html
55. Smithsonian National Museum of Natural History. n.d. 'What does it mean to be human?'; https://humanorigins.si.edu/education/frequently-asked-questions#:~:text=Humans%20and%20monkeys%20are%20both,and%206%20million%20years%20ago
56. UC Museum of Paleontology. n.d. 'The origin of tetrapods'; https://evolution.berkeley.edu/what-are-evograms/the-origin-of-tetrapods/#:~:text=And%20birds%20and%20humans%20are,lost%20their%20%E2%80%9Cfour%20feet.%E2%80%9D
57. McKie, Robin. 2008. 'So who are you calling fish-face?'. *The Guardian*. 10 February 2008; https://www.theguardian.com/books/2008/feb/10/shopping.scienceandnature
58. Press Trust of India. 'Animals are "legal persons", all citizens their parents, orders Uttarakhand HC. 4 July 2018; https://www.indiatoday.in/india/story/animals-are-legal-persons-all-citizens-their-parents-orders-uttarakhand-hc-1277559-2018-07-04
59. Soni, Preeti. 'Animals are now "legal persons", an Indian court expects citizens to be their guardians'. Business Insider. 3 June 2019; https://www.businessinsider.in/animals-are-now-legal-persons-an-indian-court-expects-citizens-to-be-their-guardians/articleshow/69586502.cms
60. BBC News. 'Orangutan with human rights to begin new life in Florida'. 27 September 2019; https://www.bbc.co.uk/news/world-us-canada-49856859

Chapter 1: The Pangolin, the Bat and the Civet Cat

1. NHS. (n.d.); https://www.nhs.uk/conditions/covid-19/covid-19-symptoms-and-what-to-do/
2. Parker-Pope, T. 'Why Days 5 to 10 Are So Important When You Have Coronavirus'. *The New York Times*. 30 April 2020; https://www.nytimes.com/2020/04/30/well/live/coronavirus-days-5-through-10.html

3. Inger Andersen. 'Preventing the next pandemic: Zoonotic diseases and how to break the chain of transmission'. United Nations Environment Programme. 6 July 2020; https://www.unep.org/news-and-stories/statements/preventing-next-pandemic-zoonotic-diseases-and-how-break-chain
4. World Wide Fund For Nature (WWF). 'Covid-19: Urgent Call to Protect People and Nature'. 17 June 2020.
5. Carrington, D. 'Coronavirus: "Nature is sending us a message", says UN environment chief'. *The Guardian*. 25 March 2020; https://www.theguardian.com/world/2020/mar/25/coronavirus-nature-is-sending-us-a-message-says-un-environment-chief
6. World Health Organization. (n.d.). 'WHO Coronavirus (COVID-19) Dashboard'; https://covid19.who.int/
7. Worldometer. (n.d.). 'Countries in the world by population (2023)'; https://www.worldometers.info/world-population/population-by-country/
8. Chan-Yeung, M., and Rui-Heng Xu. 'SARS: epidemiology'. *Respirology*, 8 Supple (Suppl 1), pp. S9–14. November 2003; doi: 10.1046/j.1440-1843.2003.00518.x. PMID: 15018127; PMCID: PMC7169193.
9. Centers for Disease Control and Prevention. (n.d.). 'CDC SARS Response Timeline'; https://www.cdc.gov/about/history/sars/timeline.htm
10. Healthline. 'COVID-19 vs. SARS: How Do They Differ?'. 29 April 2020; https://www.healthline.com/health/coronavirus-vs-sars#transmission
11. Bell D. et al. 'Animal origins of SARS coronavirus: possible links with the international trade in small carnivores'. *Philosophical Transactions of the Royal Society of London. Series B, Biological Sciences*, vol. 359, issue no. 1447, pp. 1107–14. 29 July 2004. doi: 10.1098/rstb.2004.1492. PMID: 15306396; PMCID: PMC1693393.
12. Wang, M. et al. (2005). 'SARS-CoV infection in a restaurant from palm civet'. *Emerging Infectious Diseases*, vol. 11, issue no. 12, pp. 1860–65l. December 2005; https://doi.org/10.3201/eid1112.041293
13. Bell D. et al. 'Animal origins of SARS coronavirus: possible links with the international trade in small carnivores'. *Philosophical Transactions of the Royal Society of London. Series B, Biological*

Sciences, vol. 359, issue no. 1447, pp. 1107–14. 29 July 2004. doi: 10.1098/rstb.2004.1492. PMID: 15306396; PMCID: PMC1693393.

14. Business Recorder. 'China confirms Sars case, begins civet cat cull'. 6 January 2004; https://www.brecorder.com/news/3001802
15. CBS News. 'Civet Cat Slaughter To Fight SARS'. 11 January 2004; https://www.cbsnews.com/news/civet-cat-slaughter-to-fight-sars/
16. Yardley, J. 'W.H.O. Urges China to Use Caution While Killing Civet Cats'. *The New York Times*. 6 January 2004; https://www.nytimes.com/2004/01/06/world/who-urges-china-to-use-caution-while-killing-civet-cats.html
17. Pottinger, Matt, and Ben Dolven (2003, August 14). 'China Lifts Wild-Animal Ban Despite Risk of Link to SARS'. *The Wall Street Journal*. 14 August 2003; https://www.wsj.com/articles/SB106081306319527100
18. Wang, Lin-Fa and B.T. Eaton. 'Bats, Civets and the emergence of SARS'. *Current Topics in Microbiology and Immunology*. 2007. 315. 325–44. 10.1007/978-3-540-70962-6_13.
19. Michael Worobey, et al. 'The Huanan Seafood Wholesale Market in Wuhan was the early epicenter of the COVID-19 pandemic'. *Science*, 377, pp. 951–59. 2022. DOI:10.1126/science.abp8715
20. AFP. 'Wuhan virus: Rats and live wolf pups on the menu at China food market linked to virus outbreak.' *The Straits Times*. 22 January 2020; https://www.straitstimes.com/asia/east-asia/on-the-menu-at-china-virus-market-rats-and-live-wolf-pups
21. Vox. 'How wildlife trade is linked to coronavirus'. 6 March 2020; https://www.youtube.com/watch?v=TPpoJGYlW54&t=1s
22. Holmes, E.C. 'The COVID lab leak theory is dead. Here's how we know the virus came from a Wuhan market'. The Conversation. 14 August 2022; https://theconversation.com/the-covid-lab-leak-theory-is-dead-heres-how-we-know-the-virus-came-from-a-wuhan-market-188163
23. Barnes, J.E. 'The Covid Origins Debate'. *The New York Times*. 26 July 2023; https://www.nytimes.com/2023/07/26/briefing/covid-origins-debate.html
24. Quammen, D. 'The Ongoing Mystery of Covid's Origin'. *The New York Times Magazine*. 25 July 2023; https://www.nytimes.com/2023/07/25/magazine/covid-start.html

25. Holmes, E.C. 'The COVID lab leak theory is dead. Here's how we know the virus came from a Wuhan market'. The Conversation. 14 August 2022; https://theconversation.com/the-covid-lableak-theory-is-dead-heres-how-we-know-the-virus-came-from-awuhan-market-188163
26. Maxmen, A. 'WHO report into COVID pandemicorigins zeroes in on animal markets, not labs'. *Nature*. 30 March 2021; https://www.nature.com/articles/d41586-021-00865-8
27. Michael Worobey et al., 'The Huanan Seafood Wholesale Market in Wuhan was the early epicenter of the COVID-19 pandemic'. *Science,* 377, pp. 951–59. 2022. DOI:10.1126/science.abp8715
28. Holmes, E.C. ' The COVID lab leak theory is dead. Here's how we know the virus came from a Wuhan market'. The Conversation. 14 August 2022; https://theconversation.com/the-covid-lab-leak-theory-is-dead-heres-how-we-know-the-virus-came-from-a-wuhan-market-188163
29. Temmam, S., et al. 'Bat coronaviruses related to SARS-CoV-2 and infectious for human cells'. *Nature,* 604, pp. 330–36. 2022; https://doi.org/10.1038/s41586-022-04532-4
30. Wu, K.J. 'The Strongest Evidence Yet That an Animal Started the Pandemic'. *The Atlantic.* 16 March 2023; https://www.theatlantic.com/science/archive/2023/03/covid-origins-research-raccoon-dogs-wuhan-market-lab-leak/673390/
31. Lau, S.K.P. et al. 'Isolation of MERS-related coronavirus from lesser bamboo bats that uses DPP4 and infects human-DPP4-transgenic mice'. *Nature Communications,* 12, 216. 2021; https://doi.org/10.1038/s41467-020-20458-9
32. Gupta, S.K. et al. (2022). 'Role of the Pangolin in Origin of SARS-CoV-2: An Evolutionary Perspective'. *International Journal of Molecular Sciences,* vol. 23, issue 16, 9115. 2022; https://doi.org/10.3390/ijms23169115
33. World Wildlife Fund. (n.d.); https://www.worldwildlife.org/species/pangolin
34. Page, J., B. McKay and D. Hinshaw. 'Search for Covid's Origins Leads to China's Wild Animal Farms—and a Big Problem'. *The Wall Street Journal.* 30 June 2021; https://www.wsj.com/articles/covid-origins-china-wild-animal-farms-pandemic-source-11625060088

35. do Vale, B. et al. 'Bats, pangolins, minks and other animals - villains or victims of SARS-CoV-2?'. *Veterinary Research Communications*, vol. 45, issue 1, pp. 1–19. 2021; https://doi.org/10.1007/s11259-021-09787-2
36. Xiao, X., et al. 'Animal sales from Wuhan wet markets immediately prior to the COVID-19 pandemic'. Scientific Reports, 11, 11898. 2021; https://doi.org/10.1038/s41598-021-91470-2
37. do Vale, B. et al. 'Bats, pangolins, minks and other animals - villains or victims of SARS-CoV-2?'. *Veterinary Research Communications*, vol. 45, issue 1, pp. 1–19. 2021; https://doi.org/10.1007/s11259-021-09787-2
38. Maxmen, A. 'WHO report into COVID pandemic origins zeroes in on animal markets, not labs'. *Nature*. 30 March 2021; https://www.nature.com/articles/d41586-021-00865-8
39. WWF-UK. (n.d.). 'Tackling International Wildlife Crime'; https://www.wwf.org.uk/what-we-do/projects/tackling-international-wildlife-crime
40. Bell D., S. Roberton and P.R. Hunter. 'Animal origins of SARS coronavirus: possible links with the international trade in small carnivores'. *Philosophical Transactions of the Royal Society of London. Series B, Biological Sciences*, 359, issue 1447, pp. 1107–14. 29 July 2004. doi: 10.1098/rstb.2004.1492. PMID: 15306396; PMCID: PMC1693393.
41. Nuwer, R. 'Illegal trade in pangolins keeps growing as criminal networks expand'. *National Geographic*. 11 February 2020; https://www.nationalgeographic.com/animals/article/pangolin-scale-trade-shipments-growing
42. Standaert, M. 'Coronavirus closures reveal vast scale of China's secretive wildlife farm industry'. *The Guardian*. 25 February 2020; https://www.theguardian.com/environment/2020/feb/25/coronavirus-closures-reveal-vast-scale-of-chinas-secretive-wildlife-farm-industry
43. *The Guardian*. 'China's return to wildlife farming "a risk to global health and biodiversity"'. 15 December 2022; https://www.theguardian.com/environment/2022/dec/15/chinas-return-to-wildlife-farming-a-risk-to-global-health-and-biodiversity
44. PETA India. 'Breaking Investigation: Illegal Wildlife and Dog-Meat Markets Rife in Country'. 2021; https://www.petaindia.com/features/

breaking-investigation-illegal-wildlife-and-dog-meat-markets-rife-in-country/

45. Ibid.
46. India Today News Desk. 'Gauhati High Court quashes ban on sale of dog meat in Nagaland'. *India Today*. 7 June 2023; https://www.indiatoday.in/law/story/gauhati-high-court-quashes-ban-dog-meat-sale-nagaland-2389892-2023-06-07
47. Humane Society International. (n.d.). 'Asia's Dog Meat Trade: FAQs'; https://www.hsi.org/news-resources/dog-meat-trade-faqs/
48. PETA UK. 'VIDEO: PETA Asia Goes Inside "Wet Markets", Where Diseases Like COVID-19 Originate'. 2020; https://www.peta.org.uk/features/indonesian-thai-wet-markets/
49. Eurogroup for Animals. 'Dr Anthony Fauci demands global shutdown of wet markets'. 14 April 2020; https://www.eurogroupforanimals.org/news/dr-anthony-fauci-demands-global-shutdown-wet-markets
50. Congress of the United States. 8 April 2020; https://www.booker.senate.gov/imo/media/doc/04.08.20_Booker_Graham_Quigley_McCaul_Final%20sBlock.pdf
51. Mahmoud M. Naguib et al. 'Live and Wet Markets: Food Access versus the Risk of Disease Emergence'. *Trends in Microbiology*, vol. 29, issue 7, pp. 573–81, ISSN 0966-842X. 2021; https://doi.org/10.1016/j.tim.2021.02.007. (https://www.sciencedirect.com/science/article/pii/S0966842X21000433)
52. PETA. (n.d.). 'Tell Health Officials to Shut Down Filthy NYC Live-Animal Markets'. https://support.peta.org/page/17791/action/1?locale=en-US
53. Ball, C.R. 'Commissioner Ball Letter Re Avian Flu'. 20 November 2022; https://www.scribd.com/document/609287323/Commissioner-Ball-Letter-Re-Avian-Flu#
54. Maron, D.F. 'Live animal markets in San Francisco accused of mistreatment'. *National Geographic*. 15 August 2022; https://www.nationalgeographic.com/animals/article/live-animal-markets-in-san-francisco-accused-of-mistreatment
55. Noyes, D. 'Coronovirus impact: Ban on live animal markets in California passes big hurdle'. ABC7 News. 27 May 2020; https://

abc7news.com/live-animal-markets-did-bats-cause-coronavirus-how-start-bay-area/6213914/

56. Goddard, J. 'Coronavirus: Regulation of live animal markets'. UK Parliament: House of Lords Library. 22 May 2020; https://lordslibrary.parliament.uk/coronavirus-regulation-of-live-animal-markets/
57. PETA. (n.d.). 'Footage Shows Live-Animal Markets STILL Operating in Across Asia Despite Mounting COVID-19 Death Toll'; https://www.petaasia.com/action/wet-markets-still-operating-covid-19/
58. PETA UK. 'Exposé: Suffering and Disease at Live-Animal Markets in Asia'. 2021; https://secure.peta.org.uk/page/79457/action/1?locale=en-GB
59. Vice TV. 'Wet Markets Exposed S1 E2: Peru'. 2020; https://www.vicetv.com/en_us/video/peru-1-635/5f92d479b7adf27f8d1c5224
60. Fobar, R. 'China promotes bear bile as coronavirus treatment, alarming wildlife advocates'. *National Geographic*. 25 March 2020; https://www.nationalgeographic.com/animals/article/chinese-government-promotes-bear-bile-as-coronavirus-covid19-treatment
61. Animals Asia. (n.d.). 'Bear Bile Farming'; https://www.animalsasia.org/intl/end-bear-bile-farming-2017.html
62. The Brooke Hospital for Animals. 'Chinese Company Looks to Treat Coronavirus With Donkey Skin Product'. 18 February 2020; https://www.thebrooke.org/news/chinese-company-looks-treat-coronavirus-donkey-skin-product
63. PETA. (n.d.). 'Help Stop Donkeys from Dying for Medicine in China'; https://investigations.peta.org/donkeys-heads-bashed-in-with-sledgehammers-throats-slit-in-china-for-their-skin/
64. PETA. (n.d.). 'Exposed Again: Donkeys Abused and Slaughtered for Traditional Chinese Medicine'; https://investigations.peta.org/donkeys-slaughtered-for-skin-kenya/https://doi.org/10.3201/eid1112.041293

Chapter 2: Monkey Business

1. UN Aids. (n.d.). 'Global HIV & AIDS statistics — Factsheet'; https://www.unaids.org/en/resources/fact-sheet
2. Terrence Higgins Trust. (n.d.). 'Stages of HIV infection'; https://www.tht.org.uk/hiv-and-sexual-health/about-hiv/stages-hiv-infection
3. Wadia, R. 'My brother Riyad'. *Mid-day*. 12 December 2013; https://www.mid-day.com/news/india-news/article/My-brother-Riyad-244277

4. Outlook Web Desk. 'Sands Of Time - Part 5 | What A Female Superhero Film From The 40s Had To Do With India's First Openly Gay Film'. *Outlook*. 26 December 2021; https://www.outlookindia.com/website/story/entertainment-news-sands-of-time-part-5-what-a-female-superhero-film-from-the-40s-had-to-do-with-indias-first-openly-gay-film/406768
5. Ashar, H. 'Remembering Riyad'. Mid-day. 2 December 2015; https://www.mid-day.com/mumbai/mumbai-news/article/remembering-riyad-16733166
6. HIV.gov. (n.d.). 'A Timeline of HIV and AIDS'; https://www.hiv.gov/hiv-basics/overview/history/hiv-and-aids-timeline/#year-1981
7. KFF. 'The Global HIV/AIDS Epidemic'. Global Health Policy. 26 July 2023; https://www.kff.org/global-health-policy/fact-sheet/the-global-hivaids-epidemic/
8. Ibid.
9. Centers for Disease Control and Prevention. (n.d.). 'How is HIV passed from one person to another?'; https://www.cdc.gov/hiv/basics/hiv-transmission/ways-people-get-hiv.html#:~:text=Anal%20sex%20is%20the%20riskiest,the%20body%20during%20anal%20sex.
10. HIV.gov. (n.d.). 'A Timeline of HIV and AIDS'; https://www.hiv.gov/hiv-basics/overview/history/hiv-and-aids-timeline/#year-1981
11. Bennington-Castro, J. 'How AIDS Remained an Unspoken—But Deadly—Epidemic for Years'. History. 1 June 2020; https://www.history.com/news/aids-epidemic-ronald-reagan
12. Greer, W.R. 'Violence Against Homosexuals Rising, Groups Seeking Wider Protection Say'. *The New York Times*. 23 November 1986; https://www.nytimes.com/1986/11/23/us/violence-against-homosexuals-rising-groups-seeking-wider-protection-say.html
13. Centers for Disease Control and Prevention. 'Current Trends Update on Acquired Immune Deficiency Syndrome (AIDS) --United States'. 24 September 1982; https://www.cdc.gov/mmwr/preview/mmwrhtml/00001163.htm#:~:text=Editorial%20Note,diminished%20resistance%20to%20that%20disease
14. Chamary, J. 'WHO Finally Admits Coronavirus Is Airborne. It's Too Late'. *Forbes*. 4 May 2021; https://www.forbes.com/sites/jvchamary/2021/05/04/who-coronavirus-airborne/?sh=56442e964472

15. Auerbach, David M. et al. 'Cluster of cases of the acquired immune deficiency syndrome: Patients linked by sexual contact.' *The American Journal of Medicine*, vol. 76, issue 3, pp. 487–92, ISSN 0002-9343. 1984; https://doi.org/10.1016/0002-9343(84)90668-5 (https://www.sciencedirect.com/science/article/pii/0002934384906685)
16. Bennington-Castro, J. (2020, June 1). 'How AIDS Remained an Unspoken—But Deadly—Epidemic for Years'. History. 1 June 2020; https://www.history.com/news/aids-epidemic-ronald-reagan
17. Bowcott, O. 'Thatcher tried to block "bad taste" public health warnings about Aids. *The Guardian*. 30 December 2015; https://www.theguardian.com/politics/2015/dec/30/thatcher-tried-to-block-bad-taste-public-health-warnings-about-aids
18. Florêncio, J. 'AIDS: homophobic and moralistic images of 1980s still haunt our view of HIV – that must change'. The Conversation. 27 November 2018; https://theconversation.com/aids-homophobic-and-moralistic-images-of-1980s-still-haunt-our-view-of-hiv-that-must-change-106580
19. International Labour Organization. (n.d.). 'HIV/AIDS in Africa'; https://www.ilo.org/africa/areas-of-work/hiv-aids/lang--en/index.htm
20. Pebody, Roger. 'HIV-1 and HIV-2'. NAM aidsmap. January 2021; https://www.aidsmap.com/about-hiv/hiv-1-and-hiv-2
21. Divya Jacob, Pharm .D., and Pallavi Suyog Uttekar, MD, (n.d.). 'What Is the Difference Between HIV-1 and HIV-2?'. MedicineNet; https://www.medicinenet.com/what_is_the_difference_between_hiv-1_and_hiv-2/article.htm
22. Pebody, Roger. 'HIV-1 and HIV-2'. NAM aidsmap. January 2021; https://www.aidsmap.com/about-hiv/hiv-1-and-hiv-2
23. Essex, M., and P.J. Kanki. 'The Origins of the AIDS Virus'. *Scientific American*. 1 October 1988; https://www.scientificamerican.com/article/the-origins-of-the-aids-virus/
24. Quammen, David. *Spillover: Animal Infections and the Next Human Pandemic* p. 395. 2012. New York: WW Norton and Company.
25. vervet. (n.d.). *Encyclopedia Britannica*; https://www.britannica.com/animal/vervet
26. Shoumatoff, A. (n.d.). 'In Search of the Source of AIDS'. *Vanity Fair*; https://archive.vanityfair.com/article/share/c0f19bd7-e975-4f0a-a10d-11cbbc34d80e?itm_content=footer-recirc

27. Mulder, C. 'Human AIDS virus not from monkeys'. *Nature*, vol. 333. 2 June 1988; https://www.nature.com/articles/333396a0.pdf
28. Fox, James G. et al. 'Chapter 28 - Selected Zoonoses'. In *American College of Laboratory Animal Medicine, Laboratory Animal Medicine* (Third Edition), (eds) Fox, James G., Lynn C. Anderson, Glen M. Otto, Kathleen R. Pritchett-Corning and Mark T. Whary. Academic Press, pp. 1313–70, ISBN 9780124095274. 2015; https://doi.org/10.1016/B978-0-12-409527-4.00028-6 (https://www.sciencedirect.com/science/article/pii/B9780124095274000286)
29. Quammen, David. *Spillover*, pp. 401–02. 2012. New York: WW Norton and Company.
30. Sooty Mangabey. (n.d.). New England Primate Conservancy; https://neprimateconservancy.org/sooty-mangabey/
31. Cheriyedath, S. (n.d.). 'HIV-1 versus HIV-2: What's the Difference?' News Medical Life Sciences; https://www.news-medical.net/health/HIV-1-versus-HIV-2-Whats-the-Difference.aspx
32. Quammen, David. *Spillover*, p. 406. 2012. New York: WW Norton and Company.
33. Ibid., p. 404.
34. Graham, S. 'First Case of AIDS-like Virus in a Wild Chimpanzee'. *Scientific American*. 18 January 2002; https://www.scientificamerican.com/article/first-case-of-aids-like-v/
35. Quammen, David. *Spillover*, pp. 426–27. 2012. New York: WW Norton and Company.i
36. Ibid., p. 464.
37. Keele, B. et al. 'Increased mortality and AIDS-like immunopathology in wild chimpanzees infected with SIVcpz'. *Nature*, 460, pp. 515–19. 2009; https://doi.org/10.1038/nature08200
38. Lovgren, S. 'HIV Originated With Monkeys, Not Chimps, Study Finds'. *National Geographic*. 12 June 2003; https://www.nationalgeographic.com/science/article/news-hiv-aids-monkeys-chimps-origin
39. Quammen, David. *Spillover*, p. 465. 2012. New York: WW Norton and Company.
40. Channel 4. 'Critically endangered: The plight of Cameroon's Great Apes | Unreported World'. Unreported World. 10 January 2018; https://www.youtube.com/watch?v=rgk3suYIeB0

41. Ape Action Africa. (n.d.). 'Bushmeat'; https://apeactionafrica.org/bushmeat
42. Waugh, R. (2012, May 25). 'African scientists warn that eating monkeys and apes could cause "the next HIV"'. MailOnline. 25 May 2012; https://www.dailymail.co.uk/sciencetech/article-2150033/African-scientists-warn-eating-monkeys-apes-cause-HIV-epidemic.html
43. Global Forest Watch. 'An Overview of Logging in Cameroon'. 2000; http://data.wri.org/forest_atlas/cmr/report/cmr_an_overview_logging_cameroon_eng.pdf
44. Ape Action Africa. (n.d.). 'Bushmeat'; https://apeactionafrica.org/bushmeat
45. Williams, E. 'African monkey meat that could be behind the next HIV'. *The Independent*. 26 May 2012; https://www.independent.co.uk/life-style/health-and-families/health-news/african-monkey-meat-that-could-be-behind-the-next-hiv-7786152.html
46. Sra, S. (n.d.). 'Illegal Logging in Cameroon'. The University of British Columbia; https://cases.open.ubc.ca/illegal-logging-in-cameroon/
47. Global Forest Watch. 'An Overview of Logging in Cameroon'. 2000; http://data.wri.org/forest_atlas/cmr/report/cmr_an_overview_logging_cameroon_eng.pdf
48. Williams, E. 'African monkey meat that could be behind the next HIV'. *The Independent*. 26 May 2012; https://www.independent.co.uk/life-style/health-and-families/health-news/african-monkey-meat-that-could-be-behind-the-next-hiv-7786152.html
49. Centers for Disease Control and Prevention. (n.d.). 'What is Ebola Disease?'; https://www.cdc.gov/vhf/ebola/about.html?CDC_AA_refVal=https%3A%2F%2Fwww.cdc.gov%2Fvhf%2Febola%2Fhistory%2Fsummaries.html
50. Ying, Z. 'Epidemics and Wildlife: How Ebola affects gorillas and chimpanzees'. CGTN. 9 February 2020; https://news.cgtn.com/news/2020-02-09/How-Ebola-affects-gorillas-and-chimpanzees--NW4XUMFBJe/index.html
51. Fox, M. 'Ebola has killed 5,000 gorillas, study suggests'. Reuters. 20 January 2007; https://www.reuters.com/article/science-ebola-gorillas-dc-idUKN0746373120061207

52. Hayman, D. T. et al. 'Ebola virus antibodies in fruit bats, Ghana, West Africa'. *Emerging Infectious Diseases*, vol. 18, issue 7, pp. 1207–09. 2012; https://doi.org/10.3201/eid1807.111654
53. Bajekal, N. 'Can Dogs (And Other Animals) Get Ebola?' *Time*. 8 October 2014; https://time.com/3480961/ebola-animals-transmission/
54. Barbiero, V.K. (n.d.). 'Ebola: A Hyperinflated Emergency'. *Global Health: Science and Practice*; https://www.ghspjournal.org/content/ghsp/early/2020/05/12/GHSP-D-19-00422.full.pdf
55. Ebola virus disease. World Health Organization. 20 April 2023; https://www.who.int/news-room/fact-sheets/detail/ebola-virus-disease
56. Centers for Disease Control and Prevention . 'Transmission of Yellow Fever Virus'. 13 January 2023; https://www.cdc.gov/yellowfever/transmission/index.html
57. ScienceDirect. 5.6 Ongoing Cross-Species Transmissions From Other Retroviruses From Primates to Humans. 2017; https://www.sciencedirect.com/topics/immunology-and-microbiology/simian-foamy-virus#:~:text=Primates%20to%20Humans-,Simian%20foamy%20virus%20(SFV)%20is%20infecting%20primates%20at%20high%20levels,and%20100%25%20of%20wild%20chimpanzees.&text=119%E2%80%9312
58. Vice TV. 'Wet Markets Exposed--S1 E3, West Africa'. 2020; https://www.vicetv.com/en_us/video/west-africa/5f92d59c3bb54033e07c9926
59. Reuters. 'Nigeria's wet markets thrive despite coronavirus'. 20 August 2020; https://www.youtube.com/watch?v=HJoerT4_uxg&t=2s
60. World Health Organization. 'Reducing public health risks associated with the sale of live wild animals of mammalian species in traditional food markets'. 12 April 2021; https://www.who.int/publications/i/item/WHO-2019-nCoV-Food-safety-traditional-markets-2021.1
61. Blistein, J. 'Paul McCartney Calls for an End to China's "Wet Markets"'. *Rolling Stone*. 14 April 2020; https://www.rollingstone.com/music/music-news/paul-mccartney-china-wet-market-coronavirus-983463/
62. Boyle, L. 'Ricky Gervais calls for end to wildlife "wet" markets amid coronavirus crisis'. *The Independent*. 19 May 2020; https://www.independent.co.uk/climate-change/news/ricky-gervais-animal-wet-markets-wildlife-coronavirus-china-covid-19-a9462661.html

Chapter 3: Piggy Went to Market

1. Zorn, E. 'Social media post reveals the unsettling truth about the first little piggy'. *Chicago Tribune*. 28 August 2018; https://www.chicagotribune.com/columns/eric-zorn/ct-perspec-zorn-piggies-nursery-rhyme-market-grim-0829-20180828-story.html
2. In Greger, Michael, *How to Survive a Pandemic*, p. 109, 2020. New York: Flatiron Books.
3. Devlin, H. 'Rising global meat consumption "will devastate environment"'. *The Guardian*. 19 July 2018; https://www.theguardian.com/environment/2018/jul/19/rising-global-meat-consumption-will-devastate-environment
4. Block, K. 'More animals than ever before—92.2 billion—are used and killed each year for food'. The Humane Society of the United States. 5 June 2023; https://blog.humanesociety.org/2023/06/more-animals-than-ever-before-92-2-billion-are-used-and-killed-each-year-for-food.html
5. 'Factory Farming: Assessing Investment Risks'. London: Farm Animal Investment Risk and Return (FAIRR). 2016.
6. European Commission. 'Feed ban: Commission authorises use of certain animal proteins'. 17 August 2021; https://ec.europa.eu/newsroom/sante/items/718842/en
7. Boffey, D. 'EU to lift its ban on feeding animal remains to domestic livestock'. *The Guardian*. 22 June 2021; https://www.theguardian.com/world/2021/jun/22/eu-to-lift-its-ban-on-feeding-animal-remains-to-domestic-livestock
8. In Greger, Michael, *How to Survive a Pandemic*, p. 110, 2020. New York: Flatiron Books.
9. US Food & Drug Administration. 'All About BSE (Mad Cow Disease)'. 23 July 2020; https://www.fda.gov/animal-veterinary/animal-health-literacy/all-about-bse-mad-cow-disease
10. Centers for Disease Control and Prevention. (n.d.). 'About BSE'; https://www.cdc.gov/prions/bse/about.html
11. Boffey, D. 'EU to lift its ban on feeding animal remains to domestic livestock'. *The Guardian*. 22 June 2021; https://www.theguardian.com/

world/2021/jun/22/eu-to-lift-its-ban-on-feeding-animal-remains-to-domestic-livestock

12. EFPRA. (n.d.); https://efpra.eu/about-rendering/
13. (n.d.). In Greger, Michael, *How to Survive a Pandemic,* p. 111, 2020. New York: Flatiron Books.
14. Boffey, D. 'EU to lift its ban on feeding animal remains to domestic livestock'. *The Guardian*. 22 June 2021; https://www.theguardian.com/world/2021/jun/22/eu-to-lift-its-ban-on-feeding-animal-remains-to-domestic-livestock
15. 'Antibiotics in farm animals . . . and other stories'. 10 October 2019. *BMJ*, p. 367: l5821.
16. Goldman, E. (n.d.). 'Factory farming and antibiotic resistance'. Viva!; https://cdn.viva.org.uk/wp-content/uploads/2021/03/VL76-Antibiotic-resistance-feature.pdf
17. World Health Organization. 'New report calls for urgent action to avert antimicrobial resistance crisis'. 29 April 2019; https://www.who.int/news/item/29-04-2019-new-report-calls-for-urgent-action-to-avert-antimicrobial-resistance-crisis
18. Centers for Disease Control and Prevention. 'Protecting Newborns in India from Antibiotic-Resistant Infections'. 25 July 2019; https://www.cdc.gov/ncezid/stories-features/global-stories/protecting-newborns-in-india.html
19. World Health Organization. 'New report calls for urgent action to avert antimicrobial resistance crisis'. 29 April 2019; https://www.who.int/news/item/29-04-2019-new-report-calls-for-urgent-action-to-avert-antimicrobial-resistance-crisis
20. Goldman, E. (n.d.). 'Factory farming and antibiotic resistance'. Viva!; https://cdn.viva.org.uk/wp-content/uploads/2021/03/VL76-Antibiotic-resistance-feature.pdf
21. Ibid.
22. World Health Organization. 'WHO's first ever global estimates of foodborne diseases find children under 5 account for almost one third of deaths'. 3 December 2015; https://www.who.int/news/item/03-12-2015-who-s-first-ever-global-estimates-of-foodborne-diseases-find-children-under-5-account-for-almost-one-third-of-deaths

23. Delgado, C. et al. 'Livestock to 2020: The Next Food Revolution'. *Outlook on Agriculture*, vol. 30, issue 1, pp. 27–29. 2001; https://doi.org/10.5367/000000001101293427
24. World Animal Protection. 'Silent superbug killers in a river near you'. 2021; https://www.worldanimalprotection.org/sites/default/files/2021-06/Silent-superbug-killers-in-a-river-near-you-report.pdf
25. European Public Health Alliance. 'Ending routine farm antibiotic use in Europe through improving animal health and welfare'. 28 January 2022; https://epha.org/ending-routine-farm-antibiotic-use/
26. Szűcs, István and Viktoria Vida. 'Global tendencies in pork meat - production, trade and consumption'. *Applied Studies in Agribusiness and Commerce*, vol. 11, issue 3–4, pp. 105–12. 2017; 10.19041/APSTRACT/2017/3-4/15
27. Humane Society International. 'An HSI Report: The Welfare of Animals in the Pig Industry'. May 2014; https://www.hsi.org/wp-content/uploads/assets/pdfs/hsi-fa-white-papers/welfare_of_animals_in_the_pig.pdf
28. Hess, A. 'National Hog Farmer, Genesus unveil 2019 Global Mega Producer list'. National Hog Farmer. 6 June 2019: https://www.nationalhogfarmer.com/business/national-hog-farmer-genesus-unveil-2019-global-mega-producer-list
29. Ibid., 27 May 2020.
30. *The Guardian*. 'China's 26-storey pig skyscraper ready to slaughter 1 million pigs a year'. 25 November 2022; https://www.theguardian.com/environment/2022/nov/25/chinas-26-storey-pig-skyscraper-ready-to-produce-1-million-pigs-a-year
31. Smithfield Foods. '2021: Our 20th Annual Sustainability Impact Report'. 2021; https://www.smithfieldfoods.com/getmedia/7ecf12e2-da3b-4d31-8796-d07e38b39e51/2021-Sustainability-Impact-Report.pdf
32. *The Guardian*. 'China's 26-storey pig skyscraper ready to slaughter 1 million pigs a year'. 25 November 2022; https://www.theguardian.com/environment/2022/nov/25/chinas-26-storey-pig-skyscraper-ready-to-produce-1-million-pigs-a-year
33. The Humane Society of the United States. (n.d.). The Welfare of Animals in the Pig Industry; https://www.wellbeingintlstudiesrepository.org/

cgi/viewcontent.cgi?article=1024&context=hsus_reps_impacts_on_animals

34. FAIRR: A Coller Initiative. 'Gestation Crates: A Growing Financial Risk'. 22 February 2022; https://www.fairr.org/policy/issue-briefings/gestation-crates
35. PETA India. 'West Bengal Joins Over 20 Other States and UTs in Prohibiting the Confinement of Mother Pigs to Crates Following Push From PETA India'. 24 May 2023: https://www.petaindia.com/media/west-bengal-joins-over-20-other-states-and-uts-in-prohibiting-the-confinement-of-mother-pigs-to-crates-following-push-from-peta-india/
36. Royal Stock Farms. (n.d.); https://www.royallivestock.com/livestock-farms-pig.php
37. Compassion in World Farming. 'Welfare sheet – Pigs'. 17 May 2013; https://www.ciwf.org.uk/media/5235121/Welfare-sheet-Pigs.pdf
38. Humane Society International. 'An HSI Report: The Welfare of Animals in the Pig Industry'. May 2014; https://www.hsi.org/wp-content/uploads/assets/pdfs/hsi-fa-white-papers/welfare_of_animals_in_the_pig.pdf
39. In Greger, Michael, *How to Survive a Pandemic,* p. 177, 2020. New York: Flatiron Books.
40. Centers for Disease Control and Prevention. (n.d.). '2009 H1N1 Pandemic (H1N1pdm09 virus)'; https://www.cdc.gov/flu/pandemic-resources/2009-h1n1-pandemic.html
41. In Greger, Michael, *How to Survive a Pandemic,* p. 128, 2020. New York: Flatiron Books.
42. Centers for Disease Control and Prevention. '1918 Pandemic (H1N1 virus)'. 20 March 2019; https://www.cdc.gov/flu/pandemic-resources/1918-pandemic-h1n1.html
43. In Greger, Michael, *How to Survive a Pandemic,* p. 128, 2020. New York: Flatiron Books.
44. Tanner, B. 'How a killer flu spread from western Kansas to the world'. *The Wichita Eagle.* 10 March 2020: https://www.kansas.com/news/local/article200880539.html
45. In Greger, Michael, *How to Survive a Pandemic,* p. 128, 2020. New York: Flatiron Books.

46. Ibid., pp. 128–29.
47. The Humane Society of the United States. (n.d.). 'An HSUS Report: Human Health Implications of Intensive Poultry Production and Avian Influenza'; https://grist.org/wp-content/uploads/2011/03/hsus-public-health-report-on-avian-influenza-and-poultry-production.pdf
48. Keim, B. 'Swine Flu Ancestor Born on U.S. Factory Farms'. *Wired*. 1 May 2009: https://www.wired.com/2009/05/swineflufarm/
49. In Greger, Michael, *How to Survive a Pandemic*, p. 129, 2020. New York: Flatiron Books.
50. Ibid., p. 133.
51. Ling, A.E. 'Lessons to be learnt from the Nipah virus outbreak in Singapore'. *Singapore Medical Journal*, vol. 40, issue 5, pp. 331–2. May 1999. PMID: 10489489.
52. In Greger, Michael, *How to Survive a Pandemic*, pp. 96–97, 2020. New York: Flatiron Books.
53. World Health Organization. 'Nipah virus'. 30 May 2018; https://www.who.int/news-room/fact-sheets/detail/nipah-virus
54. Patton, D. 'Swine fever surge hits small farms in China's Sichuan'. Reuters. 9 July 2021; https://www.reuters.com/world/china/swine-fever-surge-hits-small-farms-chinas-sichuan-2021-07-09/
55. Normile, D. 'African swine fever settles into Asia'. *Science*. 25 April 2023; https://www.science.org/content/article/african-swine-fever-settles-asia#:~:text=Endemic%20in%20much%20of%20Africa,in%20China%20in%20August%202018
56. AFP. 'New swine flu with pandemic potential identified by China researchers'. *The Guardian*. 30 June 2020: https://www.theguardian.com/world/2020/jun/30/new-swine-flu-with-pandemic-potential-identified-by-china-researchers
57. Centers for Disease Control and Prevention. (n.d.). 'Archived: Highly Pathogenic Asian Avian Influenza A(H5N1) in People'; https://www.cdc.gov/flu/avianflu/h5n1-people.htm
58. Gavi: The Vaccine Alliance. 'The next pandemic: H5N1 and H7N9 influenza?' 26 March 2021; https://www.gavi.org/vaccineswork/next-pandemic/h5n1-and-h7n9-influenza

59. Centers for Disease Control and Prevention. 'Archived: Public Health Threat of Highly Pathogenic Asian Avian Influenza A(H5N1) Virus'. 19 March 2015; https://www.cdc.gov/flu/avianflu/h5n1-threat.htm
60. Wiebers, D.O., and V.L. Feigin. 'What the COVID-19 Crisis Is Telling Humanity'. *Neuroepidemiology*, vol. 54, issue 4, pp. 283–86. 2020; https://doi.org/10.1159/000508654
61. Davis, N. 'WHO says avian flu cases in humans "worrying" after girl's death in Cambodia'. *The Guardian*. 24 February 2023: https://www.theguardian.com/world/2023/feb/24/who-says-h5n1-avian-flu-cases-in-humans-worrying-after-girls-death
62. Bhardwaj, M. 'India reports first human death from bird flu'. Reuters. 21 July 2021: https://www.reuters.com/world/india/india-reports-first-human-death-bird-flu-2021-07-21/
63. Centers for Disease Control and Prevention. 'Archived: Highly Pathogenic Asian Avian Influenza A(H5N1) in People'. 11 December 2018; https://www.cdc.gov/flu/avianflu/h5n1-people.htm
64. UK Health Security Agency. 'Risk assessment of avian influenza A(H7N9) – eighth update'. 8 January 2020; https://www.gov.uk/government/publications/avian-influenza-a-h7n9-public-health-england-risk-assessment/risk-assessment-of-avian-influenza-ah7n9-sixth-update
65. Centers for Disease Control and Prevention. 'Past Examples of Probable Limited, Non-Sustained, Person-to-Person Spread of Avian Influenza A Viruses'. 27 February 2023; https://www.cdc.gov/flu/avianflu/h5n1-human-infections.htm
66. United Nations. 'No bird flu risk for consumers from properly cooked poultry and eggs, says UN'. 5 December 2005; https://news.un.org/en/story/2005/12/162292
67. Centers for Disease Control and Prevention. (n.d.). 'Archived: Highly Pathogenic Asian Avian Influenza A(H5N1) in People'; https://www.cdc.gov/flu/avianflu/h5n1-people.htm
68. Gilbert, M. et al. 'Predicting the risk of avian influenza A H7N9 infection in live-poultry markets across Asia'. *Nature Communications*, 5, article no. 4116. 2014; https://doi.org/10.1038/ncomms5116

69. AFP. 'China Aims To Phase Out Sale Of Live Poultry At Food Markets'. *Barron's*. 3 July 2020; https://www.barrons.com/news/china-aims-to-phase-out-slaughter-and-sale-of-live-poultry-01593788706
70. Tawy, A.A. 'Egypt puts into effect law banning live poultry trade: Ministry'. Ahram Online. 10 October 2018; https://english.ahram.org.eg/NewsContent/1/64/313149/Egypt/Politics-/Egypt-puts-into-effect-law-banning-live-poultry-tr.aspx
71. Chan, Paul K.S. 'Outbreak of Avian Influenza A(H5N1) Virus Infection in Hong Kong in 1997'. *Clinical Infectious Diseases*, vol. 34, issue Supplement_2, pp. S58–S64. May 2002; https://doi.org/10.1086/338820
72. Schnirring, Lisa. 'Russia reports first human H5N8 avian flu cases'. CIDRAP. 22 February 2021; https://www.cidrap.umn.edu/russia-reports-first-human-h5n8-avian-flu-cases
73. Al Jazeera. 'China reports first human death due to H3N8 bird flu'. 12 April 2023; https://www.aljazeera.com/news/2023/4/12/china-reports-first-human-death-due-to-h3n8-bird-flu
74. World Health Organization. 'Human infection with avian influenza A(H10N3) – China'. 10 June 2021; https://www.who.int/emergencies/disease-outbreak-news/item/human-infection-with-avian-influenza-a(h10n3)-china
75. Clements, M. 'Europe's largest avian influenza outbreak to worsen'. WATTPoultry.com. 23 November 2022; https://www.wattagnet.com/regions/europe/article/15536729/europes-largest-avian-influenza-outbreak-to-worsen#:~:text=Along%20Europe's%20northwestern%20coast%2C%20several,the%20same%20period%20last%20year.
76. Centers for Disease Control and Prevention. 'Archived – Outbreaks of North American Lineage Avian Influenza Viruses'. 10 December 2018; https://www.cdc.gov/flu/avianflu/north-american-lineage.htm
77. In Greger, Michael, *How to Survive a Pandemic*, p. 132, 2020. New York: Flatiron Books.
78. World-Herald News Service. 'Fire destroys industrial poultry barn'. *Norfolk Daily News*. 27 February 2020; https://norfolkdailynews.com/news/fire-in-bloomfield/article_7b33c6f6-59c1-11ea-8666-fbc670795153.html

79. Global Ag Media. 'More than 500,000 US farm animals died in barn fires in 2022'. The Poultry Site. 21 December 2022; https://www.thepoultrysite.com/news/2022/12/more-than-500-000-us-farm-animals-died-in-barn-fires-in-2022
80. FAIRR: A Coller Initiative. 'Animal Pandemics'. 12 November 2019; https://www.fairr.org/resources/knowledge-hub/key-terms/animal-pandemics
81. Wiebers, D.O., and V.L. Feigin. 'What the COVID-19 Crisis Is Telling Humanity'. *Neuroepidemiology*, vol. 54, issue 4, pp. 283–86. 2020; https://doi.org/10.1159/000508654
82. Compassion in World Farming. (n.d.). 'Welfare Issues for Egg-Laying Hens'; https://www.ciwf.com/farmed-animals/chickens/egg-laying-hens/welfare-issues/
83. Animal Aid. 'New investigation reveals the reality of "enriched" cages. 16 January 2014; https://www.animalaid.org.uk/new-investigation-reveals-reality-enriched-cages/
84. Derbyshire, D. 'Up to 16,000 hens crammed into a shed, and many NEVER see daylight. But believe it or not, THESE are free-range chickens'. MailOnline. 16 November 2013; https://www.dailymail.co.uk/news/article-2508173/16-000-free-range-chickens-crammed-shed-NEVER-daylight.html
85. O'Connor, J. 'PETA Exposes This Cage-Free "Chicken Disneyland" as Hell for Hens'. PETA. 17 December 2018; https://www.peta.org/blog/chicken-disneyland-hell-hens/
86. Compassion in World Farming. (n.d.). 'Chickens Farmed for Meat'; https://www.ciwf.org.uk/farm-animals/chickens/meat-chickens/
87. Derbyshire, D. 'Up to 16,000 hens crammed into a shed, and many NEVER see daylight. But believe it or not, THESE are free-range chickens'. MailOnline. 16 November 2013; https://www.dailymail.co.uk/news/article-2508173/16-000-free-range-chickens-crammed-shed-NEVER-daylight.html
88. RSPCA Knowledge Base. 'What is beak trimming and why is it carried out?' 28 September 2022; https://kb.rspca.org.au/knowledge-base/what-is-beak-trimming-and-why-is-it-carried-out/

89. RSPCA. (n.d.). 'The Case Against Cages: Evidence in favour of alternative systems for laying hens'; https://www.rspca.org.uk/documents/1494935/9042554/Thecaseagainstcages%20(513kb).pdf
90. Humane Society International. 'An HSI Report: The Welfare of Animals in the Egg Industry'. March 2011; https://www.hsi.org/wp-content/uploads/assets/pdfs/welfare_of_animals_in_the_egg.pdf
91. National Chicken Council. 'US Broiler Performance'. February 2022; https://www.nationalchickencouncil.org/about-the-industry/statistics/u-s-broiler-performance/
92. CBC News. 'Chickens are 4 times bigger today than in 1950s'. 8 October 2014; https://www.cbc.ca/news/canada/calgary/chickens-are-4-times-bigger-today-than-in-1950s-1.2792628
93. Humane Society International. (n.d.). 'An HSI Report: The Welfare of Animals in the Egg Industry'; https://www.hsi.org/wp-content/uploads/assets/pdfs/welfare_of_animals_in_the_egg.pdf
94. Compassion in World Farming. (n.d.). 'Chickens Farmed for Meat'; https://www.ciwf.org.uk/farm-animals/chickens/meat-chickens/
95. In Greger, Michael, *How to Survive a Pandemic,* p. 180, 2020. New York: Flatiron Books.
96. Murray, L. (n.d.). 'Factory-Farmed Chickens: Their Difficult Lives and Deaths'. Saving Earth, *Encyclopedia Britannica*; https://www.britannica.com/explore/savingearth/the-difficult-lives-and-deaths-of-factory-farmed-chickens
97. Compassion in World Farming. 'Welfare Sheet: Broiler Chickens'. 1 May 2013; https://www.ciwf.org.uk/media/5235309/Welfare-sheet-Broiler-chickens.pdf
98. Davis, Karen. (n.d.). 'The Battery Hen: Her Life Is Not For The Birds'; https://www.upc-online.org/batthen.html

Chapter 4: Code Red

1. Life.Church. (n.d.). Genesis 6; https://www.bible.com/bible/111/GEN.6.NIV
2. National Center for Science and Education. 'Yes, Noah's Flood May Have Happened, But Not Over the Whole Earth'. Reports of the

National Center for Science Education, vol. 29, no. 5. September–October 2009; https://ncse.ngo/yes-noahs-flood-may-have-happened-not-over-whole-earth

3. *Encyclopedia Britannica.* (n.d.). 'Matsya: Hinduism'; https://www.britannica.com/topic/Matsya-Hinduism
4. Tharoor, I. 'Before Noah: Myths of the Flood Are Far Older Than the Bible'. *Time.* 1 April 2014; https://time.com/44631/noah-christians-flood-aronofsky/
5. Chasan, D.J. '"The Rocks Don't Lie": Debunking Noah's flood'. Crosscut. 21 August 2012; https://crosscut.com/2012/08/rocks-dont-lie-david-montgomery-chasan-flood-book
6. Zuckerman, E. 'Humane Society to honor Darren Aronofsky for using CGI animals in film'. Entertainment Weekly. 21 October 2014; https://ew.com/article/2014/10/21/humane-society-to-honor-darren-aronofsky-for-using-cgi-animals-in-noah/
7. Tharoor, I. 'Before Noah: Myths of the Flood Are Far Older Than the Bible'. Time. 1 April 2014; https://time.com/44631/noah-christians-flood-aronofsky/
8. Friend, T. 'Heavy Weather: Darren Aronofsky gets Biblical'. *The New Yorker.* 10 March 2014; https://www.newyorker.com/magazine/2014/03/17/heavy-weather-2
9. Trefil, J. 'Evidence for a Flood'. *Smithsonian.* 1 April 2000; https://www.smithsonianmag.com/science-nature/evidence-for-a-flood-102813115/
10. Carney, S. (2007, November 15). 'Did a Comet Cause the Great Flood?'. *Discover.* 15 November 2007; https://www.discovermagazine.com/planet-earth/did-a-comet-cause-the-great-flood
11. Lehnis, M. '2022 Was A Year Of Record-Breaking Extreme Weather Events'. *Forbes.* 29 December 2022; https://www.forbes.com/sites/mariannelehnis/2022/12/29/2022-was-a-year-of-record-breaking-extreme-weather-events/?sh=1e0d1f80736b
12. IFRC. 'Millions in Bangladesh impacted by one of the worst floodings ever seen'. 28 June 2022; https://www.ifrc.org/press-release/millions-bangladesh-impacted-one-worst-floodings-ever-seen#:~:text=Millions%20in%20Bangladesh%20impacted%20by%20

one%20of%20the%20worst%20floodings%20ever%20seen,-share%20on%20Facebook&text=A%20Bangladesh%20Red%20Crescent

13. Press Trust of India. '2022 Assam floods killed 197 people; Centre releases 648 crore as relief'. EastMojo. 3 August 2022; https://www.eastmojo.com/assam/2022/08/03/2022-assam-floods-killed-197-people-centre-releases-648-crore-as-relief/
14. Pirzada, S.A. 'Floods, drought, fires and cyclones: 2022, the year of extreme weather'. CGTN. 1 January 2023; https://newseu.cgtn.com/news/2023-01-01/Floods-drought-fires-and-cyclones-2022-the-year-of-extreme-weather-1gaauv7upYQ/index.html
15. Marsden, R, and L. Hull. 'Christoph-stophe! Storm batters Britain leaving homes and cars submerged and at least one person dead ahead of freezing weekend and MORE rain next week'. MailOnline. 22 January 2021; https://www.dailymail.co.uk/news/article-9174343/Christoph-stophe-Storm-batters-Britain-forcing-residents-rescued-leaving-one-dead.html
16. Fitzgerald, M., C. Angerer and P. Smith. 'Almost 200 dead, many still missing after floods as Germany counts devastating cost'. NBC News. 19 July 2021; https://www.nbcnews.com/news/world/almost-200-dead-many-still-missing-after-floods-germany-counts-n1274330
17. UN Environmental Programme. 'How climate change is making record-breaking floods the new normal'. 3 March 2020; https://www.unep.org/news-and-stories/story/how-climate-change-making-record-breaking-floods-new-normal
18. Tellman, B. et al. 'Satellite imaging reveals increased proportion of population exposed to floods'. *Nature,* 596, pp. 80–86. 2021; https://doi.org/10.1038/s41586-021-03695-w
19. Pirzada, S.A. 'Floods, drought, fires and cyclones: 2022, the year of extreme weather'. CGTN. 1 January 2023; https://newseu.cgtn.com/news/2023-01-01/Floods-drought-fires-and-cyclones-2022-the-year-of-extreme-weather-1gaauv7upYQ/index.html
20. Aldhous, P., S. Lee and Z. Hirji. 'The Texas Winter Storm And Power Outages Killed Hundreds More People Than The State Says'. Buzzfeed News. 26 May 2021; https://www.buzzfeednews.com/article/peteraldhous/texas-winter-storm-power-outage-death-toll

21. Pirzada, S.A. 'Floods, drought, fires and cyclones: 2022, the year of extreme weather'. CGTN. 1 January 2023; https://newseu.cgtn.com/news/2023-01-01/Floods-drought-fires-and-cyclones-2022-the-year-of-extreme-weather-1gaauv7upYQ/index.html
22. 88.5 WMNF. 'Hurricane Ian caused 114 deaths in Florida'. 24 October 2022; https://www.wmnf.org/hurricane-ian-caused-114-deaths-in-florida/
23. Al Jazeera. 'Millions in Japan told to evacuate from Typhoon Nanmadol'. 18 September 2022; https://www.aljazeera.com/news/2022/9/18/millions-in-japan-told-to-evacuate-as-typhoon-nanmadol-approaches#:~:text=At%20least%20four%20million%20people,paralysed%20ground%20and%20air%20transportation
24. Carrington, D. 'Climate crisis "unequivocally" caused by human activities, says IPCC report'. *The Guardian*. 9 August 2021; https://www.theguardian.com/environment/2021/aug/09/climate-crisis-unequivocally-caused-by-human-activities-says-ipcc-report
25. IPCC. 'Special Report: Global Warming of 1.5 °C'. Summary for Policymakers. 2018; https://www.ipcc.ch/sr15/chapter/spm/
26. United Nations. 'IPCC report: "Code red" for human driven global heating, warns UN chief'. 9 August 2021; https://news.un.org/en/story/2021/08/1097362
27. Harvey, Fiona. 'World likely to breach 1.5C climate threshold by 2027, scientists warn'. *The Guardian*. 17 May 2023; https://www.theguardian.com/environment/2023/may/17/global-heating-climate-crisis-record-temperatures-wmo-research
28. Biello, D. 'Did the Anthropocene Begin in 1950 or 50,000 Years Ago?' *Scientific American*. 2 April 2015; https://www.scientificamerican.com/article/did-the-anthropocene-begin-in-1950-or-50-000-years-ago/
29. Carrington, D. 'The Anthropocene epoch: scientists declare dawn of human-influenced age'. *The Guardian*. 29 August 2016; https://www.theguardian.com/environment/2016/aug/29/declare-anthropocene-epoch-experts-urge-geological-congress-human-impact-earth
30. Carrington, D. 'H-bombs or chicken bones: the race to define the start of the Anthropocene'. *The Guardian*. 6 January 2023; https://www.

theguardian.com/environment/2023/jan/06/h-bombs-chicken-bones-scientists-race-to-define-start-of-the-anthropocene

31. Wagler, Ron. 'Anthropocene extinction'. AccessScience. Last reviewed March 2023; https://www.accessscience.com/content/article/a039350
32. WWF. (n.d.). https://wwf.panda.org/discover/our_focus/biodiversity/biodiversity/#:~:text=Unlike%20the%20mass%20extinction%20events,extinction%20waves%20in%20geological%20history
33. Ceballos, Gerardo, Paul Ehrlich and Peter Raven. 'Vertebrates on the brink as indicators of biological annihilation and the sixth mass extinction'. Proceedings of the National Academy of Sciences. 2020. 117. 201922686. 10.1073/pnas.1922686117.
34. Bat Conservation Trust. (n.d.). 'Bats as pollinators'; https://www.bats.org.uk/about-bats/why-bats-matter/bats-as-pollinators
35. *Encyclopedia Britannica.* (n.d.). 'Birds'; https://www.britannica.com/science/pollination/Birds
36. Royal Botanical Gardens (Kew). State of the World's Plants and Fungi. 2020.
37. FAO and UNEP. 2020. 'The State of the World's Forests 2020: Forests, biodiversity and people'. 2020. Italy: Rome; https://doi.org/10.4060/ca8642en
38. Herrero, M. et al. 'Biomass use, production, feed efficiencies, and greenhouse gas emissions from global livestock systems'. *PNAS* USA, 110(52), p. 93. 24 December 2013; doi: 10.1073/pnas.1308149110. PMID: 24344273; PMCID: PMC3876224.
39. Poore, J., and Nemecek, T. 'Reducing food's environmental impacts through producers and consumers'. *Science*, 360(6392), pp. 987–92. 1 June 2018; doi: 10.1126/science.aaq0216. Erratum in: Science. 22 February 2019; 363(6429): PMID: 29853680.
40. Carrington, D. 'Humans just 0.01% of all life but have destroyed 83% of wild mammals – study'. *The Guardian.* 21 May 2018; https://www.theguardian.com/environment/2018/may/21/human-race-just-001-of-all-life-but-has-destroyed-over-80-of-wild-mammals-study
41. Statistisches Bundesamt (Destatis). 'Global animal farming, meat production and meat consumption'. 2022; https://www.destatis.de/

EN/Themes/Countries-Regions/International-Statistics/Data-Topic/AgricultureForestryFisheries/livestock_meat.html

42. Carrington, D. 'How the domestic chicken rose to define the Anthropocene'. *The Guardian.* 31 August 2016; https://www.theguardian.com/environment/2016/aug/31/domestic-chicken-anthropocene-humanity-influenced-epoch
43. Carrington, D. 'Earth has lost half of its wildlife in the past 40 years, says WWF'. *The Guardian.* 30 September 2014; https://www.theguardian.com/environment/2014/sep/29/earth-lost-50-wildlife-in-40-years-wwf
44. Machovina B. et al. 'Biodiversity conservation: The key is reducing meat consumption'. *Science of the Total Environment*, vol. 536, pp. 419–31. 1 December 2015; doi: 10.1016/j.scitotenv.2015.07.022; Epub 2015 Jul 29. PMID: 26231772.
45. Morell, V. 'Meat-eaters may speed worldwide species extinction, study warns'. *Science.* 11 August 2015; https://www.science.org/content/article/meat-eaters-may-speed-worldwide-species-extinction-study-warns
46. Heinrich Böll Stiftung, Friends of the Earth, Bund für Umwelt und Naturschutz. 'Meat Atlas: Facts and figures about the animals we eat'. 2021.
47. European Parliament. (n.d.). 'The European Union and forests'; https://www.europarl.europa.eu/factsheets/en/sheet/105/the-european-union-and-forests#:~:text=Forests%20in%20the%20European%20Union%3A%20valuable%20multifaceted%20and%20multi%2Dpurpose%20ecosystems&text=Taking%20the%20definition%20given%20above,world's%20
48. Cuffe, S. '2022 Amazon fires tightly tied to recent deforestation, new data show'. Mongabay. 22 November 2022; https://news.mongabay.com/2022/11/2022-amazon-fires-tightly-tied-to-recent-deforestation-new-data-show/
49. Vizcarra, N. 'Amazon fires 2021: moderate risk forecasted, but fuel enough for one of Earth's "biggest bonfires"'. Landscape News. 25 August 2021; https://news.globallandscapesforum.org/54461/amazon-

fires-2021-moderate-risk-forecasted-but-fuel-enough-for-one-of-earths-biggest-bonfires/

50. Kimbrough, L. 'The Brazilian Amazon is burning, again'. Mongabay. 3 June 2021; https://news.mongabay.com/2021/06/the-brazilian-amazon-is-burning-again/
51. Heinrich Böll Stiftung, Friends of the Earth, Bund für Umwelt und Naturschutz. "Meat Atlas': Facts and figures about the animals we eat'. 2021.
52. FAIRR: A Coller Initiative. (n.d.). 'Amazon Soy Moratorium'; https://www.fairr.org/investor-statements/amazon-soy
53. WWF. 'Brazil's Amazon soy moratorium'. 4 February 2021; http://forestsolutions.panda.org/case-studies/brazils-amazon-soy-moratorium
54. Greenpeace. (n.d.). '10 Years Ago the Amazon Was Being Bulldozed for Soy — Then Everything Changed'; https://www.greenpeace.org/usa/victories/amazon-rainforest-deforestation-soy-moratorium-success/
55. Heinrich Böll Stiftung, Friends of the Earth, Bund für Umwelt und Naturschutz. "Meat Atlas': Facts and figures about the animals we eat'. 2021.
56. Ibid.
57. Harvey, F. 'More than 3 billion people affected by water shortages, data shows'. *The Guardian*. 26 November 2020; https://www.theguardian.com/environment/2020/nov/26/more-than-3-billion-people-affected-by-water-shortages-data-shows
58. Water Footprint Network. (n.d.). 'Do you know how much water was used to grow your food and to produce your clothes and the things you buy?'; https://www.waterfootprint.org/time-for-action/what-can-consumers-do/#productwater-footprint-crop-and-animal-products/
59. Herrero, M. et al. 'Biomass use, production, feed efficiencies, and greenhouse gas emissions from global livestock systems'. *PNAS* USA, vol. 110, no. 52, pp. 20888-93. 24 December 2013; doi: 10.1073/pnas.1308149110; PMID: 24344273; PMCID: PMC3876224.
60. Grebmer, K.V. et al. 'Global Hunger Index: Food Systems Transformation and Local Governance'. October 2022. Bonn/Dublin: Welte Hunger Hilfe/Concern Worldwide.

61. Herrero, M. et al. 'Biomass use, production, feed efficiencies, and greenhouse gas emissions from global livestock systems'. *PNAS* USA, vol. 110, no. 52, pp. 20888-93. 24 December 2013; doi: 10.1073/pnas.1308149110; PMID: 24344273; PMCID: PMC3876224.
62. Greenpeace. (n.d.). 'The Amazon soya moratorium'; https://wayback.archive-it.org/9650/20200402232711/http://p3-raw.greenpeace.org/international/Global/international/code/2014/amazon/index.html
63. Cassidy, Emily S. et al. 'Redefining agricultural yields: from tonnes to people nourished per hectare'. *Environmental Research Letters*, vol. 8, no. 3. 1 August 2013; DOI 10.1088/1748-9326/8/3/034015
64. WWF. (n.d.). Amazon; https://www.worldwildlife.org/places/amazon
65. Greenpeace. (n.d.). 'The Amazon soya moratorium'; https://wayback.archive-it.org/9650/20200402232711/http://p3-raw.greenpeace.org/international/Global/international/code/2014/amazon/index.html
66. Carrington, D. 'Amazon rainforest now emitting more CO2 than it absorbs'. *The Guardian*. 14 July 2021; https://www.theguardian.com/environment/2021/jul/14/amazon-rainforest-now-emitting-more-co2-than-it-absorbs
67. Twine, Richard. 'Emissions from Animal Agriculture—16.5% Is the New Minimum Figure'. *Sustainability*. June 2021. 13. 6276. 10.3390/su13116276.
68. Mottet, A. and H. Steinfeld. 'Cars or livestock: which contribute more to climate change?' Thomson Reuters Foundation. 18 September 2018; https://news.trust.org/item/20180918083629-d2wf0
69. Milman, O. 'Meat accounts for nearly 60% of all greenhouse gases from food production, study finds'. *The Guardian*. 13 September 2021; https://www.theguardian.com/environment/2021/sep/13/meat-greenhouses-gases-food-production-study
70. Carrington, D. 'Emissions from 13 dairy firms match those of entire UK, says report'. *The Guardian*. 15 June 2020; https://www.theguardian.com/environment/2020/jun/15/emissions-from-13-dairy-firms-match-those-of-entire-uk-says-report
71. Webb, S. 'Is dairy or meat worse for the environment?'. *The Independent*. 30 October 2021; https://www.independent.co.uk/climate-change/infact/is-dairy-or-meat-worse-for-the-environment-b1891387.html

72. Environmental Protection Agency. 'Importance of Methane'. 22 May 2023; https://www.epa.gov/gmi/importance-methane
73. Ministry of Fisheries, Animal Husbandry and Dairying, India. 'India ranks first in milk production in the world contributing 24% of global milk production'. PIB Delhi. 7 February 2023; https://pib.gov.in/PressReleaseIframePage.aspx?PRID=1897084
74. Statista. 'Cattle population in India from 2016 to 2022, with an estimate for 2023'. 1 December 2022; https://www.statista.com/statistics/1181408/india-cattle-population/
75. Business Wire. 'India Dairy Industry Report 2021: Market Size, Growth, Prices, Segments, Cooperatives, Private Dairies, Procurement and Distribution - ResearchAndMarkets.com'. 31 May 2021; https://www.businesswire.com/news/home/20210531005124/en/India-Dairy-Industry-Report-2021-Market-Size-Growth-Prices-Segments-Cooperatives-Private-Dairies-Procurement-and-Distribution---ResearchAndMarkets.com
76. Guibourg, C., and H. Briggs. 'Climate change: Which vegan milk is best?' BBC News. 22 February 2019; https://www.bbc.co.uk/news/science-environment-46654042
77. Singh, S. 'Methane from Indian livestock adds to global warming'. SciDev.net. 17 January 2019; https://www.scidev.net/asia-pacific/news/methane-from-indian-livestock-adds-to-global-warming/
78. Yaffe-Bellany, D. 'The New Makers of Plant-Based Meat? Big Meat Companies'. *The New York Times*. 14 October 2019; https://www.nytimes.com/2019/10/14/business/the-new-makers-of-plant-based-meat-big-meat-companies.html
79. Coyne, A. (n.d.). 'The dairy companies also present in dairy alternatives'. Just Food; https://www.just-food.com/features/plant-based-priorities-dairy-companies-also-in-dairy-free/
80. (n.d.). 'Healthy Diets From Sustainable Food Systems: Food, Planet, Health, Summary Report'. EAT-Lancet Commission.
81. Petter, O. 'Veganism is "single biggest way" to reduce our environmental impact, study finds'. *The Independent*. 24 September 2020; https://www.independent.co.uk/life-style/health-and-families/veganism-

environmental-impact-planet-reduced-plant-based-diet-humans-study-a8378631.html

82. United Nations Climate Change. 'We Need to Talk About Meat'. 19 May 2021; https://unfccc.int/blog/we-need-to-talk-about-meat
83. Carus, F. 'UN urges global move to meat and dairy-free diet'. *The Guardian*. 2 June 2010; https://www.theguardian.com/environment/2010/jun/02/un-report-meat-free-diet
84. Melina V., W. Craig and S. Levin. 'Position of the Academy of Nutrition and Dietetics: Vegetarian Diets'. *Journal of Academy of Nutrition Dietetics*, vol. 116, issue 12, pp. 1970–80. December 2016; doi: 10.1016/j.jand.2016.09.025. PMID: 27886704.
85. Laville, S. 'UK meat tax and frequent-flyer levy proposals briefly published then deleted'. *The Guardian*. 20 October 2021; https://www.theguardian.com/environment/2021/oct/20/meat-tax-and-frequent-flyer-levy-advice-dropped-from-uk-net-zero-strategy
86. BBC News. 'Spanish ministers clash over campaign to eat less meat'. 8 July 2021; https://www.bbc.co.uk/news/world-europe-57766345
87. Valdmanis, R., and T. Cocks. 'Meat on menu, not the agenda, at COP27 climate conference'. Reuters. 15 November 2022; https://www.reuters.com/business/cop/meat-menu-not-agenda-cop27-climate-conference-2022-11-15/
88. Compassion in World Farming. 'Over 100 NGOs and high-profile figures urge world leaders to address the impact of food and animal agriculture on climate change at COP26'. 1 November 2021; https://www.globenewswire.com/news-release/2021/11/01/2324175/0/en/Over-100-NGOs-and-high-profile-figures-urge-world-leaders-to-address-the-impact-of-food-and-animal-agriculture-on-climate-change-at-COP26.html
89. Dalton, J. 'World leaders "reckless for ignoring how meat and dairy accelerate climate crisis"'. *The Independent*. 5 November 2021; https://www.independent.co.uk/climate-change/news/climate-meat-dairy-diet-food-co2-b1951760.html
90. Zarum, R.D. 'Did the ark have room for whales?' *The Jewish Chronicle*. 20 October 2017; https://www.thejc.com/judaism/features/was-there-room-for-whales-in-the-ark-1.446403

Chapter 5: In Need of a Sea Change

1. Watson, P. 'What it's like to watch a harpooned whale die right before your eyes'. *Down To Earth*. 20 October 2021; https://www.downtoearth.org.in/blog/wildlife-and-biodiversity/what-it-s-like-to-watch-a-harpooned-whale-die-right-before-your-eyes-79781
2. Greenpeace. 'Remembering Bob Hunter: Mind Bomber'. 2 May 2020; https://www.greenpeace.org/international/story/30250/bob-hunter-greenpeace-founder-memorial-mindbombs-rex-weyler/
3. Fields, D. 'Are Whales Smarter Than We Are?'. *Scientific American*. 15 January 2008; https://blogs.scientificamerican.com/news-blog/are-whales-smarter-than-we-are/
4. Kropshofer, K. 'Whales and dolphins lead "human-like lives" thanks to big brains, says study'. *The Guardian*. 16 October 2017; https://www.theguardian.com/science/2017/oct/16/whales-and-dolphins-human-like-societies-thanks-to-their-big-brains
5. Zeppetelli-Bédard, L. 'What do we know about intelligence in whales and dolphins?' Whale Scientists. 23 June 2021; https://whalescientists.com/intelligence-whales-dolphins/
6. Simon, D. '"Tour of grief is over" for killer whale no longer carrying dead calf'. CNN. 13 August 2018; https://edition.cnn.com/2018/08/12/us/orca-whale-not-carrying-dead-baby-trnd/index.html
7. Zeppetelli-Bédard, L. 'What do we know about intelligence in whales and dolphins?' Whale Scientists. 23 June 2021; https://whalescientists.com/intelligence-whales-dolphins/
8. Haney, T. 'Photos: The Culture Of Whales'. NPR. 19 April 2021; https://www.npr.org/sections/pictureshow/2021/04/19/988028339/photos-the-culture-of-whales
9. McGill University. 'Tastes differ – even among North Atlantic killer whales'. 14 April 2023; https://www.mcgill.ca/newsroom/channels/news/tastes-differ-even-among-north-atlantic-killer-whales-347500
10. Domanick, A. 'Inside the secret culture of whales, from favorite foods to family name'. KCRW. 22 April 2021; https://www.kcrw.com/news/shows/press-play-with-madeleine-brand/climate-change-homeless-nat-geo-academy-awards/secrets-of-the-whales-brian-skerry

11. Howard, B.C. 'More Big Whales in Ocean Could Mean More Fish, Scientists Find'. *National Geographic*. 12 July 2014; https://www.nationalgeographic.com/history/article/140710-whales-ecosystem-engineers-fish-conservation-science?loggedin=true&rnd=1687687593947
12. McVeigh, K. 'Iceland allows whaling to resume in "massive step backwards"'. *The Guardian*. 31 August 2023; https://www.theguardian.com/environment/2023/aug/31/iceland-allows-whaling-to-resume-in-massive-step-backwards
13. Mos. 'Japan whaling: Why commercial hunts have resumed despite outcry'. BBC News. 2 July 2019; https://www.bbc.co.uk/news/world-asia-48592682
14. Carrere, M. 'To fight climate change, save the whales, some scientists say'. Mongabay. 1 March 2021; https://news.mongabay.com/2021/03/to-fight-climate-change-save-the-whales-some-scientists-say/
15. Chami, R. et al. 'A strategy to protect whales can limit greenhouse gases and global warming'. International Monetary Fund. December 2019; https://www.imf.org/Publications/fandd/issues/2019/12/natures-solution-to-climate-change-chami
16. Editors of EarthSky. 'How much oxygen comes from the ocean?' EarthSky. 24 June 2020; https://earthsky.org/earth/how-much-oxygen-comes-from-ocean/
17. National Oceanic and Atmospheric Administration. (n.d.). 'How much oxygen comes from the ocean?'; https://oceanservice.noaa.gov/facts/ocean-oxygen.html
18. IFAW. 'whale poop and phytoplankton, the dynamic duo fighting climate change'. 2 June 2021; https://www.ifaw.org/international/journal/whale-poop-phytoplankton-climate-change
19. Howard, B.C. 'More Big Whales in Ocean Could Mean More Fish, Scientists Find'. *National Geographic*. 12 July 2014; https://www.nationalgeographic.com/history/article/140710-whales-ecosystem-engineers-fish-conservation-science?loggedin=true&rnd=1687687593947
20. Morello, L. 'Phytoplankton Population Drops 40 Percent Since 1950'. *Scientific American*. 29 July 2010; https://www.scientificamerican.com/article/phytoplankton-population/#:~:text=Researchers%20at%20

Canada's%20Dalhousie%20University,population%20between%20 1899%20and%202008.

21. Ocean Conservancy. 'Plankton: Small Organisms with a Big Role in the Ocean'. 9 August 2019; https://oceanconservancy.org/blog/2019/08/09/plankton-small-organism-big-role/
22. National Oceanic and Atmospheric Administration. (n.d.). 'What is Ocean Acidification?'; https://oceanservice.noaa.gov/facts/acidification.html
23. Barker, S. and A. Ridgwell. 'Ocean Acidification'. *Nature Education Knowledge*, 3(10):21. 2012.
24. Bassetti, F. 'Why Whales Are Important For Carbon Sequestration'. Foresight. 27 August 2020; https://www.climateforesight.eu/articles/whales-carbon-sequestration/
25. Katija K., and J.O. Dabiri. 'A viscosity-enhanced mechanism for biogenic ocean mixing'. *Nature*, 460(7255), pp. 624–6. 30 July 2000; doi: 10.1038/nature08207. PMID: 19641595
26. Carrere, M. 'To fight climate change, save the whales, some scientists say'. Mongabay. 1 March 2021; https://news.mongabay.com/2021/03/to-fight-climate-change-save-the-whales-some-scientists-say/
27. Mariani, G. et al. 'Let more big fish sink: Fisheries prevent blue carbon sequestration-half in unprofitable areas'. *Science Advances*, vol. 6, issue 44, eabb4848. 2020; https://doi.org/10.1126/sciadv.abb4848
28. Heithaus, Michael R. et al. 'Seagrasses in the Age of Sea Turtle Conservation and Shark Overfishing'. *Frontiers in Marine Science*, vol. 1. 5 August 2014; 10.3389/fmars.2014.00028. 10.3389/fmars.2014.00028
29. Sundararaju, V. 'Why we must conserve the world's seagrasses'. *Down To Earth*. 19 October 2020; https://www.downtoearth.org.in/blog/wildlife-biodiversity/why-we-must-conserve-the-world-s-seagrasses-73852
30. Milman, O. 'Global shark and ray population crashed more than 70% in past 50 years – study'. *The Guardian*. 27 January 2021; https://www.theguardian.com/environment/2021/jan/27/sharks-rays-global-population-crashed-study
31. Fleming, S. 'Growing a new coral reef in a fraction of the time with a fragment of the coral'. World Economic Forum. 7 July 2021; https://www.weforum.org/agenda/2021/07/plant-million-corals/

32. IFAW. 'how sharks keep our oceans healthy'. 12 July 2022; https://www.ifaw.org/uk/journal/sharks-keep-oceans-healthy
33. United States Environmental Protection Agency. (n.d.). 'Threats to Coral Reefs'; https://www.epa.gov/coral-reefs/threats-coral-reefs
34. National Science Foundation. 'Too much algae -- and too many microbes – threaten coral reefs'. 26 April 2016; https://new.nsf.gov/news/too-much-algae-too-many-microbes-threaten-coral
35. University of Hawai'i at Mānoa. (n.d.). 'Weird Science: Parrotfish and Sand'. Exploring Our Fluid Earth: Teaching Science as Inquiry; https://manoa.hawaii.edu/exploringourfluidearth/physical/coastal-interactions/beaches-and-sand/weird-science-parrotfish-and-sand
36. Bawden, T. 'Overfishing of Parrotfish is bad for coral reefs, research finds'. inews.co.uk. 23 January 2017; https://inews.co.uk/news/environment/overfishing-parrotfish-bad-coral-reefs-research-finds-42899
37. Environmental Protection Agency. (n.d.); https://www.epa.gov/coral-reefs/threats-coral-reefs
38. Coral Reef Alliance. (n.d.). 'Biodiversity'; https://coral.org/en/coral-reefs-101/why-care-about-reefs/biodiversity/
39. National Ocean Service: National Oceanic and Atmospheric Administration. (n.d.). 'The Importance of Coral Reefs'; https://oceanservice.noaa.gov/education/tutorial_corals/coral07_importance.html#:~:text=Scientists%20estimate%20that%20there%20may,medicines%20for%20the%2021st%20century.&text=The%20National%20Marine%20Fisheries%20Service,reefs%20is%20over%20%24100%20mill
40. Coral Reef Alliance. (n.d.). 'Biodiversity'; https://coral.org/en/coral-reefs-101/why-care-about-reefs/biodiversity/
41. Hancock, S. 'Fish "sing" as Indonesian coral reef restored back to life'. *The Independent*. 9 December 2021; https://www.independent.co.uk/climate-change/news/fish-noises-coral-reef-indonesia-b1972105.html
42. National Ocean Service: National Oceanic and Atmospheric Administration. (n.d.). 'The Importance of Coral Reefs'; https://oceanservice.noaa.gov/education/tutorial_corals/coral07_importance.html#:~:text=Scientists%20estimate%20that%20there%20may,medicines%20for%20the%2021st%20century.&text=The%20

National%20Marine%20Fisheries%20Service,reefs%20is%20over%20%24100%20mill

43. Briggs, H. 'Tuna bounce back, but sharks in "desperate" decline'. BBC News. 4 September 2021; https://www.bbc.co.uk/news/science-environment-58441142
44. Briggs, H. 'Extinction: "Time is running out" to save sharks and rays'. BBC News. 27 January 2021; https://www.bbc.co.uk/news/science-environment-55830732
45. Fairclough, C. (n.d.). 'Shark Finning: Sharks Turned Prey'. *Smithsonian*; https://ocean.si.edu/ocean-life/sharks-rays/shark-finning-sharks-turned-prey
46. Rice, D. (n.d.). 'Sharks vs. humans: At 100 million deaths against 6 each year, it's not a fair fight'. *USA Today*; https://eu.usatoday.com/story/news/2018/07/11/sharks-humans-no-fair-fight/775409002/
47. WWF. (n.d.). 'Bycatch--A Sad Topic'. Fish Forward Project; https://www.fishforward.eu/en/project/by-catch/
48. Davies, R.W.D. et al. 'Defining and estimating global marine fisheries bycatch'. *Marine Policy*, vol. 33, issue 4, pp. 661–72, ISSN 0308-597X. 2009; https://doi.org/10.1016/j.marpol.2009.01.003 (https://www.sciencedirect.com/science/article/pii/S0308597X09000050)
49. Consortium for Wildlife Bycatch Reduction. (n.d.). 'What is Bycatch?'; https://www.bycatch.org/what-bycatch
50. WWF. 'What's in the Net – Millions of turtles, seals, dolphins, seabirds and sharks killed each year'. 19 November 2020; https://sharks.panda.org/news-blogs-updates/latest-news/what-s-in-the-net-millions-of-turtles-seals-dolphins-seabirds-and-sharks-killed-each-year
51. WWF. 'Bycatch is the biggest killer of whales: Time for the world to tackle the threat'. 20 October 2016; https://wwf. panda.org/wwf_news/?281850/Bycatch%2Dis%2Dthe%2Dbiggest%2Dkiller%2Dof%2Dwhales
52. Lent, R., and M. Tarzia (n.d.). 'Opening statement from the International Whaling Commission'. Food and Agriculture Organization of the United Nations; https://www.fao.org/fileadmin/user_upload/COFI/COFI34/observers/GeneralStatement-IWC.pdf

53. Ashworth, J. (2021, October 28). 'Numbers of North Atlantic right whales fall by almost 10%'. Natural History Museum. 28 October 2021; https://www.nhm.ac.uk/discover/news/2021/october/numbers-of-north-atlantic-right-whale-fall.html
54. WWF. (n.d.). 'Dolphins and Porpoises: Vaquita'; https://www.worldwildlife.org/species/vaquita#:~:text=The%20vaquita%20is%20the%20most,ban%20throughout%20their%20entire%20habitat
55. WWF. (n.d.). 'Species/marine factsheet: Bycatch'; https://www.yumpu.com/en/document/read/33599614/wwf-bycatch-fact-sheetpdf
56. FishCount.org.uk. (n.d.). 'long line fishing'; http://fishcount.org.uk/fish-welfare-in-commercial-fishing/capture/long-line-fishing
57. PETA. (n.d.). 'Commercial Fishing: How Fish Get From the High Seas to Your Supermarke'; https://www.peta.org/issues/animals-used-for-food/factory-farming/fish/commercial-fishing/
58. Davis, J. 'Fishermen are cutting off the beaks of endangered albatrosses'. 17 November 2020; https://www.nhm.ac.uk/discover/news/2020/november/fishermen-are-cutting-off-the-beaks-of-endangered-albatrosses.html
59. Natural History Museum. 'Endangered seabirds caught by fishermen are being Intentionally killed or mutilated'. 17 November 2020; https://phys.org/news/2020-11-endangered-seabirds-caught-fishermen-intentionally.html
60. WWF. 'What's in the Net – Millions of turtles, seals, dolphins, seabirds and sharks killed each year'. 19 November 2020; https://sharks.panda.org/news-blogs-updates/latest-news/what-s-in-the-net-millions-of-turtles-seals-dolphins-seabirds-and-sharks-killed-each-year
61. Fishcount.org.uk. (n.d.). 'gillnetting'; http://fishcount.org.uk/fish-welfare-in-commercial-fishing/capture/gillnet
62. Fishcount.org.uk. (n.d.). 'purse seining'; http://fishcount.org.uk/fish-welfare-in-commercial-fishing/capture/purse-seine
63. University of British Columbia. 'Global trends show seabird populations dropped 70 percent since 1950s'. ScienceDaily. 9 July 2015; www.sciencedaily.com/releases/2015/07/150709102850.htm
64. Humane Society International. 'Scotland bans seal killing in major victory to end fish farm shootings'. 17 June 2020; https://www.hsi.org/news-resources/scotland-bans-seal-killing/

65. Hunter, R. 'Environmental Standards Scotland "ban" seal scarer devices'. *The National*. 10 August 2022; https://www.thenational.scot/news/20616554.environmental-standards-scotland-ban-seal-scarer-devices/
66. Briggs, B. 'Orkney seal killing may have broken the law'. The Ferret. 18 June 2023; https://theferret.scot/orkney-seal-killing-may-have-broken-the-law/
67. Anderson, L. 'Spare the seals'. *The Scotsman*. 9 March 2012; https://www.scotsman.com/news/opinion/letters/spare-the-seals-1639976
68. Changing Markets Foundation, Compassion in World Farming, Rethink Fish. (n.d.). 'Until the Seas Run Dry: How Industrial Agriculture is Plundering the Oceans'.
69. Monbiot, G. 'Seaspiracy shows why we must treat fish not as seafood, but as wildlife'. *The Guardian*. 7 April 2021; https://www.theguardian.com/commentisfree/2021/apr/07/seaspiracy-earth-oceans-destruction-industrial-fishing
70. Stanford University. 'Ocean study predicts the collapse of all seafood fisheries by 2050'. Phys.org. 3 November 2006; https://phys.org/news/2006-11-ocean-collapse-seafood-fisheries.html
71. Joel K. Bourne, J. 'How to Farm a Better Fish'. *National Geographic*. 2014; https://www.nationalgeographic.com/foodfeatures/aquaculture/
72. Abraham, T.J. and A. Bardhan. 'Antimicrobial Awareness Week 2021: How poor regulation threatens aquaculture'. *Down To Earth*. 17 November 2021; https://www.downtoearth.org.in/blog/agriculture/antimicrobial-awareness-week-2021-how-poor-regulation-threatens-aquaculture-80240
73. Bora, G. 'How India, the largest exporter of shrimps, lost its crown to tiny Ecuador'. *The Economic Times*. 18 March 2023; https://economictimes.indiatimes.com/small-biz/trade/exports/insights/how-india-the-largest-exporter-of-shrimps-lost-its-crown-to-tiny-ecuador/articleshow/98648967.cms
74. Ministry of Commerce and Industry, India. 'India's marine product exports record an all-time high in FY 2021-22; Grow by over 30% to Rs 57,586.48 crore (USD 7.76 billion)'. Press Information Bureau. 29 June 2022; https://pib.gov.in/PressReleasePage.aspx?PRID=1837884

75. Bhati, D. 'Antimicrobial resistance in aquaculture can hit exports, Centre warns states'. *Down To Earth*. 19 January 2022; https://www.downtoearth.org.in/news/food/antimicrobial-resistance-in-aquaculture-can-hit-exports-centre-warns-states-81176
76. TNN. 'Aquaculture: Probiotics to fight antimicrobial resistance?' *The Times of India*. 23 November 2022; https://timesofindia.indiatimes.com/city/kochi/aquaculture-probiotics-to-fight-antimicrobial-resistance/articleshow/95701803.cms
77. Schar, D. et al. 'Global trends in antimicrobial use in aquaculture'. *Scientific Reports*, 10, 21878. 2020; https://doi.org/10.1038/s41598-020-78849-3
78. Reverter, M. et al. 'Aquaculture at the crossroads of global warming and antimicrobial resistance'. *Nature Communications*, vol. 11, article no. 1870. 20 April 2020; https://doi.org/10.1038/s41467-020-15735-6
79. Alexander, A. 'One More Nasty Consequence of Factory Farming: Runaway Algae'. NRDC. 11 August 2016; https://www.nrdc.org/bio/ann-alexander/one-more-nasty-consequence-factory-farming-runaway-algae
80. United States Environmental Protection Agency. (n.d.). 'Climate Change and Harmful Algal Blooms'; https://www.epa.gov/nutrientpollution/climate-change-and-harmful-algal-blooms
81. Centers for Disease Control and Prevention. 'Illness and Symptoms: Marine (Saltwater) Algal Blooms'. 29 August 2022; https://www.cdc.gov/habs/illness-symptoms-marine.html
82. Sandy, E. 'Satellite Imagery Confirms Factory Farm Growth Is Major Cause of Lake Erie Algae Blooms'. *Earth Island Journal*. 8 July 2019; https://www.earthisland.org/journal/index.php/articles/entry/satellite-factory-farm-lake-erie-great-lakes-pollution-algae-blooms/
83. Chiu, J. 'How animal waste is helping turn China's lakes green'. *The Guardian*. 31 August 2018; https://www.theguardian.com/environment/2018/aug/31/eutrophication-algae-how-animal-waste-is-turning-chinas-lakes-green
84. One Kind, Compassion in World Farming. 'Underwater Cages, Parasites and Dead Fish: Why a Moratorium on Scottish Salmon Farming Expansion is Imperative'. March 2021. Godalming, Edinburgh.

85. Ibid.
86. Handel, N. 'Algae blooms harmful to aquaculture: UN global assessment'. Phys.org. 8 June 2021; https://phys.org/news/2021-06-algae-blooms-aquaculture-global.html
87. One Kind, Compassion in World Farming. 'Underwater Cages, Parasites and Dead Fish: Why a Moratorium on Scottish Salmon Farming Expansion is Imperative'. March 2021. Godalming, Edinburgh.
88. Tarrant, K. 'Fish farms scrutinised as antibiotic use soars'. *The Sunday Times*. 4 December 2022; https://www.thetimes.co.uk/article/fish-farms-scrutinised-as-antibiotic-use-soars-gg8jd88pw
89. Essere Animali. (n.d.). 'Undercover Investigations'; https://www.essereanimali.org/en/investigations/
90. Scalini, M. 'Our fish-farming investigations presented to members of the European Parliament'. Essere Animali. 3 November 2021; https://www.essereanimali.org/en/2021/11/fish-investigations-european-parliament/
91. Physicians Committee for Responsible Medicine. (n.d.). 'Health Concerns About Fish'; https://p.widencdn.net/zsvtil/Health-Concerns-About-Fish-Fact-Sheet
92. Winner, C. 'How Does Toxic Mercury Get into Fish?' Woods Hole Oceanographic Institute. 1 October 2010; https://www.whoi.edu/oceanus/feature/how-does-toxic-mercury-get-into-fish/
93. Physicians Committee for Responsible Medicine. (n.d.). 'Health Concerns About Fish'; https://p.widencdn.net/zsvtil/Health-Concerns-About-Fish-Fact-Sheet
94. The Biodiversity Group. (n.d.). 'About Insects'; https://biodiversitygroup.org/insects/

Chapter 6: Butterfly Effect

1. Bat Conservation Trust. (n.d.). 'Bats as pollinators'; https://www.bats.org.uk/about-bats/why-bats-matter/bats-as-pollinators
2. Lederer, D.R. (n.d.). 'Ornithology: The Science of Birds'; http://ornithology.com/birds-as-pollinators/
3. Askham, B., and L. Hendry (n.d.). 'Seven insect heroes of pollination'. Natural History Museum; https://www.nhm.ac.uk/discover/insect-pollination.html

4. Bittel, J. 'Monarch Butterflies Migrate 3,000 Miles—Here's How'. *National Geographic*. 17 October 2017; https://www.nationalgeographic.com/animals/article/monarch-butterfly-migration?loggedin=true
5. Ritchie, H. 'How much of the world's food production is dependent on pollinators?' Our World in Data. 2 August 2021; https://ourworldindata.org/pollinator-dependence
6. Bittel, J. 'Monarch Butterflies Migrate 3,000 Miles—Here's How'. *National Geographic*. 17 October 2017; https://www.nationalgeographic.com/animals/article/monarch-butterfly-migration?loggedin=true
7. Forest District Preserve Will County. 'A world without mosquitoes? It's not as great an idea as it may seem'. 3 November 2020; https://www.reconnectwithnature.org/news-events/the-buzz/world-without-mosquitoes-not-as-easy-as-it-seems
8. Bittel, J. 'Monarch Butterflies Migrate 3,000 Miles—Here's How'. *National Geographic*. 17 October 2017; https://www.nationalgeographic.com/animals/article/monarch-butterfly-migration?loggedin=true
9. Jones, B. 'The monarch is falling victim to a real-life butterfly effect'. Vox. 14 December 2021; https://www.vox.com/down-to-earth/22823993/monarch-butterflies-mexico-milkweed
10. Bittel, J. 'Monarch Butterflies Migrate 3,000 Miles—Here's How'. *National Geographic*. 17 October 2017; https://www.nationalgeographic.com/animals/article/monarch-butterfly-migration?loggedin=true
11. Miller, S. 'Why the Monarch Butterfly Migration Is Mexico's Top Natural Wonder'. Natural Habitat Adventures. 10 December 2021; https://www.nathab.com/blog/monarch-butterfly-migration-mexicos-top-natural-wonder/
12. *Encyclopedia Britannica*. (n.d.). 'Methuselah'; https://www.britannica.com/biography/Methuselah
13. University of Washington. 'Scientists crack secrets of the monarch butterfly's internal compass'. ScienceDaily. 14 April 2016; www.sciencedaily.com/releases/2016/04/160414143908.htm
14. Jones, B. 'The monarch is falling victim to a real-life butterfly effect'. Vox. 14 December 2021; https://www.vox.com/down-to-earth/22823993/monarch-butterflies-mexico-milkweed

15. Romo, V. 'Why marigolds, or cempasúchil, are the iconic flower of Día de los Muertos'. NPR. 30 October 2021; https://www.npr.org/2021/10/30/1050726374/why-marigolds-or-cempasuchil-are-the-iconic-flower-of-dia-de-los-muertos
16. Riding, A. 'A Bloody Tale of How Mexico Went Catholic.' Daily Beast. 13 April 2017; https://www.thedailybeast.com/a-bloody-tale-of-how-mexico-went-catholic
17. Romo, V. 'Why marigolds, or cempasúchil, are the iconic flower of Día de los Muertos'. NPR. 30 October 2021; https://www.npr.org/2021/10/30/1050726374/why-marigolds-or-cempasuchil-are-the-iconic-flower-of-dia-de-los-muertos
18. Monarch Joint Venture. (n.d.). 'Monarchs and Día de Muertos in Mexico'. https://monarchjointventure.org/blog/monarchs-and-dia-de-muertos-in-mexico
19. Michigan State University. 'Day of the Dead Ofrenda (Frida in Mictlan, Mictlan in Frida)'. 2007; https://museum.msu.edu/?exhibition=day-of-the-dead-ofrenda-frida-in-mictlan-mictlan-in-frida
20. Miller, S. 'Why the Monarch Butterfly Migration Is Mexico's Top Natural Wonder'. Natural Habitat Adventures. 10 December 2021; https://www.nathab.com/blog/monarch-butterfly-migration-mexicos-top-natural-wonder/
21. UNESCO. (n.d.). 'Monarch Butterfly Biosphere Reserve'; https://whc.unesco.org/en/list/1290/
22. Eltohamy, F. 'Monarch butterflies denied endangered species listing despite shocking decline'. *National Geographic*. 17 December 2020; https://www.nationalgeographic.co.uk/environment-and-conservation/2020/12/monarch-butterflies-denied-endangered-species-listing-despite
23. Echeverria, M. 'Migratory monarch butterfly now classified as Endangered'. WWF. 27 July 2022; https://www.worldwildlife.org/stories/migratory-monarch-butterfly-now-classified-as-endangered
24. Jones, B. 'The monarch is falling victim to a real-life butterfly effect'. Vox. 14 December 2021; https://www.vox.com/down-to-earth/22823993/monarch-butterflies-mexico-milkweed

25. Arnold, C. 'We're losing monarchs fast—here's why'. *National Geographic*. 21 December 2018; https://www.nationalgeographic.com/animals/article/monarch-butterflies-risk-extinction-climate-change
26. Wilkerson, J., and B. Chow. 'Why Roundup Ready Crops Have Lost their Allure'. Harvard University: The Graduate School of Arts and Sciences. 10 August 2015; https://sitn.hms.harvard.edu/flash/2015/roundup-ready-crops/
27. Arnold, C. 'We're losing monarchs fast—here's why'. *National Geographic*. 21 December 2018; https://www.nationalgeographic.com/animals/article/monarch-butterflies-risk-extinction-climate-change
28. European Chemicals Agency. 'Glyphosate'. 30 May 2022; https://echa.europa.eu/hot-topics/glyphosate
29. Carrington, D. 'Glyphosate weedkiller damages wild bee colonies, study reveals'. *The Guardian*. 2 June 2022; https://www.theguardian.com/environment/2022/jun/02/glyphosate-weedkiller-damages-wild-bumblebee-colonies
30. Eller, D. (2018, July 12). 'Iowa farmers play crucial role in monarch butterflies' survival'. The Des Moines Register. 12 July 2018; https://eu.desmoinesregister.com/story/money/agriculture/2018/07/12/monarch-iowa-needs-up-830-000-acres-habitat-save-butterfly/739653002/
31. USDA Economic Research Service. 'ERS Charts of Note'. 20 July 2018; https://www.ers.usda.gov/data-products/charts-of-note/charts-of-note/?topicId=a2d1ab41-13b3-48b5-8451-688d73507ff4#:~:text=Currently%2C%20over%2090%20percent%20of,or%20insect%20resistant%20(Bt).
32. Karges, K. et al. 'Agro-economic prospects for expanding soybean production beyond its current northerly limit in Europe'. *European Journal of Agronomy*, vol. 133, 126415, ISSN 1161–0301. 2022; https://doi.org/10.1016/j.eja.2021.126415 (https://www.sciencedirect.com/science/article/pii/S1161030121001866)
33. John Lewis Partnership. (n.d.); https://www.johnlewispartnership.co.uk/csr/our-strategy/raw-materials-sourcing.html
34. Union of Concerned Scientists. 'Soybeans'. 9 October 2015; https://www.ucsusa.org/resources/soybeans

35. Ritchie, Hannah, and Max Roser. 'Forests and Deforestation'. Our World in Data. 2021; https://ourworldindata.org/forests-and-deforestation
36. Qi, Guang-Hai. et al. (n.d.). 'Nutritional evaluation and utilization of quality protein maize (QPM) in animal feed'. Food and Agriculture Organization of the United Nations; https://www.fao.org/3/y5019e/y5019e0c.htm
37. USDA Economic Research Service. (n.d.). 'Feed Grains Sector at a Glance'; https://www.ers.usda.gov/topics/crops/corn-and-other-feed-grains/feed-grains-sector-at-a-glance/
38. American Soybean Association. (n.d.). 'Animal Agriculture'; https://soygrowers.com/key-issues-initiatives/key-issues/other/animal-ag/#:~:text=Animal%20agriculture%20is%20the%20soybean,to%20feed%20livestock%20and%20poultry
39. Cudmore, B. 'Working Together for Monarchs'. WWF. 2017; https://www.worldwildlife.org/magazine/issues/summer-2017/articles/working-together-for-monarchs
40. Loria, J. 'Factory Farming Is Killing Our Planet. Here's How'. World Animal Protection. 4 February 2020; https://www.worldanimalprotection.us/blogs/factory-farming-killing-our-planet
41. McGreal, C. 'How America's food giants swallowed the family farms'. *The Guardian*. 9 March 2019; https://www.theguardian.com/environment/2019/mar/09/american-food-giants-swallow-the-family-farms-iowa
42. WWF. Plow Print. 2021; https://files.worldwildlife.org/wwfcmsprod/files/Publication/file/5yrd3g00ig_PlowprintReport_2021_Final_HiRes_b.pdf?_ga=2.206131795.1359907129.1689509149-1283307670.1685602027
43. The World Bank. (n.d.). 'Land area (sq. km) – Lebanon'; https://data.worldbank.org/indicator/AG.LND.TOTL.K2?locations=LB
44. EcoWatch. 'Wildfires Burn Across Midwest'. 5 April 2021; https://www.ecowatch.com/wildfires-midwest-us-2651367797.html
45. Johnson, N., and J. Brooker. 'It is not just the West that is burning'. 20 October 2021; https://grist.org/burning-issue/it-is-not-just-the-west-that-is-burning/

46. Frankel, Set al. 'Forest Tree Diseases and Climate Change'. U.S. Department of Agriculture, Forest Service, Climate Change Resource Center. October 2012; www.fs.usda.gov/ccrc/topics/forest-disease
47. Strain, D. 'Climate Change Sends Beetles Into Overdrive'. *Science*. 16 March 2012; https://www.science.org/content/article/climate-change-sends-beetles-overdrive
48. Frankel, S. et al. 'Forest Tree Diseases and Climate Change'. U.S. Department of Agriculture, Forest Service, Climate Change Resource Center. October 2012; www.fs.usda.gov/ccrc/topics/forest-disease
49. Johnson, N., and J. Brooker. 'It is not just the West that is burning'. 20 October 2021; https://grist.org/burning-issue/it-is-not-just-the-west-that-is-burning/
50. University of New Mexico. 'Scientists find climate-driven tree mortality and fuel aridity increase wildfire fuel availability'. ScienceDaily. 15 December 2021; www.sciencedaily.com/releases/2021/12/211215113237.htm
51. UN Environmental Programme. (n.d.). 'Monarch Butterflies & Climate Change'; https://www.cms.int/sites/default/files/publication/fact_sheet_monarch_butterfly_climate_change.pdf
52. Cohen, I. (n.d.). 'Too Cold for Comfort: How Climate Change is Affecting the Monarch Butterfly'. UCSC Biology 136 Environmental Physiology; https://adapt136.ucsc.edu/taxa/invertebrates/too-cold-for-comfort-how-climate-change-is-affecting-the-monarch-butterfly#:~:text=A%20study%20investigating%20the%20metabolism,monarchs%20reared%20under%20summer%2Dlike
53. UN Environmental Programme. (n.d.). 'Monarch Butterflies & Climate Change'; https://www.cms.int/sites/default/files/publication/fact_sheet_monarch_butterfly_climate_change.pdf
54. University of Michigan. 'Rising carbon dioxide levels pose a previously unrecognized threat to monarch butterflies.' ScienceDaily. 10 July 2018; www.sciencedaily.com/releases/2018/07/180710071920.htm
55. Taylor, R. 'Monarch Butterflies a Canary in Coal Mine'. *The Herald Journal*. 9 May 2019; https://www.hjnews.com/opinion/letters_to_editor/monarch-butterflies-a-canary-in-coal-mine/article_85b01134-de4b-5e1c-9b4e-94c94fb1c307.html

56. Eschner, K. 'The Story of the Real Canary in the Coal Mine'. *Smithsonian*. 30 December 2016; https://www.smithsonianmag.com/smart-news/story-real-canary-coal-mine-180961570/
57. Langley, L. '450 butterfly species rapidly declining due to warmer autumns in the western U.S.'. *National Geographic*. 4 March 2021; https://www.nationalgeographic.com/animals/article/butterflies-declining-due-to-warmer-autumns-in-western-united-states?loggedin=true
58. Warren M.S. et al. 'The decline of butterflies in Europe: Problems, significance, and possible solutions.' *PNAS* USA, 118(2):e2002551117. 12 January 2021. 10.1073/pnas.2002551117. PMID: 33431566; PMCID: PMC7812787.
59. Busby, M. 'Bee-harming pesticides exported from EU despite ban on outdoor use'. *The Guardian*. 18 November 2021; https://www.theguardian.com/environment/2021/nov/18/bee-harming-pesticides-exported-from-eu-after-ban-on-outdoor-use#:~:text=The%20EU%20ban%20came%20into,use%20them%20under%20emergency%20authorisations.
60. Warren M.S. et al. 'The decline of butterflies in Europe: Problems, significance, and possible solutions.' *PNAS* USA, 118(2):e2002551117. 12 January 2021. 10.1073/pnas.2002551117. PMID: 33431566; PMCID: PMC7812787.
61. Langley, L. '450 butterfly species rapidly declining due to warmer autumns in the western U.S.'. *National Geographic*. 4 March 2021; https://www.nationalgeographic.com/animals/article/butterflies-declining-due-to-warmer-autumns-in-western-united-states?loggedin=true
62. Xerces Society for Invertebrate Conservation. (n.d.). 'About the Xerces Society'; https://www.xerces.org/about-xerces
63. van Klink, R. et al. 'Meta-analysis reveals declines in terrestrial but increases in freshwater insect abundances'. *Science*, 368(6489), pp. 417–20. 24 April 2020; doi: 10.1126/science.aax9931. Erratum in: Science. 2020 Oct 23;370(6515): PMID: 32327596.
64. duardo E. Zattara, Marcelo A. Aizen. 'Worldwide occurrence records suggest a global decline in bee species richness'. *One Earth*, vol. 4, issue 1, pp. 114–23, ISSN 2590-3322. 2021; https://doi.org/10.1016/j.

oneear.2020.12.005 (https://www.sciencedirect.com/science/article/pii/S2590332220306515)

65. Food and Agriculture Organization of the United Nations. 'Declining bee populations pose threat to global food security and nutrition'. 20 May 2019; https://www.fao.org/news/story/en/item/1194910/icode/
66. Heinrich Böll Stiftung, Friends of the Earth, Bund für Umwelt und Naturschutz. 'Meat Atlas: Facts and figures about the animals we eat'. 2021.
67. Daley, J. 'The Devastating Role of Light Pollution in the "Insect Apocalypse"'. *Smithsonian*. 25 November 2019; https://www.smithsonianmag.com/smart-news/light-pollution-contributes-insect-apocalypse-180973642/
68. Carrington, D. 'Light pollution is key "bringer of insect apocalypse"'. *The Guardian*. 22 November 2019; https://www.theguardian.com/environment/2019/nov/22/light-pollution-insect-apocalypse
69. Washington University in St. Louis. 'Four ways to curb light pollution, save bugs: Insects have experienced global declines. Flipping the switch can help'. ScienceDaily. 18 November 2019; www.sciencedaily.com/releases/2019/11/191118162938.htm
70. Kolbert, E. 'Where Have All the Insects Gone?' *The New Yorker*. 25 October 2021; https://www.newyorker.com/magazine/2021/11/01/where-have-all-the-insects-gone-e-o-wilson-silent-earth
71. Tallamy, Douglas W., and and W. Gregory Shriver, 'Are declines in insects and insectivorous birds related?'. *Ornithological Applications*, vol. 123, issue 1, duaa059. 1 February 2021; https://doi.org/10.1093/ornithapp/duaa059
72. Losey, John E., and Mace Vaughan. 'The Economic Value of Ecological Services Provided by Insects'. *BioScience*, vol. 56, issue 4, pp. 311–23. April 2006; https://doi.org/10.1641/0006-3568(2006)56[311:TEVOES]2.0.CO;2
73. Wystrach, A. 'We've Been Looking at Ant Intelligence the Wrong Way'. The Conversation. 30 August 2013; https://www.scientificamerican.com/article/weve-been-looking-at-ant-intelligence-the-wrong-way/
74. Hance, J. 'Uncovering the intelligence of insects, an interview with Lars Chittka'. Mongabay. 29 June 2010; https://news.mongabay.

com/2010/06/uncovering-the-intelligence-of-insects-an-interview-with-lars-chittka/

75. Saniotis, D.A. et al. 'Humans Not Smarter Than Animals, Just Different'. The University of Adelaide. 5 December 2013; https://www.adelaide.edu.au/news/news67182.html
76. Reader's Digest. '10 Animals with Real Superpowers That Would Make Superheroes Jealous'. 1 February 2023; https://www.rd.com/list/unusual-animal-superpowers/
77. Gorman, J. 'How Ants Sniff Out the Right Path'. *The New York Times*. 22 January 2019; https://www.nytimes.com/2019/01/22/science/ants-navigate-scent.html
78. Gorvett, Z. 'Why insects are more sensitive than they seem'. BBC Future. 29 November 2021; https://www.bbc.com/future/article/20211126-why-insects-are-more-sensitive-than-they-seem
79. Pfizer. (n.d.). 'How Genetically Related Are We to Bananas?'; https://www.pfizer.com/news/articles/how_genetically_related_are_we_to_bananas#:~:text=Fruit%20fly%3A%2060%20percent%20identical&text=These%20tiny%20winged%20creatures%20share,the%20study%20of%20human%20disease.
80. Gorvett, Z. 'Why insects are more sensitive than they seem'. BBC Future. 29 November 2021; https://www.bbc.com/future/article/20211126-why-insects-are-more-sensitive-than-they-seem
81. Zimmer, C. 'To Bee'. *National Geographic*. 25 October 2006; https://www.nationalgeographic.com/science/article/to-bee
82. University of Göttingen. 'Beetle larvae think with brain "under construction"'. ScienceDaily. 2 November 2020; www.sciencedaily.com/releases/2020/11/201102120110.htm
83. Schenkman, L. 'ScienceShot: World's Strongest Insect'. *Science*. 23 March 2010; https://www.science.org/content/article/scienceshot-worlds-strongest-insect-rev2
84. Barron, Andrew B., and Colin Klein. 'What insects can tell us about the origins of consciousness'. *PNAS* USA, vol. 113, issue 18, pp. 4900-8. 3 May 2016; doi: 10.1073/pnas.1520084113. Epub 2016 Apr 18. PMID: 27091981; PMCID: PMC4983823.

85. Gorvett, Z. 'Why insects are more sensitive than they seem'. BBC Future. 29 November 2021; https://www.bbc.com/future/article/20211126-why-insects-are-more-sensitive-than-they-seem
86. Ibid.
87. Goldman, J.B. 'I'll Bee There for You: Do Insects Feel Emotions?' *Scientific American*. 30 September 2016; https://www.scientificamerican.com/article/i-ll-bee-there-for-you-do-insects-feel-emotions/#:~:text=Bumblebees%20seem%20to%20have%20a,own%20emotions%20and%20describe%20them
88. Schultz, C. 'If Cockroaches Are Conscious, Would That Stop You From Smushing Them?' *Smithsonian*. 29 November 2013; https://www.smithsonianmag.com/smart-news/if-cockroaches-are-conscious-would-that-stop-you-from-smushing-them-180947876/
89. University of Michigan. 'Paper wasps capable of behavior that resembles logical reasoning'. EurekAlert! 7 May 2019; https://www.eurekalert.org/news-releases/708274
90. Hugo, K. 'Intelligence test shows bees can learn to solve tasks from other bees'. PBS News Hour. 23 February 2017; https://www.pbs.org/newshour/science/intelligence-test-shows-bees-can-learn-to-solve-tasks-from-other-bees
91. Andrew, S. 'Bees are better at math when they're punished for the wrong answer, a new study finds'. CNN. 11 October 2019; https://edition.cnn.com/2019/10/11/us/bees-count-study-scn-trnd/index.html
92. Dyer, A. 'Are they watching you? The tiny brains of bees and wasps can recognise faces'. The Conversation. 12 April 2018; https://theconversation.com/are-they-watching-you-the-tiny-brains-of-bees-and-wasps-can-recognise-faces-100884#:~:text=Our%20existing%20research%20shows%20that,mechanisms%20for%20wasp%20face%20processing
93. British Ecological Society. 'Ants adapt tool use to avoid drowning.' ScienceDaily. 8 October 2020; www.sciencedaily.com/releases/2020/10/201008083807.htm
94. Zeldovich, L. 'New Study Finds Insects Speak in Different "Dialects"'. JSTOR Daily. 31 July 2018; https://daily.jstor.org/new-study-finds-insects-speak-in-different-dialects/

Chapter 7: Crying over Milk

1. Dhamnetiya, D. et al. 'Trends in incidence and mortality of tuberculosis in India over past three decades: a joinpoint and age–period–cohort analysis'. *BMC Pulmonary Medicine*, 21, 375. 2021; https://doi.org/10.1186/s12890-021-01740-y
2. World Health Organization. 'Tuberculosis'. 21 April 2023; https://www.who.int/news-room/fact-sheets/detail/tuberculosis#:~:text=In%202020%2C%20the%2030%20high,Nigeria%2C%20Bangladesh%20and%20South%20Africa
3. Dhamnetiya, D. et al. 'Trends in incidence and mortality of tuberculosis in India over past three decades: a joinpoint and age–period–cohort analysis'. *BMC Pulmonary Medicine*, 21, 375. 2021; https://doi.org/10.1186/s12890-021-01740-y
4. Global tuberculosis report 2022. 'Geneva: World Health Organization'. Licence: CC BY-NC-SA 3.0 IGO.
5. Overdorf, J. 'Supercharged Tuberculosis, Made in India'. *Scientific American*. 6 July 2015; https://www.scientificamerican.com/article/supercharged-tuberculosis-made-in-india1/
6. Ministry of Health and Family Welfare. 'WHO Global TB Report 2022'. 28 October 2022; https://pib.gov.in/PressReleasePage.aspx?PRID=1871626#:~:text=India's%20TB%20incidence%20for%20the,the%20global%20average%20of%2011%25
7. Dhamnetiya, D. et al. 'Trends in incidence and mortality of tuberculosis in India over past three decades: a joinpoint and age–period–cohort analysis'. *BMC Pulmonary Medicine*, 21, 375. 2021; https://doi.org/10.1186/s12890-021-01740-y
8. Malik, Mansi et al. 'Knowledge of HIV/AIDS and its determinants in India: Findings from the National Family Health Survey-5 (2019–2021)'. *Population Medicine*, no. 13. 5 May 2023; doi:10.18332/popmed/163113
9. Dhamnetiya, D. et al. 'Trends in incidence and mortality of tuberculosis in India over past three decades: a joinpoint and age–period–cohort analysis'. *BMC Pulmonary Medicine*, 21, 375. 2021; https://doi.org/10.1186/s12890-021-01740-y

10. World Health Organization. (n.d.). 'Tuberculosis: Multidrug-resistant tuberculosis (MDR-TB)'; https://www.who.int/news-room/questions-and-answers/item/tuberculosis-multidrug-resistant-tuberculosis-(mdr-tb)
11. Centers for Disease Control and Prevention. (n.d.). 'Extensively Drug-Resistant Tuberculosis (XDR TB) Fact Sheet'; https://www.cdc.gov/tb/publications/factsheets/drtb/xdrtb.htm
12. World Health Organization. 'Tuberculosis: Totally drug-resistant TB'. 7 June 2015; https://www.who.int/news-room/questions-and-answers/item/tuberculosis-totally-drug-resistant-tb
13. Ibid.
14. Centers for Disease Control and Prevention. (n.d.). 'Extensively Drug-Resistant Tuberculosis (XDR TB) Fact Sheet'; https://www.cdc.gov/tb/publications/factsheets/drtb/xdrtb.htm
15. TB Alliance. (n.d.). 'Inadequate Treatment'; https://www.tballiance.org/why-new-tb-drugs/inadequate-treatment#:~:text=Today's%20Drugs&text=People%20with%20TB%20must%20take,are%20unable%20to%20access%20treatment.
16. Overdorf, J. 'Supercharged Tuberculosis, Made in India'. *Scientific American*. 6 July 2015; https://www.scientificamerican.com/article/supercharged-tuberculosis-made-in-india1/
17. Shivekar, S.S. et al. 'Prevalence and factors associated with multidrug-resistant tuberculosis in South India'. *Scientific Reports*, 10, article no. 17552. 2020; https://doi.org/10.1038/s41598-020-74432-y
18. American Enterprise Institute. 'Tuberculosis: Poor-Quality Medicines Contribute to Drug Resistance'. 15 February 2012; https://www.aei.org/research-products/speech/tuberculosis-poor-quality-medicines-contribute-to-drug-resistance/
19. Overdorf, J. 'Supercharged Tuberculosis, Made in India'. *Scientific American*. 6 July 2015; https://www.scientificamerican.com/article/supercharged-tuberculosis-made-in-india1/
20. Clements, M. 'India's egg producers looking to a positive future'. WATTPoultry. 17 February 2021; https://www.wattagnet.com/egg/egg-production/article/15532975/indias-egg-producers-looking-to-a-positive-future

21. Ricky Thaper. 'Indian poultry to gain from food sector modernization'. WATTPoultry. 7 January 2020; https://www.wattagnet.com/articles/39227-indias-poultry-sector-sees-bright-outlook?v=preview
22. PTI. 'PIL in HC against keeping egg-laying hens in small cages'. *The Times of India*. 3 October 2016; https://timesofindia.indiatimes.com/city/delhi/pil-in-hc-against-keeping-egg-laying-hens-in-small-cages/articleshow/54658765.cms
23. FIAPO. (n.d.). 'Animals Farmed for Food'; https://www.fiapo.org/new_site/farmed-animals/
24. Wong, E., K. Anderson and K. Kuhn. *What the Health*. Bloomington: Xlibris, 2017.
25. FIAPO. 'Hens ought to be kept in bigger cages with freedom of movement, says HC'. 5 November 2018; https://www.fiapo.org/fiaporg/news/hens-ought-to-be-kept-in-bigger-cages-with-freedom-of-movement-says-hc/
26. Sengupta, A. [Commentary] 'Factory farming for eggs impacts India's environment'. Mongabay. 3 July 2019; https://india.mongabay.com/2019/07/commentary-factory-farming-for-eggs-impact-indias-environment/
27. Humane Society International. (n.d.). 'An HSI Fact Sheet: Avian Influenza in India'; https://www.hsi.org/wp-content/uploads/assets/pdfs/hsi-fa-white-papers/an_hsi_fact_sheet_avian.pdf
28. Graber, R. 'The 6 largest poultry companies of Asia'. WATTPoultry. 31 December 2018; https://www.wattagnet.com/broilers-turkeys/article/15527231/the-6-largest-poultry-companies-of-asia-wattagnet
29. Humane Society International. (n.d.). 'An HSI Fact Sheet: Avian Influenza in India'; https://www.hsi.org/wp-content/uploads/assets/pdfs/hsi-fa-white-papers/an_hsi_fact_sheet_avian.pdf
30. Centre for Science and Environment. (n.d.). 'Antibiotics in chicken'; https://www.cseindia.org/latest-study-by-cses-pollution-monitoring-lab-finds-antibiotic-residues-in-chicken-8498
31. Pearson, N.O., and S. Limaye. 'Antibiotic Apocalypse Fear Stoked by India's Drugged Chickens'. Bloomberg. 29 March 2016; https://www.bloomberg.com/news/features/2016-03-29/antibiotic-apocalypse-fear-stoked-by-india-s-drugged-chickens#xj4y7vzkg

32. Poultry World. 'Indian government bans Colistin'. 2 August 2019; https://www.poultryworld.net/health-nutrition/indian-government-bans-colistin/#:~:text=The%20Indian%20Ministry%20of%20Health,involve%20risk%20to%20human%20beings.%E2%80%9D
33. Davies, M., and B. Stockton. 'India Bans Use of "Last Hope" Antibiotics on Farms'. The Bureau of Investigative Journalism. 22 July 2019; https://www.thebureauinvestigates.com/stories/2019-07-22/india-bans-use-of-last-hope-antibiotic-colistin-on-farms
34. Khullar, B., and R. Sinha. 'Perpetually on antibiotics'. *Down To Earth*. 10 April 2020; https://www.downtoearth.org.in/news/health/perpetually-on-antibiotics-70353
35. Sebastian, Stelvin. et al. 'Antibiotic resistance in Escherichia coli isolates from poultry environment and UTI patients in Kerala, India: A comparison study'. *Comparative Immunology, Microbiology and Infectious Diseases*, vol. 75, 101614, ISSN 0147-9571. 2021; https://doi.org/10.1016/j.cimid.2021.101614 (https://www.sciencedirect.com/science/article/pii/S0147957121000060)
36. Didyala, A. 'Antibiotics abuse in poultry comes home to roost on plate'. *The Times of India*. 24 June 2023; https://timesofindia.indiatimes.com/city/hyderabad/antibiotics-abuse-in-poultry-comes-home-to-roost-on-plate/articleshow/101229530.cms?from=mdr
37. Doriya, H. 'Chickens from intensive farms worries urban India, shows recent consumer research'. *Down To Earth*. 28 August 2020; https://www.downtoearth.org.in/blog/health/chickens-from-intensive-farms-worries-urban-india-shows-recent-consumer-research-73098
38. World Health Organization. 'Stop using antibiotics in healthy animals to prevent the spread of antibiotic resistance'. 7 November 2017; https://www.who.int/news/item/07-11-2017-stop-using-antibiotics-in-healthy-animals-to-prevent-the-spread-of-antibiotic-resistance
39. Bhati, D. 'Limiting antibiotics use in crops: What new actions did the government take'. *Down To Earth*. 6 December 2021; https://www.downtoearth.org.in/blog/governance/limiting-antibiotics-use-in-crops-what-new-actions-did-the-government-take-80543
40. Bhati, D. 'Union agriculture ministry prohibits use of TB antibiotics on crops'. *Down To Earth*. 21 December 2021; https://www.downtoearth.

org.in/news/agriculture/union-agriculture-ministry-prohibits-use-of-tb-antibiotics-on-crops-80785

41. Srinivasan, S. et al. 'Prevalence of Bovine Tuberculosis in India: A systematic review and meta-analysis'. *Transboundary and Emerging Diseases*, vol. 65, issue 6, pp. 1627–40. 8 June 2018; https://doi.org/10.1111/tbed.12915
42. Supar, T.d. (Makalah diterima 21 Agustus 2008 – Revisi 7 November 2008). 'Tuberkulosis Padi Sapi, Suatu Penyakit Zoonosis'. Balai Besar Penelitian Veteriner, Jl. R.E. Martadinata no. 30, Bogor 16114.
43. Gong, Q.L. et al. 'Prevalence of bovine tuberculosis in dairy cattle in China during 2010-2019: A systematic review and meta-analysis'. *PLoS Neglected Tropical Diseases*, 15(6), e0009502. 17 June 2021; https://doi.org/10.1371/journal.pntd.0009502
44. Supar, T.d. (Makalah diterima 21 Agustus 2008 – Revisi 7 November 2008). 'Tuberkulosis Padi Sapi, Suatu Penyakit Zoonosis'. Balai Besar Penelitian Veteriner, Jl. R.E. Martadinata no. 30, Bogor 16114.
45. Cinco, M. 'UPLB cattle herd killed to stop spread of bovine TB'. Inquirer.net. 19 November 2018; https://newsinfo.inquirer.net/1054793/uplb-cattle-herd-killed-to-stop-spread-of-bovine-tb
46. Khattak, I. et al. 'Zoonotic tuberculosis in occupationally exposed groups in Pakistan'. *Occupational Medicine* (Oxford, England), vol. 66, issue 5, pp. 371–76. 30 March 2016; https://doi.org/10.1093/occmed/kqw039
47. Islam, Md N. et al. 'Risk factors and true prevalence of bovine tuberculosis in Bangladesh'. *PLOS One*, 16(2): e0247838. 26 February 2021; doi: 10.1371/journal.pone.0247838. PMID: 33635911; PMCID: PMC7909650.
48. Cadmus, S.I.B. 'Bovine Tuberculosis in Nigeria: Historical Perspective, Burden, Risk Factors, and Challenges for Its Diagnosis and Control'. In *Tuberculosis in Animals: An African Perspective*, (eds) Dibaba, A., N. Kriek and C. Thoen. Springer, 2019; https://doi.org/10.1007/978-3-030-18690-6_17
49. Miassangoumouka, Jean et al. 'Risk Factors for the Transmission of Mycobacterium Bovis to Slaughterhouses Workers in Brazzaville, Republic of the Congo'. 2020; 10.21203/rs.3.rs-55319/v1

50. Ayele, W.Y. et al. 'Bovine tuberculosis: an old disease but a new threat to Africa'. *The International Journal Tuberculosis Lung Disease*, vol. 8, no. 8, pp. 924–37. August 2004; PMID: 15305473.
51. Eldholm, V. et al. 'Import and transmission of Mycobacterium orygis and Mycobacterium africanum, Norway'. *BMC Infectious Diseases*, 21, 562. 2021; https://doi.org/10.1186/s12879-021-06269-3
52. Duffy, S.C. et al. 'Reconsidering *Mycobacterium bovis* as a proxy for zoonotic tuberculosis: a molecular epidemiological surveillance study'. *The Lancet. Microbe*, vol. 1, issue 2, E66–E73. June 2020; https://doi.org/10.1016/S2666-5247(20)30038-0
53. Dawson, Kara L. et al. 'Transmission of *Mycobacterium orygis* (*M. tuberculosis* complex species) from a Tuberculosis Patient to a Dairy Cow in New Zealand'. *Journal of Clinical Microbiology*, vol. 50, no. 9: 3136-8. September 2012; https://doi: 10.1128/JCM.01652-12; Epub 2012 Jul 11. PMID: 22785186; PMCID: PMC3421823.
54. Parsons, Sven D.C. '*Mycobacterium orygis*: a zoonosis, zooanthroponosis, or both?' *The Lancet Microbe*, vol. 1, issue 6: e240. October 2020; doi: 10.1016/S2666-5247(20)30142-7. Epub 2020 Oct 7. PMID: 35544220.
55. Srinivasan, S. et al. 'Prevalence of Bovine Tuberculosis in India: A systematic review and meta-analysis'. *Transboundary and Emerging Diseases*, vol. 65, issue 6, pp. 1627–40. 8 June 2018; https://doi.org/10.1111/tbed.12915
56. Kakati, S. et al. 'Bacteriological quality of raw milk marketed in and around Guwahati city, Assam, India'. *Veterinary World*, 14(3), pp. 656–60. 2021; https://doi.org/10.14202/vetworld.2021.656-660
57. Rana, S. 'Should You Boil Milk Before Drinking it?' NDTV Food. 1 November 2019; https://food.ndtv.com/food-drinks/should-you-boil-milk-before-drinking-it-1695219
58. Smith, S. 'Letter to Medical Professionals about Raw Milk'. Raw Milk Institute. 3 December 2019; https://www.rawmilkinstitute.org/updates/letter-to-medical-professionals-about-raw-milk#:~:text=Raw%20milk%20has%20superior%20nutrition,immune%20system%20and%20gastrointestinal%20tract
59. Gandhi, M.S. 'Coronavirus fear shields threat of Bovine Tuberculosis'. mathrubhumi.com. 4 April 2020; https://englisharchives.mathrubhumi.

com/news/columns/faunaforum/coronavirus-fear-shields-threat-of-bovine-tuberculosis-1.4666486

60. World Animal Protection. 'Better Dairy Campaign Report'. 2020.
61. FIAPO. 'Cattle-ogue: Unveiling the Truth of the Indian Dairy Industry'. 2017.
62. The Cattle Site. 'TB (Bovine Tuberculosis)'. 29 September 2022; https://www.thecattlesite.com/diseaseinfo/185/tb-bovine-tuberculosis/#:~:text=Animals%20are%20probably%20more%20likely,a%20higher%20risk%20of%20infection
63. UK Department of Agriculture, Environment and Rural Affairs. (n.d.). 'What is Bovine Tuberculosis (TB)?'; https://www.daera-ni.gov.uk/articles/what-bovine-tuberculosis-tb
64. World Organisation for Animal Health. (n.d.). 'Bovine tuberculosis'; https://www.woah.org/en/disease/bovine-tuberculosis/
65. Gandhiok, J. 'Dairies across Delhi flout rules, flag activists'. *The Times of India*. 13 September 2021; https://timesofindia.indiatimes.com/city/delhi/dairies-across-city-flout-rules-flag-activists-list-corrections/articleshow/86149898.cms?utm_source=contentofinterest&utm_medium=text&utm_campaign=cppst
66. PETA India. (n.d.). 'Inside the Indian Dairy Industry: A Report on the Abuse of Cows and Buffaloes Exploited for Milk'.
67. Compassion in World Farming. (n.d.). 'Calves Reared for Veal'; https://www.ciwf.org.uk/farm-animals/cows/veal-calves/
68. S., Sivaraman. 'Antibiotic Use in Food Animals: India Overview'. Vellore: ReAct Asia-Pacific. 2018.
69. Mutua, F. et al. 'A review of animal health and drug use practices in India, and their possible link to antimicrobial resistance'. *Antimicrobial Resistance Infection & Control*, 9, 103. 2020; https://doi.org/10.1186/s13756-020-00760-3
70. Ibid.
71. Drugs.com. (n.d.). 'Vancomycin (Monograph)'; https://www.drugs.com/monograph/vancomycin.html#uses
72. FACLM, M.G. 'Should You Be Concerned About Bovine Leukemia Virus in Milk?' NutritionFacts.org. 29 August 2019; https://nutritionfacts.org/blog/should-you-be-concerned-about-bovine-leukemia-virus-

in-milk/#:~:text=And%20indeed%2C%20infectious%20virus%20was,it's%20causing%20human%20disease%2C%20though

73. FACLM, M.G. 'The Role of Bovine Leukemia Virus in Breast Cancer'. NutritionFacts.org. 10 October 2016; https://nutritionfacts.org/video/the-role-of-bovine-leukemia-virus-in-breast-cancer/
74. Physicians Committee for Responsible Medicine. (n.d.). 'Health Concerns About Dairy'; https://www.pcrm.org/good-nutrition/nutrition-information/health-concerns-about-dairy
75. Amy Joy Lanou, 'Should dairy be recommended as part of a healthy vegetarian diet? Counterpoint'. *The American Journal of Clinical Nutrition*, vol. 89, issue 5, pp. 1638S–1642S. May 2009; https://doi.org/10.3945/ajcn.2009.26736P
76. Sadana, D.D. 'India needs to look beyond gaushalas to address its stray cattle problem'. *Down To Earth*. 5 April 2021; https://www.downtoearth.org.in/news/wildlife-biodiversity/-india-needs-to-look-beyond-gaushalas-to-address-its-stray-cattle-problem--76189
77. BusinessToday.In. 'Vets pull out 71 kg of waste from stray cow's stomach'. 4 March 2021; https://www.businesstoday.in/latest/trends/story/vets-pull-out-71-kg-of-waste-from-stray-cows-stomach-289950-2021-03-04
78. Biswas, S. 'The myth of the Indian vegetarian nation'. BBC News. 4 April 2018; https://www.bbc.co.uk/news/world-asia-india-43581122
79. Singh, A. et al. 'Environmental and Health Impacts from Slaughter Houses Located on the City Outskirts: A Case Study'. *Journal of Environmental Protection*, vol. 5, no. 6, pp. 566–75. 2014; doi: 10.4236/jep.2014.56058
80. Ohri, R. 'Cow meat going out of India as carabeef, police investigation on'. *The Economic Times*. 20 March 2018; https://economictimes.indiatimes.com/news/politics-and-nation/cow-meat-going-out-of-india-as-carabeef-police-investigation-on/articleshow/63374600.cms?from=mdr
81. Statista. 'Distribution of leather goods exports in value worldwide in 2020, by country'. 23 February 2022; https://www.statista.com/statistics/768345/leather-goods-distribution-exports-value-by-country-world/

82. Council for Leather Exports. (n.d.). 'Indian Leather Industry'; https://leatherindia.org/indian-leather-industry/

Chapter 8: Skin in the Game

1. Theodosi, N. 'Stella McCartney Calls for Outright Fur, Leather Ban at COP26.' WWD. 3 November 2021; https://wwd.com/fashion-news/ready-to-wear/stella-mccartney-calls-for-outright-fur-ban-at-cop26-1234989591/
2. Klerk, Amy de. 'Stella McCartney is pushing for more regulation in the fashion industry'. *Harper's Bazaar*. 5 November 2021; https://www.harpersbazaar.com/uk/fashion/fashion-news/a38169578/stella-mccartney-regulation-fashion-industry/
3. The Retail Appointment. (n.d.); https://www.retailappointment.co.uk/career-advice/company-a-z/companies-f-j/handm
4. United Nations Climate Change. 'Fashion Industry Steps Up Climate Ambition with Renewed Charter'. 8 November https://unfccc.int/news/fashion-industry-steps-up-climate-ambition-with-renewed-charter
5. Conlon, S. '"Brands have been getting away with murder": Stella McCartney and leading fashion figures on the fallout of Cop26'. *The Guardian*. 26 November 2021; https://www.theguardian.com/fashion/2021/nov/26/brands-have-been-getting-away-with-stella-mccartney-and-leading-fashion-figures-on-the-fallout-of-cop26
6. CNBC International. 'Stella McCartney calls for ban on leather & tax breaks for vegan goods'. 5 November 2021; https://www.youtube.com/watch?v=s4DZe9sdKiE
7. Report from the United Nations' High-Level Expert Group on the Net Zero Emissions Commitments of Non-State Entities. 'Integrity Matters: Net Zero Committments by Businesses, Financial Institutions, Cities and Regions'. 2022.
8. United Nations. 'UN launches drive to highlight environmental cost of staying fashionable'. 25 March 2019; https://news.un.org/en/story/2019/03/1035161
9. United Nations Climate Change. 'Fashion Industry Charter for Climate Action'. Version 5 November 2021; https://unfccc.int/sites/default/

files/resource/Fashion%20Industry%20Carter%20for%20Climate%20Action_2021.pdf

10. Global Fashion Agenda and The Boston Consulting Group. 'Pulse of the Fashion Industry'. 2017.
11. Mathews, B. 'Higg Materials Sustainability Index updated'. *Apparel Insider*. 4 August 2018; https://apparelinsider.com/higg-materials-sustainability-index-updated/
12. Mathews, B. 'SAC will not suspend "unsafe" Higg scores'. *Apparel Insider*. 15 October 2020; https://apparelinsider.com/sac-refuses-to-suspend-unsafe-higg-scores/
13. Tonti, L. 'Woolly measurement: farmers say sustainable textile standard "doesn't pass the pub test"'. *The Guardian*. 28 June 2021; https://www.theguardian.com/fashion/2021/jun/29/woolly-measurement-farmers-say-sustainable-textile-standard-doesnt-pass-the-pub-test
14. Turk, R. 'How material innovation can change the fashion industry'. FashionUnited. 1 March 2021; https://fashionunited.uk/news/fashion/how-material-innovation-can-change-the-fashion-industry/2021030154038
15. Ecotextile News. 'SAC update on consumer-facing product labels'. 3 July 2023; https://www.ecotextile.com/2023070330895/labels-legislation-news/sac-update-on-consumer-facing-product-labels.html
16. PETA. (n.d.). 'These Videos Show How Sheep Suffer for Wool'; https://headlines.peta.org/wool-videos-prove-sheep-suffer/
17. The Woolmark Company. (n.d.). 'Where Wool Comes From'; https://www.woolmark.com/fibre/woolgrowers/where-wool-comes-from/#:~:text=This%20makes%20Australia%20the%20world's,Africa%2C%20the%20UK%20and%20Uruguay.
18. PETA. (n.d.). 'These Videos Show How Sheep Suffer for Wool'; https://headlines.peta.org/wool-videos-prove-sheep-suffer/
19. Grand View Research. 'Leather Goods Market Size Worth $405.28 Billion By 2030'. February 2023; https://www.grandviewresearch.com/press-release/global-leather-goods-market
20. Persistence Market Research. (n.d.). 'Wool Market'; https://www.persistencemarketresearch.com/market-research/wool-market.asp

21. Material Innovation Initiative. (n.d.). 'Environmental Fact Sheet'; https://af89fe40-1e99-4362-9d52-c39c1bba841c.filesusr.com/ugd/7db921_74aafd55d0aa43988f5a635381b27b37.pdf
22. International Wool Textile Organisation. (n.d.). 'TBC Environmental Impacts of Wool Textiles'; https://iwto.org/sustainability/tbc-environmental-impacts-of-wool-textiles/
23. Hassan, Mohammad and Jianzhong Shao. 'Chemical processing of wool: Sustainable considerations'. *Key Engineering Materials*, vol. 671, pp. 32-39. 206; 10.4028/www.scientific.net/KEM.671.32
24. Council of Fashion Designers of America, Inc. (CFDA). (n.d.). 'Alpaca'; https://cfda.com/resources/materials/detail/alpaca
25. PETA. (n.d.). 'Groundbreaking Undercover Investigation: Crying, Vomiting Alpacas Tied Down, Cut Up for Sweaters and Scarves'; https://investigations.peta.org/alpaca-wool-abuse/
26. PETA UK. (n.d.). 'Mohair: Goats Abused and Killed'; https://www.peta.org.uk/issues/animals-not-wear/mohair-goats-abused-and-killed/?utm_source=PETA%20UK::Google&utm_medium=Ad&utm_campaign=1020::gen::PETA%20UK::Google::s-grant-dsa::::searchad&gclid=CjwKCAjwloCSBhAeEiwA3hVo_cDJFs0bWAT0Q-L645fD0YlN-pkuRR1fgFb
27. Council of Fashion Designers of America. (n.d.). 'Silk'; https://cfda.com/resources/materials/detail/silk
28. Humane Society International. (n.d.). 'The Fur Trade'; https://www.hsi.org/news-resources/fur-trade/
29. Fur Free Alliance. (n.d.). 'Environment and Health'; https://www.furfreealliance.com/environment-and-health/
30. Fur Free Alliance. (n.d.). 'Public Opinion'; https://www.furfreealliance.com/public-opinion/
31. furfashion. 'The Global Fur Trade Relies on China. Is the Mood Shifting?' The International Fur Federation. 27 January 2021; https://www.wearefur.com/the-global-fur-trade-relies-on-china-is-the-mood-shifting/
32. Harrison, V. 'Fur seeks new look as traditional markets fade'. CNN Business. 28 May 2015; https://money.cnn.com/2015/05/28/luxury/fur-industry-fashion/index.html

33. Bijleveld, M., Korteland, M., & Sevenster, M. (January 2011). The environmental impact of mink fur production. Delft.
34. (Verts/ALE), R.R. (n.d.). 'Question for written answer E-005145/2012 to the Commission'. European Parliament; https://www.europarl.europa.eu/doceo/document/E-7-2012-005145_EN.pdf
35. Rastogi, S.K. et al. 'Occupational cancers in leather tanning industries: A short review'. *Indian Journal of Occupational and Environmental Medicine*, 11(1), pp. 3–5. January–April 2007; https://doi.org/10.4103/0019-5278.32456
36. Pinnock, O. 'What Is Metal-Free Leather And Why Are Brands Promoting It As Sustainable?' *Forbes*. 10 May 2019; https://www.forbes.com/sites/oliviapinnock/2019/05/10/what-is-metal-free-leather-and-why-are-brands-promoting-it-as-sustainable/?sh=3a892eba517b
37. Alliance for International Reforestation. '"Vegetable Tanned Leather" Could Cause Devastating Environmental Effects and Lead to Future Pandemics, it is NOT "Safer" or "Eco-Friendly" as Many Leather Companies Imply'. Cision. 18 June 2020; https://www.prnewswire.com/news-releases/vegetable-tanned-leathercould-cause-devastating-environmental-effects-and-lead-tofuture-pandemics-it-is-not-safer-or-eco-friendly-as-many-leathercompanies-imply-301079104.html
38. 'Chapter 9 – Industrial Examples'. In *Green Chemistry and Engineering*, (eds) Doble, Mukesh, and Anil Kumar Kruthiventi. Academic Press, pp. 245–96, ISBN 9780123725325. 2007; https://doi.org/10.1016/B978-012372532-5/50010-9
39. Yadav, K.P. 'Tangible shift'. *Down To Earth*. 15 December 2002; https://www.downtoearth.org.in/coverage/tangible-shift-15576
40. Krishnakumar, A. 'An award and despair'. *Frontline*. 3 August 2002; https://frontline.thehindu.com/other/article30245727.ece
41. *The New Indian Express*. 'Polluting units must compensate affected persons'. 20 May 2012; https://www.newindianexpress.com/states/tamil-nadu/2012/may/20/polluting-units-must-compensate-affected-persons-369642.html
42. Vellore Citizens Welfare Forum vs Union Of India & Ors on 28 August, 1996. (n.d.); indiankanoon.org: https://indiankanoon.org/doc/1934103/

43. Madhavan, D. 'Voters concerned about effluent discharge into Palar'. *The Hindu*. 17 February 2022; https://www.thehindu.com/news/national/tamil-nadu/voters-concerned-about-effluent-discharge-into-palar/article65059530.ece

44. Berke, J. 'India's holy Ganges River is devastatingly polluted, yet provides drinking water for over 400 million people — here's what it looks like'. Business Insider. 3 March 2018; https://www.businessinsider.com/photos-indias-ganges-river-pollution-2018-1?r=US&IR=T#the-ganges-begins-in-the-himalayas-as-a-crystal-clear-river-high-in-the-mountains-but-pollution-and-excessive-usage-transforms-it-into-toxic-sludge-on-its-journey-throug

45. Shukla, S. 'Uttar Pradesh: Closure of 94 tanneries ordered for polluting river Ganga'. *The Free Press Journal*. 25 March 2021; https://www.freepressjournal.in/india/uttar-pradesh-closure-of-94-tanneries-ordered-for-polluting-river-ganga

46. ANI. 'NGT constitutes 5-member committee to prevent discharge of effluents in Ganga'. *The Times of India*. 26 November 2021; https://timesofindia.indiatimes.com/india/ngt-constitutes-5-member-committee-to-prevent-discharge-of-effluents-in-ganga/articleshow/87928981.cms

47. TNN. '200 tanneries, 70 factories closed for first Magh Mela snan on Jan 6'. *The Times of India*. 4 January 2023; https://timesofindia.indiatimes.com/city/kanpur/200-tanneries-70-factories-closed-for-first-magh-mela-snan-on-jan-6/articleshow/96725331.cms

48. Common Objective. (n.d.). 'Fibre Briefing: Leather'; https://www.commonobjective.co/article/fibre-briefing-leather

49. Maksud, A.K.M. et al. 'Mapping of Children Engaged in the Worst Forms of Child Labour in the Supply Chain of the Leather Industry in Bangladesh'. CLARISSA Emerging Evidence Report 5, Brighton: Institute of Development Studies. 2021; DOI: 10.19088/CLARISSA.2021.00

50. Boseley, S. 'Child labourers exposed to toxic chemicals dying before 50, WHO says'. *The Guardian*. 21 March 2017; https://www.theguardian.com/world/2017/mar/21/plight-of-child-workers-facing-cocktail-of-toxic-chemicals-exposed-by-report-bangladesh-tanneries

51. Maurice, John. 'Tannery pollution threatens health of half-million Bangladesh residents.' *Bulletin of the World Health Organization*, vol. 79, no. 1, p. 78. January 2001. Gale Academic OneFile, link.gale.com/apps/doc/A71185975/AONE?u=anon~23b20240&sid=googleScholar&xid=539c778c
52. BizVibe. 'Global Leather Industry Factsheet 2020: Top 10 Largest Leather Producing Countries, Largest Exporters & Importers'. 29 April 2020; https://blog.bizvibe.com/blog/top-10-largest-leather-producing-countries
53. The World Bank. 'China's Transition to a Low-Carbon Economy and Climate Resilience Needs Shifts in Resources and Technologies'. 12 October 2022; https://www.worldbank.org/en/news/press-release/2022/10/12/china-s-transition-to-a-low-carbon-economy-and-climate-resilience-needs-shifts-in-resources-and-technologies#:~:text=China%20emits%2027%20percent%20of,energy%20efficiency%20and%20resource%20produc
54. World Resources Institute. 'This Interactive Chart Shows Changes in the World's Top 10 Emitters'. 2 March 2023; https://www.wri.org/insights/interactive-chart-shows-changes-worlds-top-10-emitters
55. You, L., and K. Schoenmakers. 'Why China's methane-spewing farms are a hidden climate risk'. China Dialogue. 19 January 2021; https://chinadialogue.net/en/climate/why-chinas-methane-spewing-farms-are-a-hidden-climate-risk/
56. Pitcher, L. 'New study links major fashion brands to Amazon deforestation'. *The Guardian*. 29 November 2021; https://www.theguardian.com/us-news/2021/nov/29/fashion-industry-amazon-rainforest-deforestation
57. JBS. (n.d.); https://jbs.com.br/en/about/our-business/leather/
58. PETA. (n.d.). 'Calves Dragged and Face-Branded for Leather Car Interiors'; https://investigations.peta.org/calves-face-branded-leather-car-interiors/
59. STAND.earth. 'Nowhere to Hide: How the Fashion Industry Is Linked to Amazon Rainforest Destruction'. Stand Research Group. 29 November 2021; https://stand.earth/resources/nowhere-to-hide-how-the-fashion-industry-is-linked-to-amazon-rainforest-destruction/

60. Leather Working Group. (n.d.). 'A community for responsible leather'; https://www.leatherworkinggroup.com/#:~:text=Leather%20Working%20Group%20(LWG)%20is,sustainable%20future%20with%20responsible%20leather
61. PETA. (n.d.). 'Calves Dragged and Face-Branded for Leather Car Interiors'; https://investigations.peta.org/calves-face-branded-leather-car-interiors/
62. PETA. 'The Skins Trade in India, Narrated by Pamela Anderson'. 1999; https://www.youtube.com/watch?v=3hCpz89WlUY
63. PETA India. 'PETA India Finds Appalling Cruelty at Mumbai's Deonar Slaughterhouse Before Eid'. 2019; https://www.petaindia.com/blog/peta-india-finds-appalling-cruelty-at-mumbais-deonar-slaughterhouse-before-eid/
64. PETA UK. 'Leather: Hell for Animals and Children in Bangladesh'. 2015; https://secure.peta.org.uk/page/18868/petition/1?locale=en-GB
65. PETA India. (n.d.). 'R. Madhavan Narrates "Glass Walls"'; https://secure.petaindia.com/page/86397/data/1?locale=en-GB
66. World Animal Protection. (n.d.). 'China'; https://api.worldanimalprotection.org/country/china
67. PETA. (n.d.). 'A Look Inside the Angora Rabbit Wool Industry'; https://support.peta.org/page/1846/petition/1?locale=en-US#:~:text=from%20Official%20PETA&text=Ninety%20percent%20of%20angora%20wool,the%20treatment%20of%20the%20animals.
68. PETA India. (n.d.). 'Dogs Slaughtered for Leather'; https://investigations.peta.org/china-dog-leather/
69. ACTAsia. 'China's fur trade and its position in the global fur industry'. July 2019.
70. ACTAsia. 'Report of Dog and Cat Fur Trade in China'. 2017.
71. PETA. (n.d.). 'Exposed by PETA: A Shocking Look Inside Chinese Fur Farms'; https://investigations.peta.org/chinese-fur-farms/
72. PETA. (n.d.). 'Cruelty-Assured: The Truth About "High Welfare" Fur'; https://spotlight.peta.org.uk/origin-assured-fur/
73. Maron, D.F. 'What the mink COVID-19 outbreaks taught us about pandemics'. *National Geographic*. 24 February 2021; https://www.

nationalgeographic.com/animals/article/what-the-mink-coronavirus-pandemic-has-taught-us?loggedin=true&rnd=1688730251451

74. Kesslen, B. 'Here's why Denmark culled 17 million minks and now plans to dig up their buried bodies. The Covid mink crisis, explained'. NBC News. 2 December 2020; https://www.nbcnews.com/news/animal-news/here-s-why-denmark-culled-17-million-minks-now-plans-n1249610
75. Humane Society International. 'Denmark's plan to restart mink fur farming by importing mink is branded contemptible by Humane Society International/Europe'. 15 December 2022; https://www.hsi.org/news-resources/denmarks-plan-to-restart-mink-fur-farming-by-importing-mink-is-branded-contemptible-by-humane-society-international-europe/
76. Fur Free Alliance. (n.d.); https://www.furfreealliance.com/fur-bans/
77. Fenollar, F. et al. 'Mink, SARS-CoV-2, and the Human-Animal Interface'. *Frontiers in Microbiology*, vol. 12: 663815. 1 April 2021; doi: 10.3389/fmicb.2021.663815. PMID: 33868218; PMCID: PMC8047314.
78. Fur Free Alliance. (n.d.); https://www.furfreealliance.com/fur-bans/
79. Dalton, J. 'Coronavirus: "Exotic" skins in shoe and handbag fashion stores fuel risk of further epidemics, say experts. *The Independent*. 24 April 2020; https://www.independent.co.uk/news/uk/home-news/coronavirus-wildlife-trade-fashion-shoes-boots-handbag-python-stingray-a9460811.html
80. PETA. (n.d.). 'Exotic Skins: The Animals'; https://www.peta.org/issues/animals-used-for-clothing/exotic-skins-animals/
81. Nuwer, R. 'Luxury fashion brands had thousands of exotic leather goods seized by U.S. law enforcemen't. *National Geographic*. 22 May 2020; https://www.nationalgeographic.com/animals/article/luxury-fashion-wildlife-imports-seized

Chapter 9: Testing 123

1. Associated Press, Christina Coulter, Matt McNulty. 'Last of four lab monkeys that escaped when truck towing a trailer load of 100 macaques crashed on Pennsylvania highway are caught: Three others are euthanized'. MailOnline. 23 January 2022; https://www.dailymail.

co.uk/news/article-10430309/Dont-approach-lab-monkey-missing-crash-people-told.html

2. Scarcella, F. 'UPDATE Danville woman not sick from monkey exposure'. Yahoo.com. 26 January 2022; https://finance.yahoo.com/news/danville-woman-not-sick-monkey-181700278.html?guccounter=1&guce_referrer=aHR0cHM6Ly93d3cuZ29vZ2xlLmNvbS8&guce_referrer_sig=AQAAAGvlk24FakL6MdacuARSsFKgQDft5m70kMvA5WEjYk89D1ilqMdW1VZBfJLHq3DKUw-Omnwz64BePEuKyp1QS3RHoUmjlWfDx
3. Levenson, M. 'Questions Remain After Highway Crash Involving Monkeys'. *The New York Times*. 1 February 2022; https://www.nytimes.com/2022/02/01/us/cdc-monkeys-pennsylvania-truck-crash.html
4. Metro Voice. 'What happened to the lab monkeys?' 2 February 2022; https://metrovoicenews.com/what-happened-to-the-lab-monkeys/
5. PETA. 'Monkey Crash Memorial: Where Are the Danville 97?' 2 May 2022; https://www.peta.org/media/news-releases/monkey-crash-memorial-where-are-the-danville-97/
6. PETA. 'Four Monkeys Escaped—With Viruses? PETA Statement'. 21 January 2022; https://www.peta.org/media/news-releases/1021471/
7. Levenson, M. 'Questions Remain After Highway Crash Involving Monkeys'. *The New York Times*. 1 February 2022; https://www.nytimes.com/2022/02/01/us/cdc-monkeys-pennsylvania-truck-crash.html
8. Chandna, Alka. 'PETA letter to Robert M. Gibbens, DVM'. 24 January 2022; https://www.peta.org/wp-content/uploads/2022/01/Concerns-from-PETA-re-vehicular-crash-in-Pennsylvania-w-addendum.pdf
9. PETA. 'Victory! Airline That Flew Monkeys Involved in PA Truck Crash Ends Monkey Lab Shipments'. 28 January 2022; https://www.peta.org/media/news-releases/victory-airline-that-flew-monkeys-involved-in-pa-truck-crash-ends-monkey-lab-shipments/
10. PETA. 'Monkey Crash Memorial: Where Are the Danville 97?' 2 May 2022; https://www.peta.org/media/news-releases/monkey-crash-memorial-where-are-the-danville-97/
11. PETA. 'Companies Cited After PETA Uncovers Monkeys Illegally Shipped Across the U.S., Destined for Torment in Labs'. 18 April

2022; https://www.peta.org/blog/peta-uncovers-illegal-transport-of-primates-to-us-labs/

12. PETA. 'Companies Cited After PETA Uncovers Monkeys Illegally Shipped Across the U.S., Destined for Torment in Labs'. 7 June 2023; https://www.peta.org/blog/peta-uncovers-illegal-transport-of-primates-to-us-labs/
13. European Centre for Disease Prevention and Control. 'Epidemiological update: Monkeypox outbreak'. 20 May 2022; https://www.ecdc.europa.eu/en/news-events/epidemiological-update-monkeypox-outbreak
14. Kimball, S. 'World Health Organization confirms 92 cases of monkeypox with outbreaks in 12 countries'. CNBC. 20 May 2022; https://www.cnbc.com/2022/05/20/world-health-organization-confirms-80-cases-of-monkeypox-with-outbreaks-in-11-countries.html
15. Centers for Disease Control and Prevention. '2022 Mpox Outbreak Global Map'. 5 July 2023; https://www.cdc.gov/poxvirus/mpox/response/2022/world-map.html
16. Braddick, I. 'OUTPOXXED Monkeypox: Inside dreaded outbreaks as virus first found in brain test lab monkeys leaves humans covered in blisters'. The U.S. Sun. 11 June 2021; https://www.the-sun.com/news/3060201/monkeypox-outbreaks-virus-first-found-lab-monkeys-oozing-blisters/
17. Arita I. et al. 'Outbreaks of monkeypox and serological surveys in nonhuman primates'. *Bulletin of the World Health Organization*, 46(5), pp. 625-31. 1972; PMID: 4340222; PMCID: PMC2480785.
18. NHS. 'Mpox'. 20 October 2022; https://www.nhs.uk/conditions/mpox/
19. Centers for Disease Control and Prevention. 'Mpox--How it Spreads'. 2 February 2023; https://www.cdc.gov/poxvirus/mpox/if-sick/transmission.html
20. NHS. 'Mpox'. 20 October 2022; https://www.nhs.uk/conditions/mpox/
21. Price, M. 'New Virus Jumps From Monkeys to Lab Worker'. *Science*. 14 July 2011; https://www.science.org/content/article/new-virus-jumps-monkeys-lab-worker
22. Cormier, Z. 'New Respiratory Virus Jumps from Monkey to Lab Worker'. *Scientific American*. 14 July 2011; https://www.scientificamerican.com/article/new-respiratory-virus-jumps-from-monkey-to-lab-worker/

23. Centers for Disease Control and Prevention. (n.d.). 'Symptoms'; https://www.cdc.gov/adenovirus/symptoms.html
24. Princeton University: Environmental Health & Safety. (n.d.). 'Zoonoses Associated with Old World Monkeys (Macaques)'; https://ehs.princeton.edu/laboratory-research/animal-research-health-and-safety/zoonotic-disease-information/zoonoses-associated-old-world-monkeys
25. Centers for Disease Control and Prevention. (n.d.). 'B Virus (herpes B, monkey B virus, herpesvirus simiae, and herpesvirus B)'; https://www.cdc.gov/herpesbvirus/about.html
26. CBS News. '25 years ago in Virginia, a very different Ebola outbreak'. 10 August 2014; https://www.cbsnews.com/news/25-years-ago-in-virginia-a-very-different-ebola-outbreak/
27. Cohn, D. 'Deadly Ebola Virus Found in VA Laboratory Monkey'. *The Washington Post*. 1 December 1989; https://www.washingtonpost.com/archive/politics/1989/12/01/deadly-ebola-virus-found-in-va-laboratory-monkey/d6d94b90-b44e-4fa6-a9d0-d67cc0970aca/
28. CBS News. '25 years ago in Virginia, a very different Ebola outbreak'. 10 August 2014; https://www.cbsnews.com/news/25-years-ago-in-virginia-a-very-different-ebola-outbreak/
29. 'Chapter 16 - Emerging and Reemerging Viral Diseases'. In *Essential Human Virology*. Louten, Jennifer. Academic Press, pp. 291–310, ISBN 9780128009475. 2016; https://doi.org/10.1016/B978-0-12-800947-5.00016-8 (https://www.sciencedirect.com/science/article/pii/B9780128009475000168)
30. Trachtman, P. 'Review of "The Hot Zone"'. *Smithsonian*. June 1995; https://www.smithsonianmag.com/arts-culture/review-of-the-hot-zone-96325494/
31. Joi, P. 'The next pandemic: Marburg?' Gavi the Vaccine Alliance. 22 April 2021; https://www.gavi.org/vaccineswork/next-pandemic/marburg?gclid=CjwKCAjww8mWBhABEiwAl6-2RQt4IMWYLViZBtuasBRbqjjNo_f1epMqw1h5G238g73xTfBV8RaklxoCooQQAvD_BwE
32. Centers for Disease Control and Prevention. (n.d.). 'About Marburg Virus Disease'; https://www.cdc.gov/vhf/marburg/about.html
33. Centers for Disease Control and Prevention. (n.d.). 'Marburg Virus Disease Outbreaks'; https://www.cdc.gov/vhf/marburg/outbreaks/chronology.html

34. European Centre for Disease Prevention and Control. (n.d.). 'Factsheet about Marburg virus disease'; https://www.ecdc.europa.eu/en/infectious-disease-topics/z-disease-list/ebola-virus-disease/facts/factsheet-about-marburg-virus
35. Joi, P. 'The next pandemic: Marburg?' Gavi the Vaccine Alliance. 22 April 2021; https://www.gavi.org/vaccineswork/next-pandemic/marburg?gclid=CjwKCAjww8mWBhABEiwAl6-2RQt4IMWYLViZBtuasBRbqjjNo_f1epMqw1h5G238g73xTfBV8RaklxoCooQQAvD_BwE
36. PETA. 'Monkey Imported for Lab Infected With Bioterrorism Pathogen PETA Finds; CDC Silent'. 19 December 2022; https://www.peta.org/media/news-releases/monkey-imported-for-lab-infected-with-bioterrorism-pathogen-peta-finds-cdc-silent/
37. Colley, C. 'US public not warned that monkeys imported from Cambodia carried deadly pathogens'. *The Guardian*. 18 December 2022; https://www.theguardian.com/us-news/2022/dec/18/monkeys-imported-us-from-cambodia-carried-deadly-pathogens#:~:text=Published%20last%20week%2C%20the%20case,in%20Texas%20in%20January%202021.
38. CDC Bioterrorism Agents. (n.d.); https://biosecurity.fas.org/resource/documents/CDC_Bioterrorism_Agents.pdf
39. Taetzsch, S.J. et al. 'Melioidosis in Cynomolgus Macaques (Macaca Fascicularis) Imported to the United States from Cambodia'. *Comparative Medicine*, 72(6), pp. 394–402. 1 December 2022; doi: 10.30802/AALAS-CM-22-000024. PMID: 36744511; PMCID: PMC9827603.
40. PETA. 'Monkey Imported for Lab Infected With Bioterrorism Pathogen, PETA Finds; CDC Silent'. 19 December 2022; https://www.peta.org/media/news-releases/monkey-imported-for-lab-infected-with-bioterrorism-pathogen-peta-finds-cdc-silent/
41. Centers for Disease Control and Prevention. (n.d.). 'Melioidosis'; https://www.cdc.gov/melioidosis/bioterrorism/threat.html#:~:text=Without%20treatment%2C%20up%20to%209,out%20of%2010%20people%20die.

42. PETA. 'Monkey Imported for Lab Infected With Bioterrorism Pathogen, PETA Finds; CDC Silent'. 19 December 2022; https://www.peta.org/media/news-releases/monkey-imported-for-lab-infected-with-bioterrorism-pathogen-peta-finds-cdc-silent/
43. Understanding Animal Research. (n.d.). 'Monkey'; https://www.understandinganimalresearch.org.uk/what-is-animal-research/a-z-animals/monkey
44. Desikan, S. 'Long-tailed macaques show rich tool-use behaviour'. *The Hindu*. 21 March 2020; https://www.thehindu.com/sci-tech/science/long-tailed-macaques-show-rich-tool-use-behaviour/article31129250.ece
45. Hamilton, J. 'Myth Busting: The Truth About Animals And Tools'. NPR. 23 December 2011; https://www.npr.org/2011/12/23/143833929/myth-busting-the-truth-about-animals-and-tools
46. UCL. 'Macaques' stone tool use varies despite same environment'. 29 October 2019; https://www.ucl.ac.uk/news/2019/oct/macaques-stone-tool-use-varies-despite-same-environment
47. University of Chicago. 'Humans And Monkeys Share Machiavellian Intelligence'. ScienceDaily. 25 October 2007; www.sciencedaily.com/releases/2007/10/071024144314.htm
48. Villatoro, C. 'Mapping Monogamy, Jealousy in the Monkey Mind: Uncovering the Neurobiology of Social Bonding in a Monogamous Primate'. University of California, Davis. 23 October 2017; https://www.ucdavis.edu/news/mapping-monogamy-jealousy-monkey-mind#:~:text=When%20a%20titi%20monkey%20is,from%20interacting%20with%20another%20male
49. *Nature*. 'Monkeys and Emotion'. 8 September 2011; https://www.pbs.org/wnet/nature/clever-monkeys-monkeys-and-emotion/4244/
50. University of Oxford. 'Unprecedented display of concern towards injured monkey offers hope for endangered species'. 10 July 2019; https://www.ox.ac.uk/news/2019-07-10-unprecedented-display-concern-towards-injured-monkey-offers-hope-endangered-species
51. Understanding Animal Research. (n.d.). 'Monkey'; https://www.understandinganimalresearch.org.uk/what-is-animal-research/a-z-animals/monkey

52. Zhou, V. 'China Is Running Out of Lab Monkeys To Experiment On'. Vice News. 14 May 2021; https://www.vice.com/en/article/jg8mdd/china-covid-lab-monkeys
53. Conlee, K.M., and A.N. Rowan. (n.d.). 'The Case for Phasing Out Experiments on Primates'. Ethics of Medical Research with Animals; http://animalresearch.thehastingscenter.org/report/the-case-for-phasing-out-experiments-on-primates/
54. PETA. 'Workers Electroshock Monkey Penises in Depraved Lab | PETA Investigates'. 15 September 2020; https://www.youtube.com/watch?v=mx8Yjkz4Wl4
55. PETA UK. 'Covance Pays PETA Europe £145,000'. 7 January 2015; https://www.peta.org.uk/blog/covance-pays-peta-europe/?utm_source=PETA%20UK::Google&utm_medium=Ad&utm_campaign=1120::gen::PETA%20UK::Google::s-grant-awa-dsa::::searchad&gclid=Cj0KCQjwuO6WBhDLARIsAIdeyDK7O1hPS2O00X_doorGNS-Y3JC0wv4yGe1JcWWqGwpgvORp_zAznCga
56. PETA. 'Covance Cruelty, Part One: Lab Induced Insanity'. 29 October 2018; https://www.youtube.com/watch?v=Wk7-jyLfbRc&t=37s
57. Bhalla, J.S. 'AIIMS flouts animal testing rules'. *Hindustan Times*. 7 October 2008; https://www.hindustantimes.com/delhi/aiims-flouts-animal-testing-rules/story-a2mwwWchg0shy4scYXIccI.html
58. Press Trust of India. 'Pamela urges AIIMS to retire aging monkeys'. 19 February 2011; https://www.news18.com/news/india/pamela-urges-aiims-to-retire-aging-monkeys-360987.html
59. Hindustan Times Media. 'AIIMS flouts animal testing rules'. 6 October 2008; https://www.youtube.com/watch?v=21iKH65AnW8
60. Ibid.
61. Ibid.
62. 62. PETA. 'Monkeys Retired From Experiments'. 20 June 2011; https://www.peta.org/blog/monkeys-retired-experiments/
63. AIIMS New Delhi. 'Central Animal Facility'. 13 February 2023; https://www.aiims.edu/index.php?option=com_content&view=article&id=158&catid=208&Itemid=2299&lang=en
64. PETA. (n.d.). 'VIDEO: Taxpayer-Funded Lab Torments Imprisoned Monkeys, Drives Them Mad'; https://headlines.peta.org/imprisoned-monkey-experiments-taxpayer-funded-lab/

65. Hale, T. 'The "Pit Of Despair" Was One Of The Most Unethical Experiments Of Modern Science'. IFLScience. 21 July 2021; https://www.iflscience.com/the-pit-of-despair-was-one-of-the-most-unethical-experiments-of-modern-science-60408
66. Breslow, J.M. 'What Does Solitary Confinement Do To Your Mind?' PBS. 22 April 2014; http://www.pbs.org/wgbh/frontline/article/what-does-solitary-confinement-do-to-your-mind/?fbclid=IwAR1PCcIDlNtsoDdcvvMCETypHDxCqeK2z-ZhrFRPkSilMW5L5u6oGx8Nyf0
67. PETA. (n.d.). 'VIDEO: Taxpayer-Funded Lab Torments Imprisoned Monkeys, Drives Them Mad'; https://headlines.peta.org/imprisoned-monkey-experiments-taxpayer-funded-lab/
68. Breslow, J.M. 'What Does Solitary Confinement Do To Your Mind?' PBS. 22 April 2014; http://www.pbs.org/wgbh/frontline/article/what-does-solitary-confinement-do-to-your-mind/?fbclid=IwAR1PCcIDlNtsoDdcvvMCETypHDxCqeK2z-ZhrFRPkSilMW5L5u6oGx8Nyf0
69. Bailey, J. 'Does the Stress of Laboratory Life and Experimentation on Animals Adversely Affect Research Data? A Critical Review'. *Alternatives to Laboratory Animals*, vol. 46, issue 5, pp. 291–305. 2018; doi:10.1177/026119291804600501
70. Akhtar A. 'The flaws and human harms of animal experimentation'. *Cambridge Quarterly of Healthcare Ethics*, vol. 24, issue 4, pp. 407–19. October 2015; https://doi.org/10.1017/S0963180115000079
71. Pound P. et al. 'Reviewing Animal Trials Systematically (RATS) Group. Where is the evidence that animal research benefits humans?' *BMJ*, 28;328 (7438), pp. 514–17. 28 February 2004; doi: 10.1136/bmj.328.7438.514. PMID: 14988196; PMCID: PMC351856.
72. Hajar, R. 'Animal testing and medicine'. *Heart Views*: The Official Journal of the Gulf Heart Association, vol. 12, issue 1, p. 42. 2011; https://doi.org/10.4103/1995-705X.81548
73. PETA. 'PETA Statement: Pfizer Vaccine Data'. 9 November 2020; https://www.peta.org/media/news-releases/peta-statement-pfizer-vaccine-data/
74. PETA UK. 'The Dutch Government Has Broken Promises and Made No Progress in Replacing Experiments on Animals'. 2 March 2021; https://www.peta.org.uk/blog/dutch-experiments-animals/

75. European Parliament. 'Plans and actions to accelerate a transition to innovation without the use of animals in research, regulatory testing and education'. 16 September 2021; https://www.europarl.europa.eu/doceo/document/TA-9-2021-0387_EN.html
76. Grimm, D. 'U.S. EPA to eliminate all mammal testing by 2035'. Science.org. 10 September 2019; https://www.science.org/content/article/us-epa-eliminate-all-mammal-testing-2035
77. Physicians Committee for Responsible Medicine. (n.d.). 'Human-Relevant Alternatives to Animal Tests'; https://www.pcrm.org/es/node/129693
78. PETA. 'Victory! President Signs Groundbreaking FDA Modernization Act 2.0'. 27 December 2022; https://www.peta.org/action/action-alerts/victory-congress-passes-groundbreaking-fda-modernization-act-2-0/
79. Jones-Engel, L. 'Long-tailed monkeys on the edge'. *The Jakarta Post*. 19 May 2022; https://www.thejakartapost.com/paper/2022/05/18/long-tailed-monkeys-on-the-edge.html
80. Patrick, H. (n.d.). 'Long-tailed macaques captured from wild as species listed as endangered for the first time'. *The Independent*; https://www.independent.co.uk/tv/news/endangered-monkey-long-tailed-macaque-b2129266.html
81. Goodreads. (n.d.). George Bernard Shaw; https://www.goodreads.com/quotes/34044-atrocities-are-not-less-atrocities-when-they-occur-in-laboratories

Chapter 10: The Deadly Games

1. *Encyclopedia Britannica*. (n.d.). 'venationes (Roman spectacle)'; https://www.britannica.com/sports/venationes
2. USHistory.org. (n.d.). '6e. Gladiators, Chariots, and the Roman Games'; https://www.ushistory.org/civ/6e.asp#:~:text=Some%20gladiatorial%20contests%20included%20animals,%22wild%20beast%20hunts%22)
3. *Encyclopedia Britannica*. (n.d.). 'gladiator (Roman Sports)'; https://www.britannica.com/sports/gladiator
4. USHistory.org. (n.d.). '6e. Gladiators, Chariots, and the Roman Games'; https://www.ushistory.org/civ/6e.asp#:~:text=Some%20

gladiatorial%20contests%20included%20animals,%22wild%20beast%20hunts%22)

5. Ibid.
6. Aitchison, David. 'The Hunger Games, Spartacus, and Other Family Stories: Sentimental Revolution in Contemporary Young-Adult Fiction'. *The Lion and the Unicorn*, 39, no. 3, pp. 254–74. 2015; doi:10.1353/uni.2015.0027
7. *Encyclopedia Britannica*. (n.d.). 'Spartacus (Roman Gladiator)'; https://www.britannica.com/biography/Spartacus-Roman-gladiator
8. PETA India. (n.d.); https://jallikattu.com/
9. The News Minute. 'Jallikattu announcer offers woman as prize along with bull, triggers outrage'. 16 January 2018; https://www.thenewsminute.com/article/jallikattu-announcer-offers-woman-prize-along-bull-triggers-outrage-74816
10. Annamalai, S. 'From bride to T-shirt, the Jallikattu prizes had it all'. *The Hindu*. 9 January 2016; https://www.thehindu.com/news/national/tamil-nadu/From-bride-to-T-shirt-the-Jallikattu-prizes-had-it-all/article60518818.ece
11. USHistory.org. (n.d.). '6e. Gladiators, Chariots, and the Roman Games'; https://www.ushistory.org/civ/6e.asp#:~:text=Some%20gladiatorial%20contests%20included%20animals,%22wild%20beast%20hunts%22)
12. Hardikar, J. 'With No Water and Many Loans, Farmers' Deaths Are Rising in Tamil Nadu'. The Wire. 21 June 2017; https://thewire.in/agriculture/drought-tamil-nadu-farmers-deaths
13. Indiatimes. 'In A Dramatic Move, 150 Farmers From Tamil Nadu Protest At Delhi's Jantar Mantar With Skulls Of Fellow Dead Farmers'. 20 March 2017; https://www.indiatimes.com/news/india/in-a-dramatic-move-150-farmers-from-tamil-nadu-protest-at-delhi-s-jantar-mantar-with-skulls-of-fellow-dead-farmers-273804.html
14. Warrier, S. 'Jallikattu movement is bigger than 1965 anti-Hindi agitation'. Rediff.com. 20 January 2017; https://www.rediff.com/news/interview/jallikattu-movement-is-bigger-than-1965-anti-hindi-agitation/20170120.htm
15. Andrews, E. 'The Gruesome Blood Sports of Shakespearean England'. History. 9 January 2019; https://www.history.com/news/the-gruesome-blood-sports-of-shakespearean-england

16. RSPCA. (n.d.). 'Organised animal cruelty'; https://www.rspca.org.uk/whatwedo/endcruelty/investigatingcruelty/organised
17. Walker, A. (2022, May 1). '"Killing for fun": Inside the sick world of badger baiting as bloodsport surges across Greater Manchester beauty sports'. *Manchester Evening News*. 1 May 2022; https://www.manchestereveningnews.co.uk/news/greater-manchester-news/killing-fun-inside-sick-world-23812078
18. World Animal Protection. (n.d.). 'Ending bear baiting'; https://www.worldanimalprotection.org/our-work/animals-wild/ending-bear-baiting
19. Andrews, E. 'The Gruesome Blood Sports of Shakespearean England'. History. 9 January 2019; https://www.history.com/news/the-gruesome-blood-sports-of-shakespearean-england
20. Osborn, J.F. 'Is Dog Fighting Illegal? The Dark Side of Animal Cruelty and Its Legal Consequences!' World Animal Foundation. 25 March 2023; https://worldanimalfoundation.org/advocate/is-dog-fighting-illegal/
21. *Encyclopedia Britannica*. (n.d.). 'pit bull'; https://www.britannica.com/animal/pit-bull
22. PETA India. (n.d.). 'New Investigation Reveals the Heartbreaking Cruelty of Dogfights'; https://www.petaindia.com/features/new-investigation-reveals-the-heartbreaking-cruelty-of-dogfights/
23. The Humane Society of the United States. (n.d.). The facts about dogfighting'; https://www.humanesociety.org/resources/facts-about-dogfighting
24. RSPCA. (n.d.). 'Animal Fighting'; https://www.rspca.org.uk/whatwedo/endcruelty/investigatingcruelty/organised/animalfighting
25. Humane Society International. 'About Dogfighting'. 10 January 2014; https://www.hsi.org/news-media/about_dogfighting/
26. Waggoner, M. 'Dog-fighting "legend" gets maximum of five years'. WRAL. 5 August 2011; https://www.wral.com/news/local/story/9954362/
27. Humane Society International. 'About Dogfighting'. 10 January 2014; https://www.hsi.org/news-media/about_dogfighting/

28. Quinn, D. 'Dogfight suspect now faces several child porn counts pornography'. Tucson.com. 3 May 2008; https://tucson.com/news/local/crime/dogfight-suspect-now-faces-several-child-porn-counts-pornography/article_da44d7b8-aae7-5746-91e2-a5ab6f703b90.html
29. CBS News. 'Idaho triple slaying linked to dogfighting ring, marijuana growing business, authorities say'. 8 April 2013; https://www.cbsnews.com/news/idaho-triple-slaying-linked-to-dogfighting-ring-marijuana-growing-business-authorities-say/
30. Avanier, E. 'JSO stumbles upon suspected dog fighting while attempting to execute domestic violence warrant'. News 4 Jax. 30 August 2022; https://www.news4jax.com/news/local/2022/08/30/jso-stumbles-upon-suspected-dog-fighting-while-attempting-to-execute-domestic-violence-warrant/
31. The United States Department of Justice. 'Georgia Men Sentenced to Prison for Dog-Fighting and Drug Distribution'. 1 February 2022; https://www.justice.gov/opa/pr/georgia-men-sentenced-prison-dog-fighting-and-drug-distribution
32. Stabroek News. 'Dogfighting ends in murder of man'. 27 May 2013; https://www.stabroeknews.com/2013/05/27/news/guyana/dogfighting-ends-in-murder-of-man/
33. Currie, G., and C. Galloway. 'Scots gamekeeper exposed as part of brutal dogfighting ring after SSPCA alerted to haul of sick images'. *Daily Record*. 10 May 2022; https://www.dailyrecord.co.uk/news/scottish-news/scots-gamekeeper-exposed-part-brutal-26921255
34. Humane Society International. 'About Dogfighting'. 10 January 2014; https://www.hsi.org/news-media/about_dogfighting/
35. Bacon, B. 'Inside the Culture of Dogfighting'. ABC News. 8 January 2009; https://abcnews.go.com/TheLaw/story?id=3390721&page=1
36. Animal Legal & Historical Center. 'Chart of State Dogfighting Laws'. Michigan State University College of Law. 2014; https://www.animallaw.info/article/chart-state-dogfighting-laws
37. Government of India. (n.d.). 'Section 11 in The Prevention of Cruelty to Animals Act, 1960'. Indian Kanoon; https://indiankanoon.org/doc/1763700/

38. DogsBite.org. (n.d.); https://www.dogsbite.org/
39. Mandel, B. 'No parent should have to endure the horror of their kids being mauled to death by the family pet. So when WILL pit bull owners wake up to the menace of a dog that can rip out throats, asks BETHANY MANDEL'. MailOnline. 9 October 2022; https://www.dailymail.co.uk/news/article-11291983/No-parent-endure-horror-kids-mauled-death-family-pet-BETHANY-MANDEL.html
40. PBS. (n.d.). 'Evolution of the Dog'; https://www.pbs.org/wgbh/evolution/library/01/5/l_015_02.html#:~:text=The%20dog%2C%20Canis%20familiaris%2C%20is,shorter%20muzzles%20and%20smaller%20teeth
41. ASPCA. (n.d.). 'Position Statement on Pit Bulls'; https://www.aspca.org/about-us/aspca-policy-and-position-statements/position-statement-pit-bulls
42. PETA. (n.d.). 'How You Helped the Most Abused Dogs on the Planet in 2017'; https://www.peta.org/blog/how-you-and-peta-helped-the-most-abused-dogs-on-the-planet-in-2017/
43. Anand, A. 'Unlike other breeds, Pitbulls are being abandoned at alarming rate'. 15 July 2022; https://www.indiatoday.in/cities/delhi/story/delhi-news-pitbull-dog-breeds-pitbull-attack-pitbulls-abandoned-1976103-2022-07-15
44. PETA. (n.d.). 'Why PETA Supports Pit Bull–Specific Protection Efforts'; https://investigations.peta.org/breed-specific-protection/#:~:text=PETA%20supports%20a%20ban%20on,a%20ban%20on%20chaining%20them
45. ASPCA. (n.d.). 'Pet Statistics'; https://www.aspca.org/helping-people-pets/shelter-intake-and-surrender/pet-statistics
46. Barnes, H. 'How many healthy animals do zoos put down? BBC News. 27 February 2014; https://www.bbc.co.uk/news/magazine-26356099
47. Smith, R. 'Giraffe Killing at Copenhagen Zoo Sparks Global Outrage'. *National Geographic*. 12 February 2014; https://www.nationalgeographic.com/science/article/140210-giraffe-copenhagen-science
48. Morell, V. 'Opinion: Killing of Marius the Giraffe Exposes Myths About Zoos'. *National Geographic*. 13 February 2014; https://www.

nationalgeographic.com/science/article/140212-giraffe-death-denmark-copenhagen-zoo-breeding-europe

49. Born Free Foundation. 'Conservation or Collection? Evaluating the conservation status of species'. May 2021.
50. Morell, V. 'Opinion: Killing of Marius the Giraffe Exposes Myths About Zoos'. *National Geographic*. 13 February 2014; https://www.nationalgeographic.com/science/article/140212-giraffe-death-denmark-copenhagen-zoo-breeding-europe
51. PETA. (n.d.). 'Don't zoos help to preserve endangered species?'; https://www.peta.org/about-peta/faq/dont-zoos-help-to-preserve-endangered-species/#:~:text=Most%20animals%20confined%20in%20zoos,and%20chimpanzees%20into%20the%20wild.
52. Born Free Foundation. 'Conservation or Collection? Evaluating the conservation status of species'. May 2021.
53. Zoocheck. (n.d.); https://www.zoocheck.com/zoos/
54. Ibid.
55. Born Free Foundation. (n.d.); https://www.bornfree.org.uk/zoochosis
56. Robinson, J. 'The horrifying Human Zoos: Shocking photos reveal how zoos around the world kept "primitive natives" in enclosures as Westerners gawped and jeered at them just 60 years ago'. MailOnline. 14 October 2019; https://www.dailymail.co.uk/news/article-4323366/Photos-reveal-horrifying-human-zoos-early-1900s.html
57. Newkirk, P. 'The man who was caged in a zoo'. *The Guardian*. 3 June 2015; https://www.theguardian.com/world/2015/jun/03/the-man-who-was-caged-in-a-zoo
58. Armont, Rhiona-Jade. 'Running away from the circus: A new life beneath the big top'. SBS News. 16 August 2022; https://www.sbs.com.au/news/dateline/article/running-away-from-the-circus-a-new-life-beneath-the-big-top/qkyaol7wr

Chapter 11: Creating a Monster

1. Nichols, David. 'Tell Me a Story: MMPI Responses and Personal Biography in the Case of a Serial Killer'. *Journal of Personality Assessment*, 86(3), pp. 242–62. June 2006; 10.1207/s15327752jpa8603_02

2. Davis, K. 'NEIGHBOUR FROM HELL I was Jeffrey Dahmer's neighbour – we would find cats impaled on trees, dog heads on spikes & he dissolved bones in acid'. *The Sun*. 7 October 2022; https://www.thesun.co.uk/news/20013169/neighbours-Dahmer-dahmer-cats-impaled-dogs/
3. Nichols, David. 'Tell Me a Story: MMPI Responses and Personal Biography in the Case of a Serial Killer'. *Journal of Personality Assessment*, 86(3), pp. 242–62. June 2006; 10.1207/s15327752jpa8603_02
4. Davis, K. 'NEIGHBOUR FROM HELL I was Jeffrey Dahmer's neighbour – we would find cats impaled on trees, dog heads on spikes & he dissolved bones in acid'. *The Sun*. 7 October 2022; https://www.thesun.co.uk/news/20013169/neighbours-Dahmer-dahmer-cats-impaled-dogs/
5. Federal Bureau of Investigation. 'Part 3 of 19'. 9 November 1992; https://vault.fbi.gov/jeffrey-lionel-dahmer/jeffrey-lionel-dahmer-part-03-of-19/view
6. Casey, V. et al. (n.d.). 'Jeffrey Dahmer'; http://maamodt.asp.radford.edu/Psyc%20405/serial%20killers/Dahmer,%20Jeff.htm
7. Nichols, David. 'Tell Me a Story: MMPI Responses and Personal Biography in the Case of a Serial Killer'. *Journal of Personality Assessment*, 86(3), pp. 242–62. June 2006; 10.1207/s15327752jpa8603_02
8. Nelson, K. 'The Complete Timeline Of Jeffrey Dahmer's Murders Goes Deeper Than Netflix's Monster'. *Men's Health*. 4 October 2022; https://www.menshealth.com/entertainment/a41468382/Dahmer-dahmer-victims-timeline-monster/
9. Nichols, David. 'Tell Me a Story: MMPI Responses and Personal Biography in the Case of a Serial Killer'. *Journal of Personality Assessment*, 86(3), pp. 242–62. June 2006; 10.1207/s15327752jpa8603_02
10. Federal Bureau of Investigation. 'Part 3 of 19'. 9 November 1992; https://vault.fbi.gov/jeffrey-lionel-dahmer/jeffrey-lionel-dahmer-part-03-of-19/view
11. Harrison, E. 'Jeffrey Dahmer: The true story behind Ryan Murphy's serial killer series on Netflix'. *The Independent*. 5 October 2022; https://www.independent.co.uk/arts-entertainment/tv/news/jeffrey-dahmer-netflix-true-story-victims-b2196442.html

12. Federal Bureau of Investigation. 'Part 3 of 19'. 9 November 1992; https://vault.fbi.gov/jeffrey-lionel-dahmer/jeffrey-lionel-dahmer-part-03-of-19/view
13. Ibid.
14. Johnson, Scott A. 'Animal cruelty, pet abuse & violence: the missed dangerous connection'. *Forensic Research & Criminology International Journal*, 6(6), pp. 403–15. 2018; DOI: 10.15406/frcij.2018.06.00236
15. Carlsen, A., & Chinoy, S. (n.d.). 'How to Buy a Gun in 16 Countries'. *The New York Times*; https://www.nytimes.com/interactive/2018/03/02/world/international-gun-laws.html
16. Franklin, J. 'Where AR-15-style rifles fit in America's tragic history of mass shootings'. NPR. 26 May 2022; https://www.npr.org/2022/05/26/1101274322/uvalde-ar-15-style-rifle-history-shooter-mass-shooting
17. Levin, M. 'We Need to Talk About Animal Cruelty and Mass Shooters'. *Time*. 29 June 2022; https://time.com/6191947/mass-shootings-animal-cruelty/
18. Morales, M. et al. 'Buffalo grocery store mass shooter pleads guilty to terrorism and murder charges in racist attack'. CNN. 28 November 2022; https://edition.cnn.com/2022/11/28/us/buffalo-tops-grocery-shooting-payton-gendron-plea/index.html
19. Despart, Z. et al. 'Uvalde school shooting'. The Texas Tribune. 20 December 2022; https://www.texastribune.org/series/uvalde-texas-school-shooting/
20. TMZ. 'Buffalo Shooter Tortured, Beheaded a Cat'. 18 May 2022; https://www.tmz.com/2022/05/18/buffalo-shooter-payton-gendron-beheaded-cat/
21. Weaver, M. 'Texas School Shooter Ramos "Loved Hurting Animals": Uvalde Classmate'. *Newsweek*. 29 May 2022; https://www.newsweek.com/texas-school-shooter-ramos-loved-hurting-animals-uvalde-classmate-1711242#:~:text=Texas%20School%20Shooter%20Ramos%20'Loved%20Hurting%20Animals'%3A%20Uvalde%20Classmate,-By%20Margaret%20Weaver&text=Teenage%20gunman%20Salvador%20Ra

22. The Editors of *Encyclopedia Britannica*. 'Columbine High School shootings'. *Encyclopedia Britannica*. 16 February 2023; https://www.britannica.com/event/Columbine-High-School-shootings
23. Madfis, Eric, and Arluke, Arnold. 'Animal Abuse as a Warning Sign of School Massacres'. *Homicide Studies*, vol. 18, issue 1, pp. 7–22. 2014; doi: 10.1177/1088767913511459
24. Scott-Reid, J. 'Nikolas Cruz may have never killed if society took more action on link between animal abuse and mass murderers'. *Daily News*. 7 February 2018; https://www.nydailynews.com/opinion/animal-abuse-scrutiny-stop-killers-nikolas-cruz-article-1.3826671
25. World Population Review (n.d.). 'School Shootings by Country 2023'; https://worldpopulationreview.com/country-rankings/school-shootings-by-country
26. Christensen, J. 'Why the US has the most mass shootings'. CNN. 5 October 2017; https://edition.cnn.com/2015/08/27/health/u-s-most-mass-shootings/index.html
27. Robinson, C., and V. Clausen. 'The Link Between Animal Cruelty and Human Violence'. FBI Law Enforcement Bulletin. 10 August 2021; https://leb.fbi.gov/articles/featured-articles/the-link-between-animal-cruelty-and-human-violence
28. Dalton, J. 'The link is established between serial killers and animal cruelty'. *The Independent*. 2 August 2019; https://www.independent.co.uk/news/long_reads/domestic-violence-animal-cruelty-abuse-neglect-murder-children-dogs-a9018071.html
29. PETA UK. 'Asa Rules Against PETA'S Ad Featuring Face Of Baby P Abuser Steven Barker'. 2 February 2010; https://www.peta.org.uk/media/news-releases/asa-rules-against-petas-ad-featuring-face-of-baby-p-abuser-steven-barker/
30. Lake, E. et al. 'National Outcry: What happened to Baby P?' *The Sun*. 5 May 2022; https://www.thesun.co.uk/news/4567187/baby-p-killers-tracey-connelly-steven-barker-jason-owen/
31. *Encyclopedia Britannica*. 'Ted Bundy: American Serial Killer'. 20 January 2023; https://www.britannica.com/biography/Ted-Bundy
32. Blackstock, G. 'The animal abusers who went on to kill: Investigators urged to link pet cruelty with domestic violence'. *The Sunday Post*. 12

May 2019; https://www.sundaypost.com/fp/investigators-urged-to-link-pet-cruelty-with-domestic-violenceanimal-abusers-who-went-on-to-kill/

33. Coleman, P. 'Young animal abusers can grow up to commit unspeakable violence'. *Miami Herald*. 4 April 2018; https://www.miamiherald.com/opinion/op-ed/article207997174.html
34. Mcphee, M. 'Boston Strangler Case Solved 50 Years Later'. ABC News. 11 July 2013; https://abcnews.go.com/US/boston-strangler-case-solved-50-years/story?id=19640699
35. Wade-Palmer, C. 'Serial killers who started on animals – the red flags that show murderous traits'. *The Daily Star*. 19 June 2021; https://www.dailystar.co.uk/news/world-news/serial-killers-started-animals--24327756
36. Taneja, R. 'Jisha Rape And Murder Case: All You Need To Know'. NDTV. 14 December 2017; https://www.ndtv.com/india-news/jisha-rape-and-murder-case-all-you-need-to-know-1786859
37. PTI. 'Kerala: Jisha murder accused in police custody for sexual activity with goat'. *Deccan Chronicle*. 15 July 2016; https://www.deccanchronicle.com/nation/crime/150716/kerala-jisha-murder-accused-in-police-custody-for-sexual-activity-with-goat.html#:~:text=Kerala%3A%20Jisha%20murder%20accused%20in%20police%20custody%20for%20sexual%20activity%20with%20goat,-PTI%20%7C%20
38. *Encyclopedia Britannica*. 'Veerappan: Indian Criminal'. 14 January 2023; https://www.britannica.com/biography/Veerappan
39. Montgomery, H. 'Japanese Cannibal Who Got Away With Eating and Raping a Dutch Woman Is Dead'. Vice. 2 December 2022; https://www.vice.com/en/article/7k8jnb/japan-cannibalism-murder-issei-sagawa
40. Johnson, Scott. (2018). 'Animal cruelty, pet abuse & violence: the missed dangerous connection'. *Foresic Research & Criminology International Journal*, vol. 6., issue 5. 2018; 10.15406/frcij.2018.06.00236
41. Madfis, Eric, and Arnold Arluke. 'Animal Abuse as a Warning Sign of School Massacres'. *Homicide Studies*, vol. 18, issue 1, pp. 7–22. 2014; doi: 10.1177/1088767913511459
42. Robinson, C., and V. Clausen. 'The Link Between Animal Cruelty and Human Violence'. FBI Law Enforcement Bulletin. 10 August 2021;

https://leb.fbi.gov/articles/featured-articles/the-link-between-animal-cruelty-and-human-violence

43. Teesside University. 'Animal abuse research cited in MP's campaign for tougher sentences'. 7 November 2016; https://www.tees.ac.uk/sections/news/pressreleases_story.cfm?story_id=6364#
44. Sinergia Animal. (n.d.). 'Slaughterhouse workers: What do they do and are they cruel?'; https://www.sinergiaanimalinternational.org/single-post/slaughterhouse-workers
45. Sharma, S. 'The Rise of Big Meat: Brazil's Extractive Industry Executive Summary'. Institute for Agriculture and Trade Policy. 30 November 2017; https://www.iatp.org/documents/rise-big-meat-brazils-extractive-industry-executive-summary
46. Environmental Justice Foundation. (n.d.). 'Thailand's Seafood Slaves: Human Trafficking, Slavery and Murder in Kantang's Fishing Industry'; https://ejfoundation.org/reports/thailands-seafood-slaves
47. Stauffer, B. '"When We're Dead and Buried, Our Bones Will Keep Hurting", Workers' Rights Under Threat in US Meat and Poultry Plants'. Human Rights Watch. 4 September 2019; https://www.hrw.org/report/2019/09/04/when-were-dead-and-buried-our-bones-will-keep-hurting/workers-rights-under-threat
48. Oxfam America. (n.d.). 'Lives on the Line: The high human cost of chicken'; https://www.oxfamamerica.org/livesontheline/
49. Cook, E.A. et al. 'Working conditions and public health risks in slaughterhouses in western Kenya'. *BMC Public Health*, vol. 17, issue 1, 14. 2017; https://doi.org/10.1186/s12889-016-3923-y
50. Block, K. 'More animals than ever before—92.2 billion—are used and killed each year for food'. The Humane Society of the United States. 5 June 2023; https://blog.humanesociety.org/2023/06/more-animals-than-ever-before-92-2-billion-are-used-and-killed-each-year-for-food.html
51. Heanue, O. 'For Slaughterhouse Workers, Physical Injuries Are Only the Beginning'. OnLabor. 17 January 2022; https://onlabor.org/for-slaughterhouse-workers-physical-injuries-are-only-the-beginning/#:~:text=The%20requirement%20to%20do%20violent,the%20nation's%20most%20dangerous%20occupations

52. Stauffer, B. '"When We're Dead and Buried, Our Bones Will Keep Hurting", Workers' Rights Under Threat in US Meat and Poultry Plants'. Human Rights Watch. 4 September 2019; https://www.hrw.org/report/2019/09/04/when-were-dead-and-buried-our-bones-will-keep-hurting/workers-rights-under-threat
53. BBC News. 'Confessions of a slaughterhouse worker'. 6 January 2020; https://www.bbc.com/news/stories-50986683
54. Slade, J., and E. Alleyne. 'The Psychological Impact of Slaughterhouse Employment: A Systematic Literature Review'. *Trauma, Violence, & Abuse*, vol. 24, issue 2, pp. 429–40. 2023; https://doi.org/10.1177/15248380211030243
55. Lebwohl, M. 'A Call to Action: Psychological Harm in Slaughterhouse Workers'. The Yale Global Health Review. 25 January 2016; https://yaleglobalhealthreview.com/2016/01/25/a-call-to-action-psychological-harm-in-slaughterhouse-workers/
56. Bennett, G. 'Former slaughterhouse workers killed and butchered two men in Bristol home, jury told'. Bristol Live. 9 November 2022; https://www.bristolpost.co.uk/news/bristol-news/former-slaughterhouse-workers-killed-butchered-7801760
57. Miller, M.E. '"Worst serial killer in history," who fed prostitutes to pigs, sparks rage by publishing book'. *The Washington Post*. 23 February 2016; https://www.washingtonpost.com/news/morning-mix/wp/2016/02/23/worst-serial-killer-in-history-who-fed-prostitutes-to-pigs-sparks-rage-by-publishing-book/
58. Knight, A., and K.D. Watson. 'Was Jack the Ripper a Slaughterman? Human-Animal Violence and the World's Most Infamous Serial Killer'. *Animals*, vol. 7, article no. 4, p. 30. 2017; https://doi.org/10.3390/ani7040030
59. Lebwohl, M. 'A Call to Action: Psychological Harm in Slaughterhouse Workers'. The Yale Global Health Review. 25 January 2016; https://yaleglobalhealthreview.com/2016/01/25/a-call-to-action-psychological-harm-in-slaughterhouse-workers/
60. PETA. (n.d.). 'Sex, Violence, and Vivisection: Are Some Animal Experimenters Psychopaths?'; https://headlines.peta.org/sex-violence-vivisection/

61. Mathews Hall. 'On Being Human: The Lesson of the Caterpillar'. 6 April 2018; https://matthewshall.ca/2018/04/06/human-lesson-caterpillar/

Chapter 12: How to Heal from Bites

1. Encyclopedia Britannica. (n.d.). 'Golden Rule'; https://www.britannica.com/topic/Golden-Rule
2. World Organisation for Animal Health. (n.d.). 'Animal Welfare'; https://www.woah.org/en/what-we-do/animal-health-and-welfare/animal-welfare/
3. Rowland, M.P. 'Millennials Are Driving The Worldwide Shift Away From Meat'. *Forbes*. 23 March 2018; https://www.forbes.com/sites/michaelpellmanrowland/2018/03/23/millennials-move-away-from-meat/?sh=31f5b2aba4a4
4. Rakuten Insight. 'Infographic: Plant-based food alternatives – Future or Present?' 21 January 2022; https://insight.rakuten.com/infographic-plant-based-food-alternatives-future-or-present/
5. Vegan Outreach. (n.d.); https://veganoutreach.org/vegan-mentorship-program/#:~:text=Get%20connected%20via%20email%20with,have%20been%20matched%20so%20far!
6. Physicians Committee for Responsible Medicine (PCRM) (n.d.); https://www.pcrm.org/vegankickstart
7. PETA. (n.d.). 'How to Be a Compassionate Traveler'; https://www.peta.org/features/be-a-compassionate-traveler/
8. PETA. '7 Animal-Friendly Destinations for Your Vacation'. 13 July 2016; https://www.peta.org/living/entertainment/animal-friendly-destinations-vacations/
9. US Department of Homeland Security. (n.d.). 'If You See Something, Say Something®'; https://www.dhs.gov/see-something-say-something
10. PCRM. 'A Special Report: Summer 2016'; https://www.pcrm.org/sites/default/files/2020-04/Medical%20Schools%20Report%202016.pdf
11. American Anti-Vivisection Society. 'Dying to Learn: Exposing the supply and use of dogs and cats in higher education'. American Anti-Vivisection Society. 2009; https://aavs.org/wp-content/uploads/2021/09/aavs_report_dying-to-learn.pdf
12. PCRM. (n.d.); https://www.pcrm.org/about-us/our-victories

13. PETA. 'PETA Donates Lifesaving Human Simulators to National Iraqi Surgical Training Program'. 29 November 2022; https://www.peta.org/media/news-releases/peta-donates-lifesaving-human-simulators-to-national-iraqi-surgical-training-program/
14. PETA India. 'Higher Ed Animal Use for Trainings Banned'. 20 April 2012; https://www.petaindia.com/blog/higher-ed-animal-use-trainings-banned/
15. PETA. (n.d.). 'We Never Gave Up: PETA's Triumph Over Ringling Bros'; https://www.peta.org/features/ringling/
16. Dellatto, M. 'Ringling Bros. Circus Returns—Without Animals—Five Years After Closing'. *Forbes*. 18 May 2022; https://www.forbes.com/sites/marisadellatto/2022/05/18/ringling-bros-circus-returns-without-animals-five-years-after-closing/?sh=50c5e66a79b2
17. Institute for Humane Education. (n.d.); https://humaneeducation.org/zoe-weils-books/
18. 'TEDxDirigo - Zoe Weil - The World Becomes What You Teach'. 15 January 2011; https://www.youtube.com/watch?v=t5HEV96dIuY
19. PETA. (n.d.). 'TeachKind: PETA's Humane Education Division'; https://www.peta.org/teachkind/
20. Business Plus. 'Vegetarian Dishes Gain Traction In Staff Canteens'. 6 January 2023; https://businessplus.ie/news/vegetarian-dishes-staff-canteens/
21. Arora, M. 'From filthy to fabulous: Mumbai beach undergoes dramatic makeover'. 22 May 2017; https://edition.cnn.com/2017/05/22/asia/mumbai-beach-dramatic-makeover/index.html
22. Good Food Institute. (n.d.); https://gfi.org/initiatives/
23. Wageningen University and Research. 'The future of real milk without cows'. 9 September 2022; https://www.wur.nl/en/newsarticle/the-future-of-real-milk-without-cows.htm
24. Material Innovation Initiative. (n.d.); https://materialinnovation.org/
25. Vegconomist. 'Fleather: Vegan Leather from Upcycled Temple Flowers'. 22 December 2022; https://vegconomist.com/fashion-design-and-beauty/leather-alternatives/fleather-vegan-leather-from-upcycled-temple-flowers/

26. PETA. (n.d.). 'PETA's $1 Million Vegan Wool Challenge Award'; https://www.peta.org/features/vegan-wool-award/
27. Center for Contemporary Sciences. (n.d.); https://contemporarysciences.org/
28. PETA. (n.d.). 'PETA Pays Students Who Create Alternatives to Animal Use'; https://www.peta.org/features/future-without-speciesism-competition/
29. Heinrich Böll Stiftung, Friends of the Earth Europe, Bund für Umwelt und Naturschutz. 'Meat Atlas: Facts and figures about the animals we eat'. 2021.
30. FAIRR--A Coller Initiative. (n.d.); https://www.fairr.org/about-fairr/about-us/
31. Glass Walls Syndicate. (n.d.); https://glasswallsyndicate.org/about/
32. Vegpreneur. (n.d.); https://www.vegpreneur.org/who-we-are
33. Greenpeace. 'Greenwash: what it is and how not to fall for it'. 12 April 2022; https://www.greenpeace.org.uk/news/what-is-greenwashing/#:~:text=What%20is%20greenwashing%3F,looked%20at%20in%20more%20depth
34. PETA. (n.d.). 'Patagonia's "Sustainable Wool" Supplier Exposed: Lambs Skinned Alive, Throats Slit, Tails Cut Off'; https://investigations.peta.org/ovis-lamb-slaughter-sheep-cruelty/
35. PETA. (n.d.). 'Another Patagonia-Approved Wool Producer Exposed—Help Sheep Now'; https://investigations.peta.org/another-patagonia-approved-wool-producer-exposed/
36. PETA. 'Chaining Is Prohibited in the Following Communities'. 5 November 2018; https://www.peta.org/issues/animal-companion-issues/current-legislation-tethering-dogs-prohibited-communities/
37. Humane Society International. (n.d.). 'Bullfighting'; https://www.hsi.org/news-media/bullfighting/
38. Burson, T. 'How the meat-loving city of Ghent became the veggie capital of Europe'. Mic. 31 October 2017; https://www.mic.com/articles/185650/how-the-meat-loving-city-of-ghent-became-the-veggie-capital-of-europe
39. PETA. 28 October 2020; https://twitter.com/peta/status/1321436598987378692?lang=en-GB

INDEX

ABOUT THE AUTHOR

Poorva Joshipura is the author of *For a Moment of Taste: How What You Eat Impacts Animals, the Planet and Your Health* (2020). She is the Senior Vice President of International Affairs for People for the Ethical Treatment of Animals (PETA) Foundation UK, through which she oversees numerous global PETA entity operations and projects. She is the former chief executive officer of PETA India and the former director of PETA UK. Early on in her career, she also worked in various capacities for PETA US. She is a member of the board of directors for PETA India and the former co-opted member of the government body Animal Welfare Board of India. Poorva is also an advisor to Animal Rahat, an organization that aims to help some of the most neglected animals in the world, and to the Petra Veterinary Clinic, which does similar work in Jordan.

Poorva's award-winning work involves stopping cruelty to animals used for food, clothing, experimentation, entertainment and other purposes in countries around the world. She has personally conducted undercover investigations into places where animals are used and has overseen numerous other such investigations. Her work for animals also extends to courtrooms, corporate boardrooms, government offices, police stations, college campuses, schools and on the street through rescue and emergency response efforts. Poorva has led many campaigns that have been widely covered by major news agencies around the world. She is a regular guest on television news and radio shows through which she encourages viewers and listeners to be considerate to animals. She speaks on animal rights at universities and at other events, and can usually be found in London, Mumbai, Delhi or Wadi Musa.